DIRECT
MARKETING
Success Stories

...and the
Strategies that Built
the Businesses

BOB STONE

Printed on recyclable paper

NTC Business Books
a division of *NTC Publishing Group* • Lincolnwood, Illinois USA

Library of Congress Cataloging-in-Publication Data

Stone, Bob
    Direct marketing success stories...and the strategies that built the businesses / Bob Stone.
       p.   cm.
   ISBN 0-8442-3665-9
   1. Direct marketing.   2. Success in business.   I. Title.
HF5415.126.S756   1995
658.8' 4 — dc20   94-17227
                                              CIP

Published by NTC Business Books, a division of NTC Publishing Group
4255 West Touhy Avenue
Lincolnwood (Chicago), Illinois 60646-1975, U.S.A.
©1995 by NTC Publishing Group. All rights reserved.
No part of this book may be reproduced, stored in a retrieval system,
or transmitted in any form or by any means,
electronic, mechanical, photocopying, recording or otherwise,
without the prior permission of NTC Publishing Group.
Manufactured in the United States of America.

5 6 7 8 9 VP 0 9 8 7 6 5 4 3 2 1

CONTENTS

Henry A. Johnson

Foreword

It is rather unusual for an author to call upon his publisher to write a foreword for a new book. However, in this particular case, I was both honored and eager to help out.

I was working hard and reaching for success in the mid-1960s with my advertising sales firm, The Pattis Group, when I came across a start-up advertising agency called Stone & Adler. Whereas most agencies were anxious to buy advertising space in the magazines we represented, these people had different ideas. Yes, magazines played a role in their media mix, but the real focus at Stone & Adler was in the exciting new field of direct mail and direct marketing. The men and women of this full-service direct marketing agency spoke a peculiar language with terms such as "response rate," "add-ons," "bounce-back sales," "package stuffers," and many others. At the head of this activity was an energetic, articulate, and creative innovator by the name of Bob Stone. The rest is history.

Bob has often been referred to as a pioneer of direct marketing, and he has probably won every award and recognition that has ever been given in the field. Of much greater importance, though, is the vision that this man had in the early days of the business. Personally, I have enjoyed Bob as a friend and have admired him as a professional for more than 30 years. He is truly a remarkable man who has lived a remarkable life.

In *Direct Marketing Success Stories*, Bob has assembled some of

America's most successful direct marketers to tell their stories. These people have lived through the early days of trial and error, and have developed the successful formulas that built their businesses. There is a great deal to be learned from their experiences.

Direct marketing is a strange business in that you can generally look back at results and analyze why a program was a success or failure. This ability to look back reminds me of the time in 1990 that I flew to Moscow with our Ambassador, Jack Matlock. I asked many questions about what was then the Soviet Union, and sought Matlock's views on what he thought might happen next in that rapidly-changing region. He explained that he could not even predict what would happen the next day—however, he added with a chuckle that after it happened, he'd be glad to explain why it was inevitable.

Now you can look back on some fascinating success stories that will make it easier for you to predict the outcome of your own direct marketing efforts. It's nice to be able to minimize the risk. Good luck, and happy reading.

S. William Pattis
President
NTC Publishing Group

Preface

Have you ever wondered where the idea for a new book comes from? I can tell you how this book came to be. It was a remarkable case of serendipity—*the faculty of making fortunate and unexpected discoveries by accident.*

The genesis of the idea emerged when I was lecturing at the University of Missouri—Kansas City. After one lecture, two students in the Professional Direct Marketing (PDM) program came up to me and said, "We know that you are scheduled for one more lecture. We wonder if, instead of delivering your planned remarks, you'd tell us how you built Stone & Adler (S&A) into one of the most successful direct marketing agencies of its time."

I went back to the hotel that night and proceeded to make an outline of the steps we followed to build S&A. Putting the steps on paper led to a discovery. I found that our steps were, in fact, strategies that we developed to accomplish specific objectives.

After delivering the asked-for lecture, I became obsessed with the idea of writing the whole S&A story. The further I got into the story, the more excited I got. When the task was finally completed, I said to myself, "Hey, the strategies I identified could be adapted by scores of direct marketers."

Then I moved my thought process up a notch: Suppose I were to write a cross section of truly successful direct marketers I know, give each a copy of the S&A story, and ask them if they would write their stories." Ergo, the idea for a new book was born.

The acceptance of the idea was immediate. Twelve out of thirteen invitations came back with a positive response. Everyone seemed excited about the concept. The final "yes" I needed had to come from my publisher. A verbal explanation over lunch brought an enthusiastic, affirmative response.

This book's emphasis is on strategies that solve problems or exploit opportunities. The average consumer does not realize that he or she employs strategies each day in an effort to get what he or she wants. Such strategies are instinctive for the most part.

Who among us has not seen a guy prancing through an airport with a giant Panda, big enough to fill an airplane seat? We can only guess, but is it possible that the strategy is to placate the kids and mother for being at a convention for days during which he had lots of fun? Or what about the sweet, young wife who stages a candlelight dinner, with provocative attire to match, as a prelude to telling her loving mate that she totalled the car.

Strategies—we all use them. But think how much more effective strategies can be if they are planned.

The direct marketing success stories you are about to enjoy exemplify what can be achieved when planned strategies are employed. You will be in good company when you read this book because each contributor is a certified success!

Best of success to you,

Bob Stone

1

Strategies and Direct Marketing

This is a book about strategies, strategies that have built businesses that have grown beyond the founders' wildest dreams.

Strategy Defined

For the purposes of this book, we will use a customized definition of *strategy:*

A course of action designed to achieve an identified objective.

Direct marketing, which can best be described as a marketing discipline, is, a strategy in itself. Applying our customized definition, we can express direct marketing's objective and strategy as follows:

Objective: Create a one-on-one relationship with all customers.

Strategy: Apply direct-marketing principles as the most efficient way to accomplish the objective.

As you become immersed in this book of direct-marketing success stories, you will see two types of strategies emerge: (1) strategies that led to new business startups, and (2) strategies that grew businesses.

Strategies That Launch New Businesses

The history of direct marketing is replete with examples of strategies that became the platform from which new businesses were launched. Such strategies usually develop as a result of a concerted effort to discover voids in the marketplace. These discoveries lead to *niche marketing*.

Going back over 100 years, both Sears Roebuck and Montgomery Ward discovered a tremendous void in the marketplace: Farmers and rural residents did not have access to "big-city" merchandise. The basic strategy these two companies developed was to bring big-city merchandise directly to farmers and rural residents through the medium of a catalog.

There are scores of examples of strategic niche marketing in modern-day direct marketing. Three of our stories exemplify how identifying voids in the marketplace can lead to new business startups.

Spiegel

Chapter 2 is the fascinating story of an old business on the road to extinction that was turned into an entirely new business.

The miraculous turnaround started in January 1976, when Spiegel hired Henry Johnson, an outstanding catalog marketer, in a last-ditch effort to save the company. Johnson's first act was to identify Spiegel's strengths in contrast to their glaring weaknesses. He then set out to uncover voids in the marketplace.

Being a visionary, Johnson foresaw a rapidly emerging market of huge size: *women entering the business and professional world in record numbers.* They were better educated than previous generations and were acutely aware of social, business, and fashion issues. They also had little time to shop.

Having identified this huge void, Johnson set out to offer products and services exclusively for this new market. The existing company had none of the products and services needed, so a slow death was dictated for the old Spiegel: The new business would grow as the old business died.

The strategies that Johnson and his associates created and applied turned the company completely around. Today, sales are in excess of $1 billion a year.

Leo Burnett

The story of Leo Burnett's entry into direct marketing (Chapter 4) is unique. The strategies the firm created in order to have a direct-marketing presence were drastically different than strategies employed by other members of the top ten general advertising agencies. The other agencies all employed an identical strategy: start or acquire a direct-marketing agency as a separate profit center, letting the direct-marketing arm service general advertising clients as well as clients outside these accounts.

Burnett's strategy was to integrate direct marketing into all of the agency's disciplines, including general advertising, sales promotion, and public relations. The company opted not to set direct marketing up as a separate profit center, and it likewise restricted direct marketing to Burnett clients only.

The basic strategy proved to have inherent advantages: (1) Direct marketing didn't have to compete for budget dollars; and (2) Burnett could include direct marketing, where appropriate, in total advertising programs it presented to its clients. Consequently, Burnett was in the forefront of advocating *integrated communications,* a concept that has won wide acclaim in the advertising fraternity.

The Loo Brothers

Chapter 6 demonstrates the power of strategic thinking as it applies to growing a business. It is the story of how the Loo brothers, Dusty and Gary, took over a small family greeting-card business and grew it from $1,840,000 in 1968 to $102.4 million in 1986.

Two strategies that the Loo brothers and their associates applied account for the dramatic growth over the 18-year period. The strategies can be expressed as follows:

1. Continuing explorations of new market niches is a sound course to follow in growing a business.

2. Product line extension is a major key in growing a business.

When Dusty Loo graduated from the University of Kansas in January of 1961, he entered the family business immediately. Their fledgling mail-order business catered to one market niche—Methodist ministers.

The product they offered was called "Post-A-Note." "Post-A-Notes" came 40 to the box at a cost of 55 cents. Church women sold them for $1.00 a box. This proved to be a successful product because it filled an ongoing need to raise funds, which is common to all churches. Recipe cards became the second product offered for fund-raising purposes.

Based on their success with churches, the Loo brothers looked to other market niches that could use fund-raising products. They were successful with 4H groups, schools, and Campfire Girls. Each new niche helped to grow the business.

But, quite by accident, they learned that their market segments went far beyond organizations wanting to raise funds. What they learned over time is that they were getting group orders from military wives, school teachers, secretaries in large corporations, and women astute at pooling orders with friends to earn maximum discounts. This discovery opened a huge universe of women mail-order buyers. From that point forward, sales skyrocketed.

With receptive niche markets expanding at a rapid pace, product line extension became imperative. The product mix had to expand as the company became more of a mail-order card shop for individuals and less of a place to buy a lot of single products for fund raising.

The first major product extension occurred in the mid-1970s when a Valentine line was introduced. It was a tremendous success and led to other event-oriented products for occasions such as Easter, back-to-school, Halloween, Thanksgiving, and Mothers' Day.

Until the late 1970s all product line extensions were created by the company. That policy changed at a dramatic meeting spearheaded by Dusty and Gary. The decision was made to double the number of products and thereby greatly expand the size of their catalog. Outside sources were used for the first time to make the expanded product line possible.

The strategy to double the product line was a resounding success. Gross volume ballooned from $25 million to $50 million in 12 months' time. The growth pattern continued until it reached $102.4 million at the time the business was sold.

Strategies That Grow Businesses

It's one thing to develop a strategy that will launch a business; it's quite another to develop strategies that grow a business.

The Strategies We Inherit

Marketers who embrace direct marketing inherit a rich legacy—timeless strategies that have been developed over time. Examples of such strategies are as follows:

Free trial offers. This strategy puts a product or service in the prospect's hands without obligation, under the assumption that using the product or service will convince a large percentage of prospects that the product is worth the cost.

Optional features. The strategy here is to sell the basic product or service at a set price but to offer the added value of optional features, thereby increasing the amount of the sale.

Credit options. Based on the premise that people resist sending payment with an order, the strategy is to make it easy for the consumer to buy. Allowing the customer to charge to a credit card reduces resistance.

Free gifts. Free gifts constitute incentives to try or buy. The strategy is that people are more likely to try a product or service if an attractive gift is offered as an incentive.

Time limits. An inherent problem facing all direct marketers is human inertia. The strategy behind setting time limits is that it will force the prospect to make a decision *now* rather than later (or never).

Sweepstakes. There are two strategies behind every sweepstake: (1) The lure of winning a big prize increases the chance that the prospect will read the letter or ad used to announce the product; and (2) many people erroneously believe that if they buy something, they have a better chance of winning the sweepstake.

Strategies and Product Life Cycles

Everyone has access to the well-established strategies that are part and parcel of direct marketing, but to grow a business at a steady pace, customized strategies are essential. The strategies you develop should relate to your competition and the point at which your product stands in the product life cycle. Each product or product line you develop goes through the four stages shown in Exhibit 1.1: (1) introduction, (2) growth, (3) maturation and saturation, and (4) decline.

The following case involves a product category, pianos, that definitely qualifies as being in the last stage of its product life cycle. The steps Yamaha took to combat a serious downward trend is a classic example of how a customized strategy can and does reverse a trend.

Exhibit 1-1 The Product Life Cycle

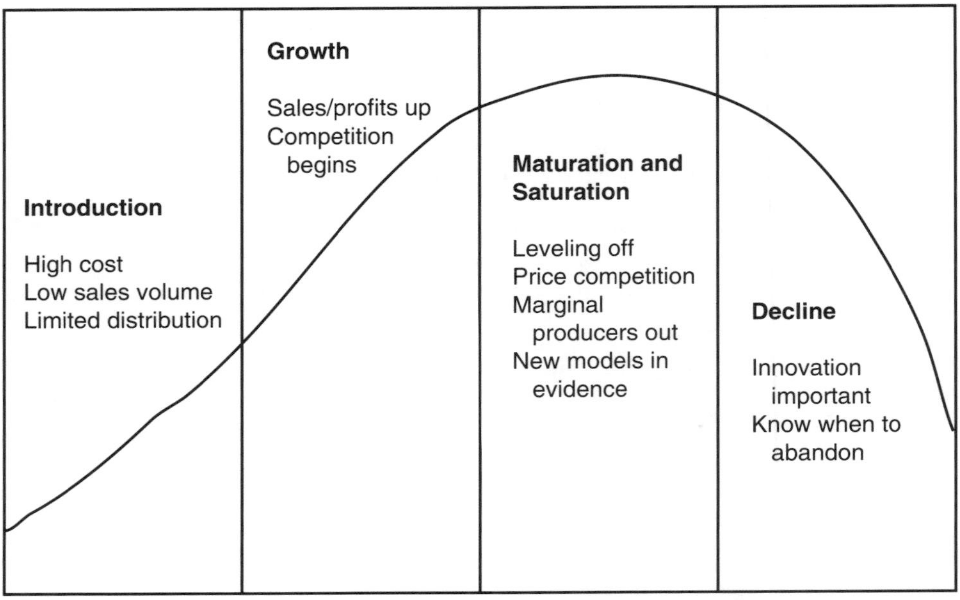

Growth

Sales/profits up
Competition
begins

Introduction

High cost
Low sales volume
Limited distribution

**Maturation and
Saturation**

Leveling off
Price competition
Marginal
  producers out
New models in
  evidence

Decline

Innovation
  important
Know when to
  abandon

Yamaha Piano

Situation Analysis. Yamaha had succeeded in capturing 40 percent of the
global piano market. Unfortunately, just when Yamaha became the market
leader, the overall demand for pianos started to decline by 10 percent a year.
There are some 40 million pianos around the world, in living rooms, dens, and
concert halls, and for the most part, they just sit and gather dust. As head of
Yamaha, what would you do? Some American analysts would say, "Get out of the
piano business!"

Solution to the Problem. Yamaha's marketers determined that one possible
way to solve the problem was to add value to the millions of pianos already
sold. They remembered the old player piano—a pleasant idea with a not very
pleasant sound. Using a combination of sophisticated digital and optical technology, they developed a "player" program that can distinguish 92 degrees of
key touch speed and strength. With this technology, piano owners could
record live performances by the pianists of their choice, or they could buy
such recordings on a computer-like disk. So for an expenditure of around
$2,500, piano owners could retrofit their idle, untuned, dust-collecting pieces

of oversized furniture to make great artists play for them in the privacy of their homes.

End Result of the Value-Added Concept. Owners of 40 million more or less idle pianos became a vibrant market for retrofitting sales. Yamaha started marketing this technology in April 1988, and sales since then have been explosive. This new technology has even created new interest in learning to play the piano.

Techniques for Developing Strategies

The Hollywood version of marketing and advertising executives shows dynamic individuals who go into a trance until a light bulb goes on over their heads. Then, presto; a brilliant new strategy is born! Well, those of us who function in the real world know differently.

Real-world ideas, concepts, and strategies come about as a result of identifying problems and opportunities, establishing objectives, and creating plans to accomplish those objectives. Rarely does this exercise involve just one person. More often than not it is a team effort.

SWOT Analysis

It has been said that you can't grasp opportunities or solve problems if you don't know what your opportunities and problems really are. Likewise, you can't counteract weaknesses and threats if you haven't established their existence. These facts dictate SWOT analysis, an acronym for

S = strengths

W = weaknesses

O = opportunities

T = threats

The direct marketing success stories in this book prove the value of SWOT analysis. Referring again to the Spiegel story in Chapter 2, we see that Henry Johnson dealt with each step of the analysis process. He identified the following five strengths for Spiegel:

The ability to produce catalogs

Knowledge about buying merchandise, processing orders, and warehousing merchandise

▪ Good credit (the company was owned by Beneficial Finance)

▪ Many good, hardworking employees

▪ Widespread awareness of the Spiegel name

Weaknesses were rampant, but the most serious weakness was that the company's strategy was better suited to the 1940s and 1950s. Offering utilitarian merchandise at low prices was fine decades ago, but in 1976, it was a "me-too" strategy that placed Spiegel a distant fourth behind Sears and Roebuck, Montgomery Ward, and JC Penney. Along with its unproductive strategy, Spiegel was burdened with indecisive leadership and poor morale.

Johnson saw an opportunity to cater to women entering the business and professional work force. Their numbers were increasing rapidly; they were fashion conscious and had the money to buy.

There were many serious threats to Spiegel's success in the new marketplace. The profile of its customer base at the time was totally contrary to the upscale market Johnson envisioned. Profitable categories, such as automotive parts, had to be eliminated because they interfered with the new image Spiegel was trying to build. Mail-order stores had to be closed because upscale women didn't shop that way. Buyers had to be trained to buy upscale goods and identifiable brands, and the company had to convince upscale vendors that the new Spiegel was worthy of offering their top-of-the-line brands. The strategies developed to overcome these threats bordered on genius.

Brainstorming

Once you identify your strengths, weaknesses, opportunities, and threats, you are ready to create objectives and develop strategies to meet your goals. Different companies develop strategies in different ways. Some appoint an executive committee to develop strategies; others appoint teams. The company's size and culture usually dictates the best route to follow.

Whatever the procedure, it is essential that breakthrough (really big) ideas result. *Brainstorming* is an excellent way to generate such ideas, because it produces a large number of ideas and often leads to gangbuster strategies that surpass those reached through other procedures. The rules for brainstorming are simple but precise.

Selecting a Leader. The first step is for the group to select a leader and have him or her take all responsibility for keeping a realistic outlook; everyone else in the brainstorming meeting is to "think wild." In the brainstorming meeting, the leader plays a low-key role. It's important to avoid influencing the partici-pants. The duties of the leader are

- To see that detailed notes are taken on all ideas expressed

- To see that the agenda and time schedule are adhered to

- To admonish any critical thinkers in the group; no negative thinking is allowed during the brainstorming session

- To see that the group takes time to "build up" each idea

- To keep all participants involved and contributing

House Rules for Brainstorming. The brainstorming session itself needs to follow these guidelines:

1. Suspend all critical judgment of ideas. Don't ask if this is a *good* idea or a *bad* idea. Accept it and keep looking for ways to improve the concept.

2. Welcome "freewheeling," off-the-wall thinking. Wild, crazy, funny, far-out ideas are important. Why? Because they frequently shock us into seeing a totally new perspective of the problem.

3. Quantity, not quality, is the objective during the brainstorming session. This may sound contradictory, but it's not. Remember, every member of the group has been briefed on the problem in advance. You have a carefully planned agenda of material to cover. Consequently, your group's thinking is well directed toward the problem. Therefore, you can say, "Go for quantity in the idea session."

4. Build up each idea. Here's where most brainstorming sessions fail. They just collect ideas as fast as they come and let it go at that. The leader should carefully slow the group down so they stop with each idea and help build it up. Enhance each idea, no matter how crazy or offbeat it may seem.

It's the leader's responsibility to see that these four guidelines are adhered to in every meeting, but he or she should do this in a very low-key, informal manner. It is important that the leader not become a dominant, authority figure in meetings.

Brainstorming is part of a three-phase process:

1. Before starting, create an agenda and carefully define the problem(s) in writing.

2. Set quotas for ideas and a time limit for each section of the agenda.

3. Review the house rules with participants before each brainstorming session.

When the session is over, then, and only then, use your normal, everyday judgment to logically select ideas with the most potential from all of the available alternatives.

How to Profit from This Book

Before you delve into the success stories, here are a couple of suggestions on how I feel you can profit most from this book.

Every time you come upon a strategy that particularly appeals to you, ask yourself this simple question: How can I adapt that idea to my line of business? For example, the Book-of-the-Month Club concept can be adapted to Fruit-of-the-Month, Gadget-of-the-Month, Print-of-the-Month, and so on.

Also, take a few minutes to review the commentary at the end of each chapter, checking off the strategies that you would like to pursue for your business. If you do this, you will have a rich storehouse of strategies by the time you finish the book.

Having said all this, let the success stories begin!

CHAPTER

2

From Mass to Class
The Spiegel Story

Henry A. Johnson, President,
Henry A. Johnson & Associates

*H*enry A. (Hank) Johnson's career spans 40 years—all of it in the catalog direct-marketing industry. After 25 years at Aldens, Johnson joined Spiegel in 1976 as president and chief executive officer. He retired as vice chairman in December, 1987, and was named to the Direct Marketing Association's Hall of Fame in 1991. He is the author of The Corporate Dream.

In 1975, Beneficial Finance received the results of a disheartening study conducted by consulting firm Booz Allen Hamilton. The study focused on Spiegel, the catalog company owned by Beneficial. For a number of years, Beneficial had been dissatisfied with Spiegel's performance and profits that had dwindled to almost nothing. They commissioned the study to determine what options were available. Booz Allen concluded that Beneficial had three alternatives:

- Sell Spiegel

- Liquidate its assets

- Make a last-ditch effort to resurrect the company

But Booz Allen did not hold out much hope of success for any of these options. The firm determined that if Beneficial put Spiegel on the market, it was highly unlikely anyone would buy it. It also concluded that Beneficial would lose hundreds of millions of dollars if Spiegel were liquidated. Although Booz Allen didn't believe that Beneficial could do much with the company, resurrection was preferable to the other two strategies.

Beneficial began a search for a CEO who could bring fresh ideas to the moribund organization. After a series of interviews and discussions, I was hired as Spiegel's chief executive in January 1976. It was immediately apparent that the company's overall strategy was better suited to the 1940s and 1950s than to the current era. Offering utilitarian merchandise at low prices and easy credit was fine decades ago, but in 1976 it was a "me-too" strategy that placed the company a distant fourth behind Sears Roebuck, Montgomery Ward, and JC Penney. Along with this unproductive strategy, Spiegel was burdened with indecisive leadership and poor morale.

To an outsider (such as Booz Allen), the situation might have seemed hopeless. But rather than dwell on the company's weaknesses, I focused on its strengths, recognizing that if a turnaround strategy were possible, it would begin there. These strengths included

- The ability to produce catalogs

- Knowledge about buying merchandise, processing orders, and warehousing merchandise

- Good credit because of Beneficial ownership

- Many good, hardworking employees

- Widespread awareness of the Spiegel name

It struck me that if we could get away from Spiegel's me-too direction, capitalize on its strengths, and serve a new or overlooked market, we might be able to catalyze a turnaround. The question became, where do we find such a market?

We didn't look for it in the traditional way. Typically, companies develop a product or service and then search for a market. But I preferred an "outside-in" approach. We would identify a new market and then develop our product and services exclusively for that market.

At the time, a market was emerging that helped us implement this outside-in strategy. Women were entering the business and professional world in record numbers; they were better educated than previous generations, and they were acutely aware of social, business, and fashion issues. Television and other media fostered this awareness faster and more graphically than ever before.

I envisioned a different type of woman, one who had more to do than ever before and less time in which to do it. She would naturally search for a better way of shopping that would save her time, that would be convenient, and that would offer her the fashionable name brands that her job and lifestyle demanded.

The Dream Strategy

During the next few months, a plan emerged. Not only would we target this emerging market of working women, but we would offer them an upscale catalog that reflected their lifestyle.

It was a daring plan for a company that was on the verge of collapse and that had previously served a completely different market. In fact, few people inside or outside of Spiegel believed this plan had a chance of succeeding. Not only weren't there any upscale catalogs such as the one I'd conceived (the only possible exceptions being Horchow's and Neiman-Marcus, though they had a much narrower audience and product range), but my concept represented a 180-degree change of direction for Spiegel—from mass to class.

Yet I was convinced that my concept would work, and I set out to convince others. It was not a textbook strategy. Instead, my strategy was a dream set to numbers: a dream of a beautiful department store in print. I can't overemphasize the dream's importance to our success. Unlike a pure strategy, a dream isn't inflexible and tied to numbers. Too many good ideas get bogged down in financial priorities and strategic time frames. When the focus shifts from the core concept to return-on-investment and meeting quarterly goals, the concept is in trouble. I wanted to keep things flexible and flowing, to get people involved and excited. A dream would meet those objectives far better than a by-the-book strategy.

All this is not to say that we dispensed with budgets and time frames. I promised our owners I wouldn't ask for a major cash infusion or make out-of-the-ordinary expenditures. But to avoid the bottom-line mentality, we established less rigid "vital signs."

When I was a boy and told my mother I felt sick and couldn't go to school, she felt my forehead. If it wasn't too warm, she told me I was fine and to get dressed. Analogous vital signs were instituted for our business; they were barometers that gave us a sense of how a given action affected the business. Like a hand to the forehead, these barometers gave us a generalized, but generally accurate, reading of where the company was heading. My feeling was that if everything that was supposed to go up went up and everything that was supposed to go down went down, the bottom line would take care of itself.

Communicating the Dream

Before we did anything with the catalog, I wanted our people to understand and share the dream. To that end, I articulated it at every possible opportunity, in one-on-one discussions and to large groups of employees. I talked to them about how women were searching for a better way to shop, better quality goods, and identifiable brands. I explained how if we could provide those things and make it easier and faster to buy, we'd corner that market. Our goal, I preached, was to create a beautiful department store in print.

Typically, when new CEOs talk to employees about major change, people are terrified about not fitting in or even losing their jobs. But rather than scare people into changing, I insisted that not only would the changes be good for them, but that the coming years would be the most exciting time in their work lives.

I required the enthusiastic participation of all our people, and for that reason, I never confined my remarks to what I wanted them to do; I told them why. In many organizations, managers say they don't have time to explain why and just want to make sure the job gets done. My feeling was that unless people understood the why, their work, would never have the value that was crucial for the dream to materialize.

Evolutionary Instead of Revolutionary Change

From the beginning, we knew that everything had to change: the way the catalog looked; the merchandise; the procedures for shipping, handling and billing;

and the customers. But we also recognized that everything couldn't change at once. If we tried to go from mass to class overnight, we would go out of business. Our strategy, therefore, was to segue gradually from the old Spiegel to the new one. That way, we could buy ourselves time to acquire new customers without driving our old customers away all at once.

To that end, we had to transform our merchandise through a series of steps rather than in one fell swoop. One of the first steps was to establish guidelines for the types of products we wanted to eliminate and the types we wanted to acquire. For the latter, we established a relatively simple standard: Each product must be the type that would be carried by a beautiful department store. In terms of the former, purely utilitarian items we carried, such as mufflers and hot water heaters, had to go, despite the fact that such items accounted for about $60 million worth of our $250 million sales volume. Over time, we would replace these utilitarian items with merchandise that had some element of fashion—even appliances such as toasters and blenders wouldn't be allowed unless they were fashionable.

A Method to the Madness

To follow these guidelines without creating chaos, we needed to establish an orderly process for our buyers to follow, a process that would provide them with benchmarks for getting rid of utilitarian products and buying fashionable ones. The process that we developed was simple and effective.

We asked our buyers to pretend that they were acquiring merchandise for Marshall Field's department store, to determine the highest and lowest line in a category, and then to compare it to Spiegel's line. Typically, where Marshall Field's line started, Spiegel's ended. For instance, their low-end $19.95 blouse represented our top of the line.

We instructed our buyers not to go after Field's high-end merchandise. Not only was it doubtful that their high-end sources would sell to us, but, even if they did, our traditional customers wouldn't buy it, and word would spread throughout the industry of our failure with that line. We told our buyers to go after Marshall Field's low-end line, and it would become our high-end line. Once our buyers secured that, they could drop our lowest line in the category.

This process wasn't always easy. I remember how our buyers balked at eliminating a ladies stretch pants line that accounted for millions of dollars in sales. In that instance, we phased the line out by removing it from our big catalog and carrying it only in our sales catalog. It was painful to do even this, but it was absolutely essential to our dream strategy. If we hung on to unfashionable-but-profitable lines, our transition period would drag on indefinitely.

The Service of the Dream

The changes at Spiegel weren't limited to merchandise. We realized that it wasn't simply better products that our new customers were searching for, but a better way of shopping. Products were available in many places; it was the combination of product, service, and image that would differentiate us. For that reason, our strategy called for a number of new and improved services and image-related changes, including the following:

- **Offering customers 24-hour, toll-free ordering.** In 1976, toll-free ordering was still in its infancy. We were one of the first catalog companies to make it available to our customers, giving busy, professional women a more convenient way of shopping.

- **Bringing UPS in to deliver our merchandise.** Prior to 1976, United Parcel Service (UPS) was primarily a business-to-business alternative to the post office. Its biggest customer was General Motors (GM), delivering parts from factory to dealers. The delivery service's strength was its speed, and we required that speed in order to offer our customers a better way of shopping. After a few years, Spiegel became UPS' second biggest customer next to GM.

- **Improving customer service.** Rude and unhelpful customer service representatives were the rule rather than the exception in the mid-1970s. When people called to complain or ask if they could get their money back, service representatives would often treat them like criminals. We made compassionate, humanistic customer service a priority, adopting a no-questions-asked refund policy. In the following years, we were able to resolve over 80 percent of complaints or inquiries during the first call, an extremely high percentage.

- **Upgrading the "look" and "sound" of the catalog.** Like most catalogs at the time, Spiegel's projected an overhyped, unsophisticated image, illustrated in Exhibit 2.1. We extracted all the puffery from the book, creating the following copy guideline: "If it's devious, don't say it." Just as importantly, we stopped shooting merchandise and models in the studio with large cameras; the look was staged and antiseptic. We hired hot freelance photographers who used high-speed cameras, shooting on the steps of New York museums and other locations and capturing the natural lifestyle look we desired. An example of our final product is shown in Exhibit 2.2.

Exhibit 2-1 Page from a 1976 Spiegel Catalog

gabardine pantsuits
of woven, texturized Visa® polyester by Milliken

MILLS HY.

Suit also in Petite, Tall sizes

Suit also in Tall, Half sizes; Shirt also Larger

Photographed at the Mills Hyatt House, Charleston, S.C., a contemporary example of gracious Southern hospitality.

MANDARIN-COLLARED SUIT ties with sash. pants have zip fly. Visa® polyester gabardine. machine wash. Color: Blue. Miss. Irs. 7,8,9. 10,11,12,13,14,15,16,17,18. (2 lbs. 11 oz.)
A15 R 1641—State size **39.95**
PETITES(5'3" under) 5,6 to 15,16.
A15 R 1642—State size **39.95**
TALLS(5'7½" over) 10,12,14,16,18,20.
A15 R 1643—State size **41.95**

BOW-TIED BLOUSE of acetate/nylon jersey. Long cuffed sleeves. button front. Machine wash. Blue Multi. Bust 32,34,36,38 sq.
A15 R 1644—State size (13 oz.) **12.98**

BUCKLE-TRIMMED SHIRT-JAC SUIT with zip fly pants. Belt not incl. Visa® polyester gabardine. machine wash. Color: Rust Miss. Irs. 7,8,9. 10,11,12,13,14,15,16,17,18. (2 lbs. 11 oz.)
A15 R 1636—State size **39.95**
TALLS(5'7½" over) 10,12,14,16,18,20.
A15 R 1637 .... **41.95**
HALFS(5'4" under) 16½,18½,20½,22½,24½,26½.
A15 R 1638 .... **43.95**

STRIPED SHIRT in woven polyester crepe by Klopman. Machine wash, dry. Rust (13 oz.)
A15 R 1639—Bust 32,38 in. State size **12.98**
A15 R 1640—LARGER 40,42,44,46 in **13.98**

SPIEGEL • 21

Exhibit 2-2 Page from a Recent Spiegel Catalog

A. THE CARDIGAN. Placed cable stitch all around. Button front, shoulder pads, front pockets. Pistachio. Acrylic/wool. Dry clean. Imported.
Misses: S(4-6); M(8-10); L(12-14); XL(16).
A93 932 1046—State size letter.
(1 lb. 6 oz.) 98.00

B. THE CREWNECK. Sleeveless knit sweater in allover cable stitch; with rib trim at neck, armholes. Pistachio. Acrylic/wool. Dry clean. Imported.
Misses: S(4-6); M(8-10); L(12-14); XL(16).
A93 932 1047—State size letter. (14 oz.) 59.00

C. THE SKIRT. Cut long and slim with an elastic waist. Approx. length from natural waist 32½". Pistachio. Acrylic/wool/nylon/other fiber. Dry clean. Imported. (1 lb. 5 oz.)
Misses: S(4-6); M(8-10); L(12-14); XL(16).
A93 932 1048—State size letter. 98.00

D. THE TURTLENECK. Allover-placed cable stitch with a tunic silhouette. Shoulder pads. Pistachio. Acrylic/wool. Dry clean. Imported.
Misses: S(4-6); M(8-10); L(12-14); XL (16).
A93 932 1051—State size letter.
(1 lb. 5 oz.) 88.00

E. THE SKIRT. Cut shorter and slim. Approx. length from natural waist: 19". Elasticized waistband. Pistachio. Acrylic/wool/nylon/other fiber. Dry clean. Imported. (1 lb. 1 oz.)
Misses: S(4-6); M(8-10); L(12-14); XL(16).
A93 932 1052—State size letter. 88.00

F. STONE BRACELET. From Kate Hines. Marbleized ivory-colored stones are embellished with matte gold-tone metal. 7½" L.
N21 932 6472T—(6 oz.)† 65.00

G. BUTTON EARRING. From Kate Hines. Marbleized ivory color stones are encased in matte gold-tone detail. Clip style.
N21 932 6249T—(4 oz.)† 39.00

H. SACHA LONDON™ PLATFORM PUMP. Updated with a full ¾" platform bottom. Snipped toe and and slightly dipped sides. Nubuck leather upper; leather sole and padded insole. 3¼" heel. Available in full and half sizes. (1 lb. 14 oz.)
B(Medium): 6-10; 11.
W20 932 1712—Taupe. W20 932 1713—Black.
State color, size and B width. 115.00

J. SACHA LONDON™ LOW HEEL PLATFORM. U-shaped throat; snip toe. Nubuck leather upper; leather sole. Padded leather insole. ½" platform bottom; 1¼" heel. (1 lb. 14 oz.)
B(Medium): 6-10; 11.
W20 932 1715—Taupe. W20 932 1716—Black.
State color, size and B width. 105.00

K. OFF-SHOULDER SWEATER. Allover chunky cable stitch. Tunic shape with a rib knit cowl neck. Pistachio. Acrylic/wool. Dry clean. Imported. (2 lb. 9 oz.)
Misses: S(4-6); M(8-10); L(12-14); XL(16).
A93 932 1049—State size letter. 118.00

L. KNIT PANT. Slim legs taper to ankle. Pull on; elastic waistband. Pistachio. Acrylic/wool/nylon/other fiber. Dry clean. Imported. (1 lb. 4 oz.)
Misses: S(4-6); M(8-10); L(12-14); XL(16).
A93 932 1050—State size letter. 98.00

†Del. from mfr.; allow 14 days plus transit

theomiles

Reorganizing for Change

None of these changes could have taken place without a dramatically different organizational structure. Our traditional pyramid structure could not quickly and effectively deploy the dream strategy; the bureaucratic layers ensured that all decision-making power was at the top and that messages would be distorted as they passed from one layer to the next.

I decided to flatten the organization. Although a common practice today, this was an unusual move in the mid-1970s. It violated the common assumption that a CEO should not have more than three or four people reporting to him—an assumption I didn't share, especially if the CEO refrained from running everyone else's department. Very quickly, I created a structure in which there were only seven vice presidents, each directly linked to the manager level. All the senior supervisory positions between these two levels no longer existed.

Similarly, I pushed decision-making responsibility down to the lowest level where people had the necessary information to make decisions. My feeling was that everything happens at the manager level; managers and the people who work for them are the ones who get things done. It would be useless to have a grand dream at the top of the organization and be unable to translate that dream into appropriate tactics.

Though the term was not widely used back then, we were empowering our employees. For instance, Spiegel's planning meetings for the catalog used to consist only of vice presidents and managers. In our flattened organization, not only did buyers become involved in these meetings, but so did assistant buyers and advertising people.

This new structure facilitated all the innovations discussed previously. We were able to make major changes in the catalog because the right people were empowered to make those changes. In addition, our structure enabled us to change far more quickly than a company with multiple organizational layers would have done.

We made one very dramatic structural change relatively early on that was perceived as a major risk but was essential to our strategy. Spiegel's 200 order stores accounted for 40 percent of our business, but they had to be closed. I had worked long and hard to communicate my dream to everyone at Spiegel, and the order stores stood in the way of that dream.

For one thing, they symbolized the inconvenience and mass-merchandise approach we were attempting to jettison. Customers had to pick up their merchandise at order stores that were usually located in the worst section of town; credit was given freely and often ill-advisedly; the assembly operation for the stores was antiquated and costly.

Still, no one likes to lose 40 percent of their business, and some of my people worried that closing the stores could destroy the company. But I knew that as real as that risk was, we would also gain significant payroll and operational savings by closing the stores and reducing credit losses. As it turned out, we broke even during this massive restructuring that took two years to complete.

Selling the Customer Last

Changing people's perceptions is difficult. Despite all the changes we made—closing the order stores, upgrading the catalog, improving operations—we recognized that creating a new image for Spiegel would take time. We also realized that we couldn't simply convince customers that we had changed; first, we had to change the way other groups perceived Spiegel. We identified the following four groups:

- Employees
- Suppliers
- Media
- Customers

We targeted our own people first. We had to convince them we were serious about our dream strategy. If they thought we were all talk and no action, we'd never get anywhere. Dramatic moves like eliminating profitable but unfashionable lines certainly showed we were serious. But it was an event completely divorced from remaking the catalog that really changed our people's attitudes.

Spiegel used to be located in an old, decrepit, converted warehouse on the southwest side of Chicago. It was dirty, dusty, and lacked air conditioning. If any building represented mass rather than class, this was it. I decided we had to move.

After a search of the area, we found a wonderful building in Oakbrook (a suburb of Chicago) with surprisingly reasonable lease terms. When we moved, we told everyone that they could only take what they could carry; everything else should go in the trash and be replaced with new equipment and furnishings. We took six floors in the new building. No one had an office; I wanted an open, flowing floor plan that made everyone feel like a part of the company.

A few months after we moved in, I said to my personnel director, "It seems like we have a lot of new people around here."

He responded that we didn't.

"Well," I said, "they look different."

"They are different," he said. "They're working in a beautiful setting, they feel like dressing better when they come to work, they're smiling and happier. That's what's different."

The next group we targeted were suppliers. They were a tough nut to crack at first. With the old Spiegel, our buyers called upon tried-and-true sources and were warmly greeted by vice presidents. When they called on new sources who represented better lines, a sales representative would come out and brusquely inform the buyers that they didn't sell to catalog houses. We had to change their perceptions, and we created an effective, if somewhat unusual, tool for doing so.

That tool was a picture of a three-layer cake in the shape of the United States. Each layer represented a demographic slice of the country. Candles were placed on top of the cake, representing the locations of major department stores. Armed with this cake, buyers went into sources and made the following argument:

> You claim you want to reach the top layer of the cake, the highest demographic slice. But as you well know, department stores hit all three layers; their newspaper advertising reaches everyone in their area. Look at all the people you're missing. You can see by the location of the candles that there are huge sections of the country where these department stores aren't located. Not only does Spiegel reach those sections, but we target the top-third layer you say is your primary market.

This argument often secured the lowest-priced line from a better supplier. When that line sold well through our catalog, they gave us a slightly higher-priced one. Each move up was easier than the one before. Soon, the sources were bragging, "We got more business out of Spiegel than we did out of XYZ store, and I don't have to ship our merchandise to multiple locations when I deal with Spiegel." Word spread, and perceptions changed.

The third group was the media. Working with our public relations agency, we started with the trade media and moved on to the general media. We had a great story to tell them: the story of a catalog doing an unprecedented 180-degree shift. Each new designer we picked up was news, scores of stories were written about the shock of seeing a Liz Claiborne or Norma Kamali outfit in the Spiegel catalog.

After changing the way everyone else perceived Spiegel, we were ready for our customers. Only now would our message be credible. We were prepared to acquire new customers and convince them that a new Spiegel had been created to meet their needs. In eight years, we gradually let go of over 1.5 million customers while acquiring 2 million new ones. These new customers were professional, educated women looking for name brands and a better way to shop. Convincing these women that Spiegel offered them both was the result of numerous tactics.

First, we hired a new advertising agency. Our previous agency had a great deal of direct-marketing expertise, but they knew very little about image advertising. Our new agency was inexperienced with both direct marketing and catalogs, but they were savvy image marketers. After we educated them about our business, they did a terrific job of helping us put together a nontraditional ad campaign. It was nontraditional in a number of respects, including the following:

- **Choice of media.** We eschewed placements in magazines frequently used by catalog marketers such as *TV Guide* and *People* and chose more upscale publications, such as *Vogue* and *Better Homes & Gardens.*

- **Types of ads.** Rather than showing typical catalog items at sale prices, our ads created a distinct image designed to appeal to our new customers. If we showed a catalog item, we made sure it was a brand-name, highly fashionable one.

- **Unprecedented offers.** Response cards with the ads invited readers to return the cards and receive a catalog. That in and of itself wasn't unusual. What was unusual, and what startled the industry, is that we were asking customers to pay for the privilege of receiving a catalog. Our reasoning was that you get what you pay for. If something costs nothing, that's the value people place on it.

Besides advertising, we were doing sophisticated database marketing in order to create a mailing list that reflected the demographics and psychographics of our new customers. We were also doing everything possible to retain customers once their perceptions about Spiegel had changed.

For instance, our service representatives overwhelmed customers with kindness and compassion. We instituted a policy that made it extraordinarily easy for customers to return unwanted merchandise. Our critics thought we had lost our minds; making it easy to return merchandise seemed like financial suicide, sure to boost an already high return rate. But while the rate did rise, so did customer loyalty. Just as important, our customers weren't left with Spiegel merchandise they didn't want. If such merchandise was in their homes, every glimpse of the unwanted product would remind them of how much they resented Spiegel.

Over the years, we launched a number of highly successful customer loyalty programs. One year for Christmas, we sent our 20,000 best customers a cookbook by a famous chef (which cost $30 at most stores). Though the program didn't raise the average customer purchase, it more than satisfied our customers, as one letter I received attests: "I was so thrilled to get that beautiful book. I have been shopping at XYZ store for years, and they've never even said so much as thank you."

Completing the Turnaround

By 1987, we were a $1 billion company, light years removed from the near-bankrupt $250 million organization we had been in 1976. Not only had we turned an unprofessional, me-too, utilitarian catalog into the most beautiful one on the market, we had also changed the assumptions and rules of the catalog business. The flood of specialized catalogs that appeared in our wake—and the demise of Ward's and Sears' catalogs, as well as others that took a "be all things to all people" approach—demonstrated the effectiveness of our dream strategy.

That strategy encompassed many tactics that I've only touched upon or neglected entirely because of space restrictions. I would be remiss, however, if I didn't note the following aspects of our dream strategy:

- **Total-look pages.** Catalogs used to plunk merchandise down on a page almost indiscriminately, the sole criteria being the category of merchandise designated for a given page. We moved away from this approach toward a "total look," one that graphically integrated a variety of products based on lifestyle. Instead of simply focusing a shot on a bed we were selling, we'd show and sell the nightstand, lamp, wall hanging, and everything else that went with the lifestyle look of the bed.

- **The pace of change.** Some of our people wanted to remake the catalog and its customer base overnight. Others wanted to move at a snail's pace. I set the speed of change between those extremes and insisted that everyone move together. It would do us no good if one buyer was purchasing top-of-the-line merchandise while another kept buying from old Spiegel sources. Our forward movement had to be synchronized, and I was continually urging some people to speed up and others to slow down so that we'd arrive at our goal together.

- **Inspirational, enthusiastic leadership.** I sold my people the dream with evangelical fervor. As odd as it might sound, that was a critical part of my leadership strategy. It was absolutely essential that everyone in the organization believe in the Spiegel I envisioned. We would never be able to convince others that Spiegel had changed unless we first convinced ourselves. For that reason, I preached my vision of the future constantly and passionately to individuals as well as large groups. I made it my business to explain why and how the mass-to-class strategy would work.

One last point about our turnaround: It was not the perfectly smooth process it might seem. There were bumps in the road. When we installed a state-of-the-art, computerized order-processing system, glitches in that system cut our profits to the bone. A catalog company without a working order-processing system is a company in serious trouble. But we didn't panic or look for scapegoats. Instead, we renewed our faith in the dream strategy, recognizing that the glitches in the computer system did not represent a flaw in the strategy, and that sooner or later we'd be back on course.

The Future

Since I left Spiegel, it has continued to grow in new and mostly positive directions. The catalog business and associated strategies have changed significantly from when I took over. Most significantly, the Spiegel strategy is now the rule rather than the exception. Specialized catalogs for affluent, niche markets are everywhere.

In fact, there's a glut of these catalogs. People who fit certain demographic and psychographic profiles are on lists that many catalog companies purchase. Not only are these people inundated with catalogs, they often are inundated inappropriately: For instance, the person who lives in a townhouse receives a gardening catalog.

It's time for the industry to confront this problem. One solution might be including a postage-paid return card with every catalog, allowing the recipient to state if he or she wants to continue receiving the book. The prospect of lowering an already low response rate might frighten some catalog marketers. But it is preferable to the current catalog glut we've created (not to mention the ecological harm of overproducing catalogs). Our best customers are the ones who are receiving the most catalogs, and they're getting fed up.

It is time for someone to come up with a new strategy—a strategy that takes the customer's point of view into consideration. The company with the courage to replace its me-too strategy with a dream will be the one that breaks from the pack and sets the pace for catalog marketers in the 1990s.

Bob Stone's

Bob Stone's
Commentary

The Spiegel story will probably be used as a classic case study for marketing students for decades to come.

In the 1980s, the American business community watched with horror as powerful giants (IBM, Chrysler, General Motors, and others of their ilk) were toppled from their mountaintops, heading for an abyss fraught with the danger of extinction.

Economists and industry experts predicted the demise of Chrysler with certainty. They only disagreed on how long it could survive. But then Lee Iococca stepped forward, and, as they say, the rest is history.

So it was in the catalog industry. Of the falling giants in that industry—Montgomery Ward, Sears, and Spiegel—Spiegel was by far the weakest. There was no doubt in hardly anyone's mind that the company was history. But then Henry Johnson stepped in. He had a dream, a vision, a determination that turned a terminally ill patient into a new person who was vibrant, healthy, and profitable.

The lesson to be learned from the Iococcas and Johnsons of American business is that one person, no matter how large the company, can make the *big* difference. A vision or a dream, coupled with strong leadership, overcomes seemingly impossible odds.

The strategies Johnson employed to make his dream a reality can be applied to any business.

- Identify your strengths.

- Identify new markets, and products and services exclusively for those markets.

- Don't let financial priorities and strategic time frames kill dream concepts.

- Institute vital signs as a barometer to get a sense of how a given action impacts your business.

- Share your dream with your employees. Show how the dream will be good for them.

- Revolutionary plans should be evolutionary. Segue gradually from the old to the new.

- Differentiate yourself from your competition with the right combination of product, service, and image.

- Eliminate bureaucratic layers of decision-making power from the top; push decision-making responsibility to the lowest manager level where people have the necessary information to make decisions.

- Have the courage to eliminate major marketing channels if they are in conflict with your dream concept.

- Before you can sell your prospect and customer on a new concept, you must first sell your employees, suppliers, and the media.

- When you provide a clean, attractive environment, employees dress better, smile more, and feel better about themselves.

- The best way to convince new suppliers to accept you is to demonstrate your ability to reach markets they are not currently reaching.

- New concepts make news. Tell your story to your trade press and to the media that reach your markets.

- Know the demographics and psychographics of your customer base.

- Make it easy for your customers to order and return your products or services.

- Create customer loyalty by treating customers in a special way.

- If you are selling merchandise via a catalog, give your pages a "total look," one that graphically integrates a variety of products based upon a specific lifestyle.

- Manage the pace of change. Don't move too fast or too slow.

- To convince others that change is good for them, we must first convince ourselves that change is good for us.

CHAPTER

3

Strategies That Made Us Successful
Stone & Adler

Bob Stone, Chairman Emeritus, Stone & Adler, Inc.

*B*ob Stone is a member of the Direct Marketing Association (DMA) Hall of Fame. He is an eight-time winner of the DMA's Best of Industry Award and has received two Gold Echo awards, as well as numerous other industry awards. Stone has spent 12 years as a professor of direct marketing. He is the author of Successful Direct Marketing Methods, *now in its fifth edition, and* Successful Telemarketing, *now in its second edition.*

"The time is ripe," said Aaron Adler, "to start a full-service direct-marketing agency in the Midwest." With these prophetic words (the year was 1966) the decision was made to go into business together.

This wasn't a spur-of-the-moment decision. Aaron and I had become acquainted through direct-marketing circles in Chicago. We shared a passion for direct marketing and lunched often at the M&M Club in the Merchandise Mart, sharing our dreams of a future that we felt was full of promise and opportunities.

In 1966, Aaron Adler was a partner in a medium-sized advertising agency by the name of Gourfain, Loeff & Adler. He was the direct-marketing arm of the agency. I was president of National Communications Corporation, a firm I founded to sell sales training material to business firms. A second mission was to take on direct-marketing accounts.

In assessing what each of us could contribute, we felt that together we could provide our new agency with an impressive array of accounts. Aaron could bring Central Security Insurance Co.; American Oil Company; Americana, an encyclopedia company; and Sloan-Ashland, America's most successful syndicator of merchandise at the time, among others. I, on the other hand, could bring in at least two accounts: Sunset House in Los Angeles, a catalog firm that sold low-cost gadgets to millions of consumers, and Baldwin Cooke Co., which sold desk diaries and atlases to business firms for gift-giving.

Melding Our Experiences and Talents

There probably never were two partners with more diverse personalities. Aaron was shy and humble; I was described as gregarious. Aaron was a merchant in the true sense, a genius in selecting mail-order merchandise; I had little feel for this activity. Aaron had a number of years' experience in the advertising agency business; I had none. While Aaron's forte was merchandise, mine was business-to-business direct marketing.

Aaron wasn't well known nationally; I was well known because of the many speeches I had made before direct-mail clubs around the country. Also, I had served on the board of the Direct Mail Advertising Association and had written a book titled *Successful Direct Mail Advertising and Selling,* which went through eight printings. If it was true that opposites attract, we couldn't miss. We certainly complemented each other.

The Strategy that Made Stone & Adler a Reality

Having made the big decision to get married, so to speak, all that remained was to draw up the papers. A snap, we thought. But such was not the case.

The question before us was, considering the business each was to bring into the new agency, what amount should each party invest? Our respective accountants couldn't agree; Aaron and I couldn't agree either. We had reached an impasse that could have been a deal breaker.

We wanted to get married, but we couldn't work out a prenuptial agreement. What was needed, I felt, was an agreement that would filter every dime of profits on Aaron's accounts to Aaron and every dime of profits on my accounts to me. That way neither of us would come up on the short end.

I went through a long gestation period, often necessary for developing a sound strategy. But one day the bell rang loud and clear. Suppose we set up our respective accounts as Stone & Adler (S&A) accounts, but pay 100 percent of the profits from designated accounts to each partner as earned. This arrangement would continue as long as those accounts remained with the agency. The contract would further stipulate that, from day one, income from all new accounts would accrue to the agency. I presented the plan to Aaron, and we were in business.

Advantages Inherent in the Strategy

Now we had a complete plan that offered the following advantages to both of us:

1. Neither of us had to invest to compensate for the other's accounts.

2. Since both of us would have our own sources of income going in, neither of us would have to draw a salary from the fledgling agency at the outset.

3. We didn't have to rent new space or buy office furniture. The fact that I had an office for National Communications Corp. enabled me to propose that we start the new agency on those premises. I also had all the office furniture and typewriters we would need, so I threw furniture and equipment in as part of the deal.

These strategies practically eliminated the need for substantial investment. It's laughable today, but our total investment was $500.00 each, and that was the last investment either of us ever made.

Strategies for the Agency Launch

We used the intervening weeks between our decision to go for it and our launch date (December, 1, 1966) to develop our strategies for positioning the agency.

Fees and Client Duration

Back in 1966, most startup direct-marketing agencies were willing to take on new accounts on a "try-us" basis. They'd do a mailing package at a set price just to get a foot in the door. Aaron and I decided such offers showed weakness, a lack of confidence in their abilities and a deterrent to long-term relationships.

Instead we opted for a $1,000-a-month retainer fee and a 12-month contract that gave either party the right to cancel at the end of six months. Time would be charged on an hourly basis, and if the billable hours equated to more than $1,000, the client would be billed for the difference.

Did this gutsy approach meet resistance at the time? Yes, but we stuck to our guns, actually turning down one-time assignments from two potentially juicy accounts, Fingerhut and General Electric.

Aaron and I were determined to distance ourselves from the others. We had case histories to prove our track record. Combined, we had experience in both consumer and business-to-business direct marketing. We could show examples of our work in direct mail, catalogs, radio, and television. We presented ourselves as a full-service agency at all times.

Looking back at our strong stand later, we had to say we did it with mirrors. But the bottom line was that the strategy worked.

Startup Personnel

While the two unpaid principals were to be the backbone of S&A, we couldn't do everything by ourselves. A support staff had to be put in place before we could start.

Aaron and I both needed a secretary. Aaron brought his with him, and I pressed my long-time secretary into service. Aaron also brought a production manager and an account executive with him, and I pressed my bookkeeper into service. Our total staff was seven people.

We did not opt for an art director. Our rationale was that art needs would be sporadic at the outset, so why pay an art director to sit around? Instead, we used several outstanding art studios.

Publicity

Our agency was now in place. Unfortunately, only we knew that. We had to get the word out. Not having a budget for paid advertising, we resorted to a news release. *Advertising Age* and *Direct Marketing Magazine,* among others, gave us the needed publicity.

The First One Hundred Days

Stone & Adler came off the launching pad at a speed that led us to believe we might indeed realize our dreams within our lifetime. Within days, we acquired our first new account—WinCraft of Winona, Minnesota. The company sold fundraising items to high schools via a catalog. (Fifteen years later, it was still on our client roster.) Our second account was Amsterdam Printing and Lithograph Co. of Amsterdam, New York. They sold printed specialties to business firms.

An event that shouldn't go unmentioned is the issuance of our first operating statement. It showed that we made $125.00 the first month. Our $1,000 investment was still intact!

After we acquired the Amsterdam Printing account, we decided we needed a second account executive. We hired Jim Kobs, a young man I knew at *Success Unlimited* magazine. This motivational magazine was published by W. Clement Stone, the insurance tycoon and prime advocate of positive mental attitude (PMA). Jim was making $8,000 a year at the time; We offered him $11,000. He joined S&A and brought his PMA with him.

Our limited staff shared in every account win. Each victory called for popping a bottle of champagne. But accounts were coming so fast that I called a halt to passing around the bubbly, fearing that we'd all end up as alcoholics.

By the end of the first 100 days, we had won seven new accounts. By the end of the first year, we had a before-tax profit of $25,000.00. We were well on our way to becoming a force in the exciting world of direct marketing. And Aaron and I started to draw a modest salary.

Strategies for Building an Authority Image

Although we were in a frequent state of euphoria over our early success, we didn't delude ourselves into thinking S&A had become a household word. Our goal down the line was to establish our agency as a prime authority for the direct-marketing discipline. The problem before us was, how do you create such an image?

We brainstormed the problem and came up with five concrete strategies:

1. Develop a "hit list" of desirable prospects and send them an informative newsletter each month.

2. Become active members of the Chicago Association of Direct Marketing (CADM): Serve on committees, help build the club, attend monthly meetings without exception, and network with potential clients.

3. Attend all national DMA conventions: Get speaking slots for our key people and network with fellow registrants.

4. Get on the speakers' circuit of direct-marketing clubs around the country.

5. Become the direct-marketing authority for *Advertising Age,* the leading advertising and marketing journal in the country.

We were sure strategies one through four were doable, but the real plumb would be accomplishing strategy five. *Advertising Age's* imprimatur could boost our image a hundredfold.

As luck would have it, I had had lunch with Sid Bernstein, publisher of the magazine, just a few weeks previously. At the time, Sid wasn't too happy with the coverage of direct marketing in his publication. So I knew the door was open at least a crack.

In preparation for my approach to Sid Bernstein, I developed a list of 52 article titles and one complete article exemplifying what I could provide. Sid approved, and the column started a life of its own.

The first column appeared in the fall of 1967. Favorable letters to the editor indicated we had struck a chord. Subsequent articles appeared every other week for a number of years, later dropping to once a month. The final of over 200 articles appeared in the April 9, 1984, issue of *Advertising Age.*

My editorial goal throughout the series was twofold: (1) to cater to the information needs of established direct marketers, and (2) to inform nontraditional direct marketers about the opportunities in direct marketing. From an agency standpoint, the second goal was more important than the first. We considered nontraditional direct marketers to be an untapped gold mine.

There's no way I can put a dollar figure on the value of the magazine series. However, I have no doubt that we achieved our goal to build an authority image.

As for attracting major nontraditional marketers, I can't document the influence of the column, but by the second year of publication, we acquired four such major accounts: Polaroid, United Airlines, Allstate Insurance, and Hewlett-Packard.

Of the four, Hewlett-Packard (H-P) was the most exciting. Company representatives came to us with a secret Product X. Before they would reveal their invention, we had to sign a nondisclosure form. The invention was the first-ever scientific pocket calculator. Its proposed selling price was $399.95.

Stone & Adler was invited to make a presentation at H-P headquarters in California in competition with four major agencies. Jim Kobs and I presented before a core of H-P executives, including Bill Hewlett, the brilliant president and engineer. When Jim and I got back to Chicago, there was a sign on my office door. It read: "We've got the Hewlett-Packard account!"

Looking back on this big win, I'm convinced that it was the creative genius of Aaron Adler that won the account. The sample mailing package that Aaron did for our presentation contained a pop-up. When the mailing package was opened, a replica of the pocket calculator opened to the exact size and dimension of the product being offered. I can still see Bill Hewlett, the consummate engineer, taking the gadget in and out of his shirt pocket throughout the presentation.

Our campaign for H-P went over like gangbusters. One of our inquiry ads converted to $40,000 in sales for each 1,000 inquiries. But innovative direct-mail packages, especially those carrying Aaron's pop-up, were the work horses. If memory serves, by the third year, H-P was doing close to $100 million in calculator sales: all by direct marketing.

Lightning Strikes Twice

The authority image, built through the editorial pages of *Advertising Age,* gave us enough favorable exposure to gain a national reputation. But our good luck continued.

Sid Bernstein called me one day out of the blue and said he'd like to talk to me about the Crain Books division. Sid wanted to know if I'd be interested in writing a book on direct marketing for them. Interested? You bet!

At the time there were several good books in print on the subject of direct mail, as well as a number of mail-order books. However, none were devoted to direct marketing as a whole. I felt Sid had a great idea; I signed a contract immediately. A book on the totality of direct marketing had the potential of greatly enhancing the authority and image of Stone & Adler.

It took me 14 months to write the book, which we titled *Successful Direct Marketing Methods.* Stone & Adler prepared a mailing package and double-spread ad which went to 60,000 *Advertising Age* readers. Results for both were way above expectations. The first printing in 1973 sold out in weeks.

Over the next 20 years, four more editions were published, each updating the previous edition. Since the first edition, the book has been translated into

Japanese, French, German, Italian, Spanish, Portuguese, and Swedish. Approximately 200,000 copies are in print in the United States, and the book is the prescribed text in over 100 colleges and universities.

Care and Feeding of the Stone & Adler Staff

I believe it was Fairfax Cone of Foote, Cone & Belding who first said, "The advertising business is the only business in the world in which all of your major assets go down in the elevator each night." What a truism. Without our talent pool, we wouldn't have clients.

By 1969, we had a staff of close to 40 people. Direct marketing was growing by leaps and bounds, and there was more need for talent then there was talent. Top S&A talent was being wooed by competition. Loss of quality talent presaged regression rather than expansion.

Determined to avoid a possible calamity, we came up with the following seven strategies, all of which were executed.

1. **Establish an "Aaron Adler Award."** Among those most sought after by our competition were our creative people. All of our creative people were trained and nurtured by Aaron. We wanted them to know we cherished their talent.

   In recognition, we set up a cash-award program for best creative work by a team as well as awards for outstanding creativity by individual artists and writers. The "Aaron Adler Award" plaque became a centerpiece for our reception room.

2. **Establish profit-sharing and bonus plans for all employees.** Stone & Adler contributed 15 percent of salary after one year of employment to all eligible employees. A bonus pool was put into the hands of each department head at year's end. Amounts distributed were at each department head's discretion, based on his or her evaluation of each employee's performance.

3. **Make stock available to key people, people we wouldn't want to lose under any circumstances.** Aaron and I decided upon three "must-keep" people: Jim Kobs, Don Kanter, and John Machella. Each was offered treasury stock at book value which could be paid for over time.

4. **Develop an annual weekend off-site retreat dedicated to creativity.** All account supervisors, account executives, creative people, and art and production people were invited to participate in a cre-

ative workshop at Harrison House, a seminar center in a northern Chicago suburb. A chairman was selected to develop the program, and lectures were given by industry leaders and a number of S&A top performers.

But the big excitement grew out of competition between S&A teams charged with solving a client problem. Although evenings were designated as leisure time, many teams used the allotted time to sharpen their presentations. Competition was intense.

The payoffs of the retreats were scores of new creative ideas and pride in being an S&A staff member. The creative workshop became the event of each year.

5. **Form an executive committee to deal with the big issues.** At this point in our growth, it became obvious that Aaron and I should no longer be the sole decisionmakers; we had to bring more brain power to the decision-making process. Our answer was to form an executive committee consisting of Jim Kobs, Don Kanter, John Meccalla, Aaron, and myself.

We met monthly, attacking such problems as profit ratios by accounts, salary levels, personnel evaluations, new business opportunities, equipment needs, and so forth. Each meeting closed with a "to-do" list, a designated person assigned to each task, and a due date for the task's completion.

6. **Bring the rank-and-file employees into the loop.** We felt we had the answers to giving recognition to and getting involvement from our top people. But we were doing a lousy job of bringing the rank and file into the loop. We weren't tuning them into the excitement of S&A.

To fill the void we started an agency newsletter. It reported birthdays, company anniversaries, new hires, awards, account wins, company outings, everything that was going on.

The house organ did its job. But I determined that a one-on-one relationship was necessary to create a closeness second to no other agency. So I hosted a series of dinners in a private room at the M&M Club where it all started for Aaron and me. The agendas were carefully structured and followed some basic rules: Invite no more than eight people at a time; mix the guest list so that no more than two executives appear at any one dinner, the balance being rank and file; make no speeches, just talk about current events at the agency (good and bad); invite questions; answer all questions frankly; trade jokes; and maintain a social dinner atmosphere.

As I look back on the one-on-one dinners, I must conclude that they brought a better understanding and appreciation of each other than anything we had ever done. The thank-you notes received after each dinner made it all worthwhile.

7. **Develop an in-house training program.** Strategies one through six were designed to help keep the people we had. But, in spite of the strategies, we knew we'd lose some, and if we were to continue to grow, we'd need more. So where would these people come from? We decided to grow our own.

A direct-marketing course was announced. Anyone in the agency from office boy on up, was eligible to enroll. Classes would be held one evening a week, and instructors would be top agency personnel.

The course paid off in a big way. One secretary became a writer. Another secretary became a traffic person. A bookkeeper became a production assistant. Several assistant account executives became full-fledged account executives.

Care and Feeding of Stone & Adler Clients

If you don't have a happy, competent staff, you can't grow. And if you don't have a happy, satisfied client list, you can't survive. The two go hand in hand.

The proper care and feeding of a client list is an imperative. Stone & Adler developed a number of strategies that seemed to keep most of our clients happy most of the time.

Assigning the Right Account Team

Chemistry, we found, plays a major role in keeping clients happy. A good relationship develops only when members of the agency team match well with counterparts on the client team. Our dictum was: If poor chemistry exists between an agency person and the client counterpart, remove the agency person and introduce a new one.

Being Proactive Rather than Reactive

We drilled our account teams on the necessity of being proactive at all times. In order to do this, they had to constantly come up with a stream of new ideas, new directions for the client to pursue. A reactive stance would relegate the agency to the status of a boutique, getting assignments only at the client's discretion.

Pursuing Monthly Structured Meetings

While account executives were in almost daily phone contact with their clients, the key to growing an account was a scheduled formal meeting each month, complete with an agreed-upon agenda. Part of every meeting was a review of current campaign results and creative presentations for new campaigns. (It was rare to return to the office without any new assignments.) Within 48 hours after each meeting, a detailed report was on the client's desk.

Staying Out of Client Politics

Relationships between agency and client personnel often grow to social friendships. That's good on the surface, but there's a real danger too. The danger is that the client friend may share his company's political problems with his agency friend, asking for support. Our policy at S&A was firm: *Don't get involved in client politics.* The reason behind the policy was simple: If the client friend lost his or her job, chances were the agency would lose the account.

Recognizing Clients in a Special Way

One of the best ideas we ever came up with in pursuit of client happiness was an annual client party at the site of the annual DMA convention.

Most of our competitors, who likewise had parties, invited prospects whom they would like to serve. We wanted to be different, so we established a policy of clients only from the outset.

We'd carefully select a five-star restaurant away from the convention hotel. The food and drink were the best; entertainment was lively; and there were no speakers, just conviviality.

The effect was magical. An Allstate executive sitting next to an American Oil executive, a Hewlett-Packard marketing executive chatting with a United Airlines marketing executive. All tables were peopled by clients and agency personnel. The net effect was that our clients were selling each other on our agency. Each guest left impressed with the assemblage.

Branching Out

Our growth continued right through 1970. But we were still a Midwest agency; we had no presence in New York City. Admittedly, we were no match for Wunderman, Ricotta & Kline, the largest direct-marketing agency in the world, which was recently acquired by Young & Rubicam. Ogilvy & Mather Direct wasn't far behind.

We had a decision to make. Should we start a New York office from scratch, or should we explore a merger with an existing New York direct-marketing agency? We opted for the latter alternative.

After reviewing existing independent direct-marketing agencies in the Big Apple, we identified Rapp & Collins as the logical merger candidate. I knew Stan Rapp and Tom Collins well. Stan was a brilliant strategist with a creative background; Tom was a renowned copywriter. Rapp & Collins had several gilt-edged accounts; there were no client conflicts between us.

We invited Stan and Tom to have dinner with us in Chicago and told them of our desire for a New York presence. To our surprise, they told us of their desire for a Chicago presence. The chemistry between us was great. We agreed to exchange balance sheets.

A balance sheet comparison showed that S&A was far more profitable at the time. The disparity in profits was explained by the fact that Stan and Tom, who originally started the direct-marketing operation at Foote, Cone & Belding, had purchased the franchise in order to form Rapp & Collins. Paying off the purchase cut deeply into profits.

So if stock was exchanged in the new corporation—Rapp, Collins, Stone & Adler (RCS&A)—in ratio to balance sheet figures, Aaron and I would end up with far more stock. Understandably, this wasn't acceptable to Stan and Tom.

The solution to the problem came to me like a thunderbolt: Use the identical strategy that brought Aaron and me together in 1969. Rapp & Collins would keep all income from their existing accounts, and S&A would do likewise. From day one, all new accounts would accrue to the new agency. It was a deal.

The launch date for the new agency was set for October 1, 1971. The four principals met to map out strategies for the launch. We agreed unanimously that we should announce the formation with a flourish. The decision was made to prepare a full-page ad to appear in the September 8, 1971, issues of both the *New York Times* and the *Chicago Tribune.* The banner headline of the ad read:

Announcing a new force in direct marketing advertising for the 1970s

The subhead read:

Rapp & Collins, Inc., New York, and Stone & Adler, Inc., Chicago,
are joining hands to form a new advertising agency:
RAPP, COLLINS, STONE & ADLER, INC.
Effective October 1, 1971

Body copy spoke of the opportunities and growth of direct marketing as well as the combined strengths of the two agencies, and the officers of RCS&A were listed as follows:

> Bob Stone, Chairman; Stan Rapp, President; Aaron Adler, Executive Vice President (Chicago); Thomas F. Collins, Executive Vice President (New York)

The ad closed with the complete client lists of both Rapp & Collins and Stone & Adler.

The announcement ad, plus our joint appearance at the national DMA convention the same month, resulted in leads from 14 prospects, an incredible number for a one-month period. The very first account signed by the new agency was *Psychology Today,* a hot magazine at the time. The second account was Old American Insurance Co. of Kansas City.

Mergermania Starts Up

Rapp, Collins, Stone & Adler became a force in a short period of time. The quasi-merger of the two agencies was in the forefront of a growing trend toward major general agencies acquiring direct-marketing agencies. We were among those being pursued.

Of those pursuing, Doyle, Dane, Bernbach showed the most interest. There were no client conflicts between them and our New York accounts, but such was not the case with our Chicago accounts. There were three conflicts, one of which was United Airlines, our largest Chicago account.

I wish that I could say we came up with a great strategy to solve the problem. We didn't. So in the fall of 1975, the four principals, who had become good friends, made a practical business decision. Rapp & Collins would be acquired by Doyle, Dane, Bernbach; Stone & Adler would return to being an independent.

Mergermania Heats Up

Even though S&A lost a New York presence, there was no loss of accounts. Direct marketing had entered a golden era, and S&A was riding the waves. Mergermania was heating up. General agencies continued to acquire direct-marketing agencies. Stone & Adler stood out as one of the largest still independently owned.

By 1978, Aaron was 64 years old, and I was 60. Stone & Adler accounted for the major portions of our estates. If either or both of us went to that big direct-marketing agency in the sky, our beneficiaries would have hell to pay. Jointly, we decided to listen to our pursuers.

Over the course of several months, we heard from seven of the top ten general agencies. The strategy we took with each agency was to state a non-negotiable price up front. The price was based upon an extremely high earnings multiple.

One could make a case that this approach was risky, even foolish. But I was counting on two factors: (1) S&A's reputation, and (2) the almost frantic determination of major agencies to own reputable direct-marketing agencies. I lucked out. No one quibbled over the price.

A late entry in the derby was Young & Rubicam (Y&R). This came about as a result of a phone call from Lester Wunderman, chairman of Wunderman Ricotta & Kline, who was a member of the Y&R board. Les told me that the board was interested in acquiring a direct-marketing agency in the Midwest. He wanted to know if S&A might be interested.

I told Les his call was timely since we were talking to a number of agencies. Furthermore, I told him I was scheduled to be in New York the very next day. Les arranged for me to meet with Jim Mortensen, a member of the Y&R executive committee.

At the meeting I presented the S&A financials and clearly stated our non-negotiable selling price. Jim told me he'd visit us in Chicago within two weeks with a proposition in hand.

True to his word, Jim Mortensen came to Chicago with a specific proposal. Young & Rubicam offered stock at book value equal to our stipulated selling price. Stock would be redeemed for cash in two years for Aaron and in five years for me. Aaron and I would both get employment contracts for durations equal to our pay-out dates.

Advantages of the Proposal

Comparison of the Y&R proposal with others we had on the table clearly indicated that the Y&R proposal was to our best interest for the following reasons:

1. Young & Rubicam had owned a direct-marketing agency for five years. Therefore, they had a far superior knowledge of how direct marketing fits into the total marketing mix than did other members of the big ten.

2. Because Y&R was the biggest advertising agency in the country, S&A would benefit from its prestige.

3. All Y&R stock was employee owned. Value per share was at book value. If Y&R earnings continued to compound at 15 percent a year, the value of each share would practically double at the end of five years.

4. Stone & Adler would now have access to all Y&R training programs, reputed to be the best in the field.

5. Stone & Adler would now have access to a superb media department and a 45-person research department.

6. Stone & Adler would have an array of new business opportunities with Y&R accounts.

The advantages of going with Y&R were overriding. A deal was made. The merger date was set for December 1, 1978, exactly 12 years from the day Aaron and I had opened our humble office on North Clark Street in Chicago. To paraphrase a cigarette ad of the time—"We'd come a long way, baby!"

The Young & Rubicam Experience

Young & Rubicam brought us into a culture we had not known before. It was my good fortune to be appointed to the Y&R U.S.A. Board of Directors. There I learned firsthand the inner workings of a major advertising agency. It was a learning experience just to observe Alex Kroll, the Y&R president, perform as chairman of the board.

The S&A staff, back in Chicago, were moved quickly into the new culture. They were introduced to new systems, new procedures, and new disciplines: business plans, budgeting, mission statements, media and creative work plans, brand-personality statements, "stopping power" procedures, and strategy-selection outlines. In short, a whole new world.

Stone & Adler benefitted tremendously from the Y&R training programs. The jewel was the Y&R Creative Workshop, an intensive six-week program staffed by top-ranking Y&R personnel. We enrolled the one person each year who we considered to be superstar material. The learning curve of each enrollee was dramatic.

There's a saying that when you are acquired by a big corporation, you shake hands with the CEO the day the deal is signed and never see him again. Such was not the case with Edward N. Ney, the Y&R chairman. Ed Ney was the epitome of what a CEO should be—handsome, personable, caring, perceptive, inspirational, and decisive. Ed made it a point to visit Y&R's 27 worldwide offices on a regular basis. His visits to S&A were regarded as career highlights by many of our people. Unlike so many CEOs who are inaccessible, Ed always took my phone calls, always put his prestige on the line to help solve my problems.

The Payoff

The Y&R experience was great, but the true measure of its success was our bottom line. Before being acquired, our capitalized billing was at $24 million annually. Three years later, it had reached $78 million.

By the end of 1981, our profits exceeded $1 million for the first time in our 15-year history. One year later, our profits exceeded $2 million, all of which goes to prove that the second million is easier to make than the first.

It would be logical to assume that our dramatic growth was due primarily to business we got from Y&R accounts, but such was not the case. Most new business from Y&R accounts went to Wunderman in New York, where most new business opportunities arose. So an advantage we had anticipated really didn't materialize.

But an advantage we didn't anticipate came to the fore. The unexpected advantage was the dynamics of a well-established principle: *Big attracts big.*

Stone & Adler had a number of Fortune 500 accounts, but we certainly didn't have the biggest of the big. The two biggest, which we coveted, were AT&T and Sears. Our strategy was to present ourselves as an integral part of Y&R, the country's largest advertising agency. We got both accounts; big attracted big.

A Fond Farewell

On December 31st, 1983, I relinquished my chair at Stone & Adler, closing out 17 years of strategies, chills, and thrills. I left with a plan for the rest of my life: teach and write.

I'm happy teaching in the professional direct-marketing program at the University of Missouri and having taught in the master's program at Northwestern University. In between I serve on several boards and put on seminars in the United States, Europe, and South America. I've revised two of my books, and I'm working on another. Aaron was so right. The time was ripe to start a full-service direct-marketing agency in the Midwest!

Bob Stone's
Commentary

This commentary gives me an opportunity to set the record straight. In no way was I the sole architect of the strategies that built the business of Stone & Adler. Tremendous credit must be given to Aaron Adler; our executive committee; our account groups; and our production, media, art, and financial groups. Strategic planning and execution was a team effort.

Having said this, I take pleasure in recounting the strategies that built the business.

☐ Timing is a key factor in business success. Good timing involves discovering a void in the marketplace and structuring to fulfill the identified need.

☐ If you're starting a new business, seek a partner who complements your talents and experience rather than one who is a mirror of yourself.

☐ When you enter into a partnership make sure both sides win.

☐ If you are convinced that you have more to offer than your competition, set prices and terms that are consistent with your perceived value.

☐ If you can't afford to advertise your new business at the outset, resort to news releases in publications that serve your target market.

☐ Newsletters to desirable markets convey authority.

☐ To gain recognition in your industry, participate actively in local clubs and national trade associations.

☐ Your authority image will be enhanced if you and selected associates deliver speeches before clubs and conventions.

- [ ] The ultimate in establishing an authority image is to write a book or to be a regular contributor to an industry trade publication.

- [ ] Profit-sharing and bonus plans motivate achievers to do their best work.

- [ ] The desire to own a piece of the business is inherent in all ambitious executives: A generous stock plan promotes loyalty and achievement.

- [ ] Off-site meetings and seminars create a feeling of belonging and camaraderie.

- [ ] The more a business grows, the more important it becomes to bring executives other than the founders into the decision-making loop.

- [ ] Rank-and-file employees lose interest unless they are told regularly what's going on. The best way to keep them informed is in small groups or one-on-one discussions.

- [ ] In-house training programs are superior to hiring outside talent at inflated prices.

- [ ] Make sure the chemistry is right between your representative and his or her customer/client counterpart. If it's not, appoint a different representative.

- [ ] Make sure your representatives don't relegate themselves to being "order takers." Instead, school them to be proactive in presenting new ideas and new concepts during the course of each customer/client contact.

- [ ] Avoid customer/client politics like the plague. A neutral stance is always safest.

- [ ] Customers/clients are your most priceless assets. Give your customers/clients special recognition at festive occasions.

- [ ] A strategy that proved successful in solving one problem can be equally successful in solving a similar problem.

- [ ] If the major portion of your estate is tied up in

your business as you grow older, it is time to consider selling to a friendly suitor.

☐ If you decide to sell your business, it is wise to set a firm price.

☐ If you are going to retire, make sure you know what you are going to do with the rest of your life.

CHAPTER

4

What's This Big "R" Doing in My Revolution?

Leo Burnett Company

Tom Collinger, Senior Vice President
Jerry Reitman, Executive Vice President,
Leo Burnett Company

Tom Collinger was named senior vice president of Leo Burnett Company and the company's director of direct marketing in 1990. His responsibilities cover all Burnett clients. Collinger has been a guest speaker at Direct Marketing Association (DMA) conferences, the Professors' Institute of the DMA's Educational Foundation, the Advertising Research Foundation, and Northwestern University's Kellogg Graduate School of Business.

Jerry Reitman joined Leo Burnett Company as executive vice president in 1987 to fully integrate worldwide direct marketing into the agency's general advertising function. He has lectured on direct marketing, creativity, and advertising in 32 countries, and his articles have appeared in Advertising Age, Fund Raising *magazine,* Folio, Direct Marketing, *and the Dutch advertising magazine,* Adformatie.

It didn't happen overnight. No one waved a magic wand and said, "Let there be direct marketing at Leo Burnett Company." In fact, the evolution has been traced as far back as circa 1950, when our founder, Leo Burnett, lectured the National Association of Advertisers on a topic he called the "Magic Advertising Lantern." In his speech, Leo admonished his listeners to develop a working knowledge of *all* marketing disciplines, saying, "These techniques…are tools of the trade. In my opinion, the modern agency should be completely familiar with each of them."

Leo knew that there was more to the strategic marketing equation than just print and television. Yet historically, as with most agencies, Burnett generally regarded direct marketing as a subsidiary to general marketing—instigated only to reinforce television and print advertising, and implemented by specialists who typically worked outside the agency.

Then came the 1980s and perhaps the biggest revelation in the history of modern advertising: The mass market consumer was disappearing. The huge, accessible population so important in the 1960s and 1970s had been replaced by a nation of individuals who were beginning to actively explore their roots, examine their identities, and celebrate their diversity. At the same time, media outlets were proliferating, research tools were improving, database capabilities were expanding, a global market was emerging, and consequently, the marketing landscape was being completely renovated.

Naturally, these developments did not go undetected at Burnett. In fact, they were being closely monitored by a management task force whose charge was to prepare Burnett for the 1990s and beyond.

Burnett is not an agency where overnight revolutions occur. Future CEOs are painstakingly homegrown. Clients are nurtured. Brands are built. Research is pioneered. And the business is, as it will remain, privately held. So naturally, in preparation for the future, Burnett proceeded thoughtfully, purposefully, and with strict regard for its corporate mission, which is a simple but lucid objective:

The mission of the Leo Burnett Company is to create superior advertising. In Leo's words: 'Our primary function in life is to produce the best advertising in the world, bar none. This is to be advertising so interrupting, so daring, so fresh, so engaging, so human, so believable and so well-focused as to themes and ideas that, at one and the same time, it builds a quality reputation for the long haul as it produces sales for the immediate future.

This mission has given Burnett a standard against which to judge every management decision. And that's how Burnett weighed its decision to provide direct-marketing services to its clients as a discipline in and of itself. The shifting marketplace had precipitated consideration of the idea, and a few clients were indicating that they wanted to consolidate efforts with one agency that could maintain brand equities across all forms of communications, including direct marketing.

After careful evaluation, the executive committee decided that direct marketing could, indeed, be a tactical and strategic amplification of the agency's mission, if it were embraced without disrupting the agency's work or alienating clients and personnel. In short, the timing and configuration had to be orchestrated so that the corporate mission was not compromised but expanded to embrace direct marketing.

Heeding these concerns, Burnett decided that direct marketing would not be acquired or built as a separate profit center. Instead, it would be established within the agency as a distinct discipline, yet integrated into the general advertising arena. There would be no fighting over ad budgets, and no client would ever hear conflicting recommendations from two sets of account or creative teams. Instead, the direct and general marketing professionals would work in tandem to optimize the potential of each and every advertising dollar spent.

The Search

Rick Fizdale, then president and chief creative officer of Leo Burnett USA, volunteered to conduct a search for two experienced direct professionals, one with a marketing background and one with creative expertise. According to Fizdale, he met with people from nearly every prestigious direct-marketing company in the industry and grew increasingly enthused about the rich potential of direct marketing. He also received an earful of the frustration and dissension felt by many professionals at the time. Fizdale recalls the experience in this way: "I asked everybody the same opening question, 'Why did you agree to meet with me?' And I was shocked by the similarity and frequency of the negative responses. Most complained that the general advertising people didn't really understand direct, and that communication was almost nonexistent, making it impossible to develop a coordinated marketing program that would benefit the clients' brands."

Fizdale listened, shared his learning with his management team, and a plan evolved. The two veteran direct-marketing professionals hired to provide immediate expertise were to subsequently hire as many specialists as needed to service clients. Those specialists, in turn, would be assigned to a client group and would work within that group. There would be no tug of war over budget or turf issues, but rather a "one-team/one-voice" approach to building brands. It was also determined that the direct-marketing experts could serve as teachers, charged with educating the general account group about the fundamentals and nuances of direct-to-consumer advertising.

Perhaps the most unique aspect of the integrated plan was the fact that direct profits would not be measured separately. Everyone agreed that there wouldn't even be a breakout of the billings. The proof would be evidenced by brand-building results.

Industry Doubts

Burnett officially announced the integration of its direct services on October 23, 1986. The advertising community tittered. "Buying an established firm would be the quickest way to gain credibility in the business," *Crain's Chicago Business* challenged. Other skeptics emerged within the advertising community, and the prediction on the street was that Burnett—so big and well established— would not convince its general advertising people to embrace direct. The prognoses ranged from mass exodus to chronically low morale.

But Burnett's managers knew better. They had faith in the above-and-beyond caliber of their employees. Plus, on a small but significant scale, they had watched the successful integration of disciplines for many years: Creatives who had produced award-winning campaigns had also designed everything from product packages to belt buckles; and account people were constantly recommending promotions and other unique opportunities to their clients.

The two veteran direct professionals came on board and set up shop within the Burnett walls. And, as management predicted, they were generally welcomed by a curious staff eager to tap the new direct resource.

Building Blocks

Several factors contributed to the successful integration of direct marketing at Burnett. The first was that the board of directors had already launched plans to distill and publish the agency's operating principles. This decision was precipitated by the fact that the existing management team would be the last to have worked directly with Leo, and the directors wanted to ensure his legacy.

The operating principles provided clear-cut directives on day-to-day business operations and, in publishing those principles, Burnett galvanized the entire organization behind its mission.

Shortly after the direct integration was announced, management also decided to isolate and break down any existing barriers to change. A questionnaire exploring obstacles was administered to 1,000 members of the professional staff. Nine hundred and sixty people responded, and Burnett used the feedback to incite a renewed commitment to interdisciplinary teamwork.

Then, to manifest that teamwork, management coordinated its multinational accounts so that each network of people working on one piece of business could manage their brands from a global perspective. This not only allowed every office to benefit from the combined experiences of the extended organization, but it also induced a general spirit of collaboration among "Burnetters." Management sensed that, in light of these developments, the agency was poised to embrace a broader implementation of direct marketing.

Revolution from Within

If there was a revolutionary aspect to the integration of direct marketing at Burnett, it was defined by the pace at which everyone in the agency became versed in direct marketing and exposed to its potential. The key was careful management of the transition.

The first stage was exploratory: The direct specialists ventured out into the corridors of Burnett to confer with general-advertising specialists on a client-by-client basis, learning the inherent equities of various brands. Some account teams sought out the direct experts more quickly than others, but ultimately the connection was made across all account teams. Together, these fortified teams explored opportunities, and direct projects were chosen judiciously after careful analysis of brand-building potential.

As soon as an opportunity was identified, the combined general/direct team developed a plan of action and copresented the idea to the client. With client approval, the account team worked jointly to implement the program, with strategies and tactics designated to create optimum impact across the strategic mix of media.

The successes began to mount, and almost immediately the power of direct began to affect some of Burnett's biggest campaigns.

Direct Marketing on Tap

One of the first brands to benefit from the new services was McDonald's. The client asked Burnett to help with a crew recruitment program because the fast-food giant was experiencing difficulty recruiting employees in some markets. Initial research revealed that teenagers, a shrinking but important segment of McDonald's employee population, had misconceptions about McDonald's employees. A television commercial, "Hip To Be Crew," was created to capture the vitality of the McDonald's environment. It also invited inquiries, and the fulfillment package communicated to respondents that "kids just like you" work at McDonald's.

At the same time, mothers and senior citizens, ideal McDonald's crew candidates, were targeted. Two commercials, "Home for Lunch" and "New Kid," aimed at alleviating target audience concerns: Mothers would have flexible hours so that they could be home when their kids were, and senior citizens would not be out of place in the McDonald's environment. Both commercials solicited responses and were followed up by direct-mail pieces, one that included a letter from a working mom to others, and the other a letter and profile from Bill, the senior citizen featured in "New Kid." Using a different message for each segment made the campaign more relevant to each and enhanced the likelihood that the target audience would remember and respond to it.

Proctor and Gamble's Cheer Free detergent was another brand to receive direct support. Developed for people with sensitive skin, the product had an unidentified audience. Two television commercials, "Man in Chair" and "Use the Phone," solicited responses by broadcasting a 1-800-FOR-ITCH number offering a free sample. Print ads announced a similar sample opportunity in an effort to generate names of people with sensitive skin. Respondents received a fulfillment kit accompanied by the sample, a letter, and a questionnaire requesting information about skin sensitivity.

Responses were in the millions and the brand, which went national in January 1990, quickly became one of the most successful detergent flankers in Proctor and Gamble's history.

Another direct success was orchestrated on behalf of Merit cigarettes. Print ads in leading consumer magazines announced the "Blind Challenge," offering smokers two free packs of mystery cigarettes to compare to their current brand. Research had indicated that smokers consistently preferred Merit to their own brands in blind tests, but had typically stuck to their own cigarettes when the brand names were evident.

Shortly after the participants received the unidentified packs, a follow-up letter revealed Merit as the mystery cigarette. Enclosed in the letter were computer-coded, trackable coupons that helped measure the program's success. It was subsequently determined that Philip Morris had been able to get Merit into the hands of 2.5 million competitive smokers within three years.

The results of these and other direct efforts did as much to bolster the success of Burnett's direct-marketing integration as did any other factor. Clients and agency people got the message quickly: Direct worked. Direct marketing could accomplish brand-building objectives not achievable with other media.

Within three years of Burnett's direct-marketing integration, there was evidence of the following:

- More than 70 professionals with direct-marketing experience were hired to provide technical expertise in database management, direct media, production, and telemarketing.

- Nearly all of the general agency professionals received training of one kind or another, whether in the form of brief seminars or in-depth workshops.

- More than 600 Burnett people had benefitted from on-the-job exposure to direct through client-related activities.

- Twenty-one of Burnett's clients had added direct to their portfolio of Burnett-provided services.

No Bad News?

Every good success story has some drama, and no one should believe that the integration of direct marketing at Burnett proceeded without some difficulty. There was more client demand than management had initially anticipated, which made preliminary training a bit of a tactical challenge. There was also a deficit in database information for most of the agency's packaged-goods clients, which meant Burnett and its clients often had to build one—a painstaking process when done right.

Burnett also discovered that consumer, and even agency, perceptions of direct as "junk mail" were slow to die. Plus, there was a handful of seasoned professionals who had a difficult time accepting direct as a canvas on which they could paint.

But Burnett had a lot working in its favor, not the least of which was our mission and culture. There is a palpable sense of family and teamwork here that even the skeptics acknowledge, and that spirit paved the way for broad acceptance of the direct-marketing specialists and their ideas. Additionally, direct marketing has always been held to the "best-in-the-world" standards inherent in Burnett's corporate mission: Every project had to pass the agency's stringent creative review committee standards prior to client presentation.

Burnett 2000

Significant to this case history is that the successful integration of direct marketing as a total discipline laid the groundwork for a broader implementation of integrated communications.

As the 1990s dawned, the marketing landscape continued to transform beyond recognition. Network television, a long-time marketing behemoth that had once commanded a 99-percent share of the prime-time viewing audience, was commanding only 64 percent of its former share and was dwindling. Cable television, video cassette recorders, rental movies, video games, and remote controls were no longer luxuries, but standard operating equipment in most households. What's more, by the early 1990s, more than 350 kinds of media were available to marketers who had the talent and expertise to use them effectively.

In response to the proliferating opportunities, we implemented a proactive agenda to integrate a broad spectrum of marketing disciplines within the agency. In essence, we wanted to provide clients with one-stop expertise, but we had to make sure that our services were top-shelf.

The concept was simple: Clients' lives would be greatly simplified, and their ability to guarantee synergies and maximize brand merit enhanced, if they could partner primarily with one general agency that intuitively understood the brands *and* had multidisciplinary skills. Burnett wanted to be just such a partner, able to create, manage, and nurture brand merit through a highly disciplined thought process designed to facilitate the integrated planning, execution, and evaluation of a brand's communication effort.

To make this goal a reality, we enlisted assistance from Northwestern University, an internationally respected institution that had just developed a master's program in integrated marketing communications. Working with experts from Northwestern, we developed a curriculum to disseminate required skills and knowledge to our employees.

In 1991 and 1992, agency seminars were conducted for nearly 200 U.S. Burnetters at the director level. The seminars, each with a maximum of 30 people, were opened by Rick Fizdale, who led the group through an introduction and overview of the integrated communications objective. Participants, collectively and in small groups, then learned about the integration planning process and new concepts such as *behavioral segmentation*—a broad understanding of what distinguishes and motivates brand purchasers—and *brand contacts*—the various points at which a message can reach a specific potential brand user. Part of that learning involved a hypothetical case study which was presented to small groups. Each group was asked to analyze the situation, develop an integrated program, and present the plan to a theoretical client who was actually a Northwestern University professor.

The second half of the seminar encouraged participants to practice *media-neutral thinking,* an openness to all media possibilities, and provided a quick course in strategic uses of integrated disciplines, including direct marketing, sales promotion, event marketing, and public relations.

In 1992 and 1993, we took a modified version of the training seminars on the road and used it throughout the agency's five worldwide regions.

Much as we had done with direct marketing, we integrated new and existing disciplines, services, and experts within the agency. Local area marketing, retail marketing, database management, event marketing, sales promotion, retail planning, and public relations (many of which had existed as independent departments) were similarly integrated within the agency. They are now on our menu of strategic-marketing disciplines, yet none of them exist as a separate profit center, and all are managed by individuals or teams who operate within the structure of the general account teams. We wanted our account teams to be solution-neutral, with no advocacy for a particular medium. Our only advocacy was to build brands for our clients.

At the close of 1993, there were more than 90 professionals overseeing Burnett's integrated services throughout the client service, research, creative, media, and production departments. Twenty-five U.S. clients—80 percent of the domestic roster—were using two or more of these services, more than 160 clients world-wide were benefitting from the expanded services.

As with direct marketing, results such as the following provided the primary impetus for the broad acceptance of integrated communication:

- Hallmark created a niche for its "Windows" line of cards, introducing it with a television commercial, supporting it with print ads, and encouraging sales through direct-mail couponing and two freestanding inserts offering the consumer three kinds of Hallmark cards for $3.

- The Beef Industry Council reversed a downward trend in beef consumption by orchestrating a campaign via television image commercials plus print ads, direct marketing, and point-of-purchase materials that included 30-minute beef recipes.

- Oldsmobile successfully positioned its Eighty Eight LSS against comparable luxury imports using direct-response television and print, and offering a fulfillment kit that included a videotape of a competitive test drive featured in the advertising.

- Jenn-Air exceeded launch expectations for its new wall oven by using print ads, public-relations efforts that generated coverage in consumer and trade publications and television programs, special events, direct marketing, and point of purchase.

All around the globe, integrated communication success stories developed. Burnett's Mexican office used events, promotions, television commercials, and print ads to generate a huge consumer response and surge in sales for Nintendo. The success of the integrated campaign inspired Nintendo to assign its business to Burnett in other markets in Latin America. Reebok gained a competitive edge in Tokyo thanks to an integrated campaign by Leo Burnett Kyodo, which involved print, direct mail, event sponsorship, point of purchase, and promotions. The Asian success contributed to Reebok assigning its global advertising to Burnett. And Vidal Sassoon enhanced its image and bolstered its database in Frankfurt when Burnett added direct marketing to its existing campaign.

And the successes keep mounting. Will integrated communication work at Burnett? It already has. Will it flourish? Absolutely, as long as we continue to create innovative new tools designed to successfully deal with the realities of a dynamic marketplace. And there is another equally compelling question: Can other agencies institute our approach to integration?

That answer is not so clear. Many smaller to medium-sized agencies have succeeded in launching integrated communications. But for larger agencies, the transition requires a radically new approach. In essence, all of the old tenents of advertising have been broken down. It's a brand new world, and change doesn't come quickly or easily. Frankly, ours might be a difficult blueprint for some to emulate. We have the benefit of a history-rich corporate culture and a succession of management teams who have heeded our founder's warning not to behave "too big."

Our early commitment to integrated communications may have widened our competitive advantage in the industry. As *Fortune* magazine wrote in the November 15, 1993, issue: "What marketers must do, amid the change and confusion, is align with…partners that…are fully adaptable to the broadly expanding needs of their clients. And are highly creative, of course. Some agencies are up to the task already." That Burnett was listed in an accompanying chart as one of those agencies already "up to the task," confirms what the intrinsically biased authors of this chapter suggest: Burnett is uniquely poised to successfully guide its clients through the winds of a changing, global-integrated, interactive marketplace.

Bob Stone's
Commentary

They said it couldn't be done. So Burnett did it. The revelation of how Burnett integrated direct marketing into the total fabric of a great agency is a case study of what an agency with a defined culture and a clear mission can accomplish.

The Burnett story is the result of one central strategy:

The best way for a general-advertising agency to capitalize on direct marketing is to integrate the discipline into the general-advertising arena. Integration eliminates fights over ad budgets and conflicting recommendations from two sets of account or creative teams.

The one-team, one-play strategy, as the authors show, is not limited to direct marketing; it applies to a broad spectrum of marketing disciplines. Thus, Burnett is ideally positioned to move into the interactive super highway as the dream becomes reality.

Collinger and Reitman have provided us with a mini-case history that exemplifies the results of integrated communications. For a better understanding of how integrated communications is orchestrated, we close this chapter with a full-scale case history from Burnett.

Heinz Pet Products' Amore Cat Food

Market Conditions

The ultra-gourmet 3 oz. segment of the canned cat food category has been one of the primary driving forces behind the growth of the overall canned category. On a 52-week basis (most recent period ending 3/24/90), the ultra-gourmet 3 oz. segment accounts for approximately 14.2 percent of total canned cat food volume, up almost 8 percent vs. year-ago. More significantly, by virtue of its incredible price premium, this segment accounts for approximately 28 percent of total canned category sales.

Given the relatively high profit margins attainable (operating income roughly 18 percent to 20 percent of gross sales), the ultra-gourmet 3 oz. segment has experienced a tremendous influx of new entrants within the past 20 months, including Sheba (Mars Company), Fresh Catch (Carnation), 9-Lives 3 oz., Alpo 3 oz., and Whiskas Select Entrees (Mars Company). Additionally, the media spending allocated in support of these introductions has been significant, and is expected to increase through calendar 1990.

As a result of the increasingly competitive ultra-gourmet 3 oz. environment, innovative and effective media vehicles have become an essential marketing ingredient for success. Given the tremendously indulgent and involving nature of cat owners who serve ultra-gourmet 3 oz. canned cat food, and the ability to isolate a significant number of these potential purchasers, use of direct marketing evolved as a critical component of Amore's overall advertising effort.

Amore Direct-to-Consumer Background

Purchasers of ultra-gourmet 3 oz. canned cat food tend to be incredibly indulgent individuals who disregard the 100 percent price premium (of 3 oz. canned cat food) in order to serve their cats the best cat food available.

Through a Dunham and Marcus research study fielded in the summer of 1989, two salient findings were uncovered which suggested the use of a direct-to-consumer program for Amore:

1. *Finding:*
   Eighteen percent of the purchasers of 3 oz. canned cat food account for 62 percent of total 3 oz. volume. There are approximately 1.5 million of these individuals in the United States.
   Implication:
   A significant identifiable, and isolatable target audience could be reached.

2. *Finding:*
   These heavy purchasers of 3 oz. canned cat food were incredibly indulgent, involving cat owners.
   Implication:
   Amore's emotional, involving positioning could be effectively communicated to this target audience via a warm, personalized direct-to-consumer approach.

Target Audience

- *Demographic:* Women 35–64. Tend to be employed, with slightly higher income (skew $50 thousand and over) and small household size (2 people, on average). As mentioned, these heavy purchasers (although only 18 percent of total purchasers) account for roughly 62 percent of total 3 oz. volume.
- *Purchase Motivation:* These women are *heavy* purchasers of 3 oz. canned cat food. They are indulgent cat owners committed to doing the best they can for their cat. The relationship they enjoy with their cats is a fundamental component of their lives.

Direct-to-Consumer Objectives

Overall, the purpose of Amore's Direct program is to increase usage of Amore. The objectives of Amore's Direct-to-Consumer program are as follows:

- Compel targeted individuals to purchase more Amore (including incremental consumption among loyal users as well as trial among competitive users).
- Enhance Amore's image among indulgent cat owners.
- Support and enhance communication of Amore's emotional, involving positioning against the target of indulgent, heavy users of 3 oz. canned cat food: "By serving Amore, you will feel like a more loving cat owner...."

Strategies

The strategic initiatives for Amore's Direct-to-Consumer program are as follows:

- Initiate relevant dialog with heavy 3 oz. purchasers, via personal letters from Barbara Chapman (sponsored by Amore), an involved cat owner who is employed by Heinz Pet Products.
- Provide compelling trial purchase incentives, as well as response incentives.
- Provide compelling continuity premium offer through which brand-loyal purchase behavior can be generated by extending the impact of the Direct-to-Consumer program beyond its three-mailing scope.

Program Structure/Creative Material

The Amore Direct-to-Consumer program is in the form of Amore-sponsored letters from Barbara Chapman, an employee of Heinz Pet Products who is an avid Amore purchaser. Barbara's letters are intended to initiate a dialog between her and consumers, primarily focused on cat-owner relationships. Consumers will become involved in the program by responding to the *Crazy About Cats* survey, asking cat owners about how their cats behave as well as the various ways in which they interact with their cats.

Consumers will feel a sense of affiliation with Barbara and with other cat owners involved in the program. The intention is to make the consumer feel positive about Amore through the communication from Barbara Chapman, and ultimately consider Amore an important component of the fundamental relationship between cat and owner.

The program consists of three mailings, as follows:

- *Mailing 1:* Mailed nationally to 500,000 heavy purchasers of 3 oz. canned cat food, the initial mailing includes the following components:
  - —Outer folding piece, with teaser copy enticing recipients to open the mail
  - —Letter from Barbara Chapman (see Exhibit 4.1)
  - —*Crazy About Cats* survey (see Exhibit 4.2)

Exhibit 4.1 Two-Page Letter and Manufacturer's Coupon Included in Mailing 1

Barbara Chapman/P.O. Box 609/Bellwood, Illinois 60104

9999-999

Dear Sample A. Sample:

You're on a luxury cruise liner in the Caribbean. A wave smashes over the deck, washing your husband and your cat overboard.

Who would you save first?

If you're like me, you either thought about it for a minute, or chose the cat right off. Because you know, as well as I do, that the love between you and your cat is as strong and as real as any other kind of love in the world.

Maybe even stronger.

Sure, many people love their cats. But there are those, such as myself, and maybe you, that go even a step further. We're crazy about them.

That's why I'm writing -- to find out more about your relationship with your cat. Why? Because for the past 14 years, I've had one of the most amazing relationships. He watches for me to come home every day, faithfully perched on the windowsill overlooking my street. He becomes extraordinarily attentive and affectionate when I am upset -- he knows when I need him most.

Mischief is so much a part of my life that, even when I'm away from him, I spend hours just talking about him, what he does, and how he makes me feel. And I've found that other people who love their cats enjoy sharing the same stories and exploits of their most significant "others."

That's what brought me to Amoré. I've been working for them for the past few years. And when they found out more about it.

The more I shared with them, the more they wanted to know about the loving relationships others wanted to know about. (After all, the name "Amoré" means share with their cats.

"love" in Italian. That's why they put such care into making Amoré cat food.)

So they helped devise this Crazy About Cats Survey. It's fun to do, and will help you discover just how much you really love your cat, and how much your cat really loves you. Are we crazy? Or just crazy about our cats? That's what's in store with these 21 fun questions.

Then, you'll get a chance to learn how other cat lovers feel. Once you're done, send the finished survey back to me. I'll compile them all and send you the results in time for the holidays this December, sharing the fun and feelings from all over the country.

Everyone who sends in their survey by June 30 will receive the results, plus the folks at Amoré will send you a terrific gift.* You've already received a coupon for a free can of Amoré, just for taking the time to read this letter. You can use the coupon to buy your cat's favorite flavor (Mischief likes Ocean Whitefish and Tuna).

So what are you waiting for? Curl up with your better half, and let me know how you feel about your cat. Mischief and I will be waiting impatiently!

In the meantime, I wanted to leave you with a thought. The last time I went on a business trip, I left extra food and water for Mischief. I was only gone a day, but when I came home, he wasn't waiting for me. He wasn't talking to me. In fact, he wouldn't even acknowledge my presence. Oh, about dinner time he began to realize something, and that's when I started to forgive me. He didn't care, he wouldn't be angry. So why give someone who cares enough to be mad anything less than Amoré? Isn't he worth it? I think so!

Sincerely,

Barbara and Mischief

*You'll have to allow 4 to 6 weeks for delivery of the gift, and the offer's only good while supplies last! So hurry! © 1990 Maine Pet Products

Exhibit 4.1 (continued)

Exhibit 4.2 Twenty-One Question Survey Included in Mailing 1

Exhibit 4.2 (continued)

_____   ( )
Name   Area Code   Phone Number

_____
Address   City   State   Zip

_____
What type of cat(s) do you have?

_____
What is/are your cat's name(s)   Cat's Birthday

AMORÉ CRAZY ABOUT CATS SURVEY
(Check appropriate box. Write in your own comments where necessary.)

1. Which best describes the personality of your cat?
   - ☐ *Mother—he/she takes care of me*   ☐ *Shy—hides from strangers*
   - ☐ *Teenager—always bouncing off the walls* ☐ *Lover—attentive and demanding*
   - ☐ *Other_____*

2. Does your cat get jealous?
   - ☐ *Yes*   ☐ *No*

3. If so, of whom?
   - ☐ *Boyfriend/Girlfriend* ☐ *Family Members* ☐ *Other_____*
   - ☐ *Husband/Wife*   ☐ *Other Pets*

4. When I'm sad or down, my cat comforts me. Does your cat comfort you?
   - ☐ *Yes*   ☐ *No*

5. If so, how does he or she go about doing it? _____

_____

6. When your cat gets angry, does he/she:
   - ☐ *Hide*   ☐ *Ignore you*   ☐ *Knock things over*
   - ☐ *Other_____*

7. Has your cat ever made you cry?
   - ☐ *Yes*   ☐ *No*

Exhibit 4.2 (continued)

8. If yes, tell us how it happened: _____
   _____
   _____

9. If your cat is like mine, he or she loves gourmet cat food. Which, if any, do you serve your cat?
   Serve *(Check all that apply.)*   Most often *(Check one.)*
   ☐ *Amoré*   ☐
   ☐ *Fancy Feast*   ☐
   ☐ *Sheba*   ☐
   ☐ *Fresh Catch*   ☐
   ☐ *Other (specify)*_____   ☐

10. What does your cat like to play with most?
    ☐ *Yarn balls*   ☐ *Cat toys (Which types?)* _____
    ☐ *Scratching posts* ☐ *Other*_____

11. When you have to leave town, do you:
    ☐ *Put your cat in a kennel*   ☐ *Leave your cat with a friend*
    ☐ *Hire cat sitters to come in*   ☐ *Take your cat with you*
                    ☐ *Other*_____

12. Pretend that you were offered a job overseas, but found you couldn't take your cat.
    Which best describes your considerations?
    ☐ *You'd never go*   ☐ *You'd think about it, but still not go*
         ☐ *You'd go only if your best friend kept your cat*

13. What do you think your cat does when you're away from home? _____
    _____

(over)

Exhibit 4.2 (continued)

14. Mischief sleeps curled up next to me. Where does your cat sleep?
☐ *In your bed*   ☐ *In his/her bed*   ☐ *On the couch*   ☐ *On the floor*
☐ *Other* _____

15. Cats love to hide. Where is your cat's favorite hiding place?
☐ *Underneath furniture*   ☐ *In the kitchen*
☐ *Behind the bed*   ☐ *Other* _____

16. Mischief loves to play, and I love to play with him! What are
your cat's favorite games or activities which you share with your cat? _____
_____

17. Does your cat snub his/her food if it's not fresh?
☐ *Yes*   ☐ *No*

18. How often would you say you serve three-ounce cans of cat food?
☐ *Daily*   ☐ *2—6 times a week*   ☐ *Once a week, for a treat*

19. Does your cat talk to you?
☐ *Yes*   ☐ *No*

20. Every cat communicates in their own special way.
How does your cat tell you when he or she is hungry? _____
_____

How about when he or she is happy? _____
_____

21. Does your cat kiss you?
☐ *Yes*   ☐ *No*

0369-002   201137577   © 1990 Heinz Pet Products

—Buy 2, get 1 free coupon
—Business reply envelope (with postage paid), for ease in returning the survey

• The initial mailing is designed to accomplish the following objectives:

—Introduce the program.
—Communicate why Barbara Chapman is writing, and why the recipient should be interested in the program.
—Request and elicit response to the survey. The survey includes both open-ended and close-ended questions, through which responders can convey usage information as well as discuss various aspects of their relationship with their cat.
—Deliver promise of a free gift (cat poster) and survey results.

• *Mailing 2:* This mailing includes two versions:

Responder mailing: Sent to all individuals who respond to the survey, it consists of the following:

—Thank-you note from Barbara Chapman
—Cat poster (free gift promised in initial mailing)
—Buy 2, get 1 free coupon
—Promise of survey results by Thanksgiving

Nonresponder mailing: Sent to all individuals who do not respond to the survey distributed in the initial mailing, this mailing consists of the following:

—Letter from Barbara Chapman
—Buy 2, get 1 free coupon
—*Crazy About Cats* survey
—Business reply envelope (postage paid)
—Promise of survey results by Thanksgiving

• *Mailing 3:* Mailed to all program responders, this mailing consists of the following:

—Survey results
—Letter from Barbara Chapman
—Premium gift offer

(See Exhibit 4.3.)

Incentives/Offers

Consumers were provided with several purchase incentives and rewards:

- Buy 2, get 1 free coupon (1 million to be distributed during the course of the program)
- Free cat poster, for responding to the survey (distributed in the second mailing to all initial mailing responders)
- Premium offer (distributed to all responders in the third mailing)
- Survey results (distributed to all responders in the third mailing)

Media

Strategically, Amore's Direct-to-Consumer program works synergistically with Amore's television and print creative campaigns. Each of these campaigns is focused around the theme "Isn't He/She Worth It?," emphasizing the special relationship between cat and owner. Additionally, Amore's print and television media flighting was tailored to enhance the potential impact of Amore's Direct program, by running/airing simultaneously with the projected receipt of Amore's initial Direct-to-Consumer mailing. Perhaps most significantly, *Cat Fancy* magazine was used not only as a source of list names for receipt of the Direct program, but also as the primary vehicle for Amore's print advertising.

Executionally, Amore's print campaign is perfectly synergistic with Amore's Direct-to-Consumer campaign, utilizing identical creative material in an effort to enhance the overall impact of Amore's advertising. Similarly, one of Amore's three television executions visually depicts Amore's Direct creative material, also in an effort to enhance

Exhibit 4.3 Two Components of Mailing 3

Barbara Chapman/P.O. Box 609/Bellwood, Illinois 60104   001-238

Dear Sample:

If you fell in love with the stationery I used on the letters, notes, and surveys (which many of you did, judging from the number of requests and questions I received about the custom-made letterhead), then here is something especially for you.

Amoré is offering a custom-made "Crazy About Cats" stationery kit, just like the one in the picture, for only $9.99 and 10 Amoré proofs of purchase. (If Bijou enjoys Amoré as much as Mischief, that won't take too long to collect!)

Just send your check or money order along with 10 Amoré UPCs (those funny-looking straight lines on the label) in the enclosed envelope for each kit, and you'll receive the complete Amoré stationery kit(s) in four to six weeks. (Wouldn't it be a great holiday gift?)

Our lawyers told me to tell you that the offer is void where prohibited, and that the kits are only available until January 31, 1991, or while supplies last, so hurry!

Sincerely,

Barbara and Mischief

Send me _____ Stationery Kit(s) at
$9.99 each (shipping and handling
included).

Amount enclosed: _____.

UPCs enclosed: _____.
(10 Amore UPCs per each kit).

Please make check or money order payable
to AMORE, and send along with UPCs to:
Barbara Chapman, P.O. Box 659, Bellwood, Ill. 60104.
Do not enclose cash.

_____
name

_____
address

_____
city   state   zip

1 2 3 4 5 6 7 8 9

Exhibit 4.3 (continued)

A Note from Barbara:

Many of you wrote to tell me of friends or relatives who were as "Crazy about Cats" as you and I. And they wanted to share in the fun. Well, here's their chance.

If you know anyone who would like to be included in our feline fun, just jot their name and address down on this note. Or, just give this form to any interested cat lover and they can request to be included themselves.

Use the enclosed envelope to send this back to me. You can put it in with your stationery order form, or just send it by itself.

NAME			CAT'S NAME	
ADDRESS	CITY		STATE	ZIP

NAME			CAT'S NAME	
ADDRESS	CITY		STATE	ZIP

NAME			CAT'S NAME	
ADDRESS	CITY		STATE	ZIP

NAME			CAT'S NAME	
ADDRESS	CITY		STATE	ZIP

the impact of Amore's Direct-to-Consumer advertising by stimulating survey response. (See Exhibit 4.4.)

In total, Amore's Direct-to-Consumer, print, and television campaigns work in strategic and executional harmony in an effort to enhance the overall impact of Amore's advertising campaign.

List Name Sources

Amore's 500,000 targeted individuals were derived from three sources, in order of priority as follows:

- Select and Save (heavy users of canned cat food)
- *Cat Fancy* subscriber list
- Amore promotion sweepstakes responders

Timing

Amore's three Direct-to-Consumer mailings were scheduled for distribution as follows:

Mailing 1: w/o May 15

Mailing 2: w/o July 15

Mailing 3: w/o October 22

Amore's initial mailing was distributed on May 15 to 487,000 targeted heavy purchasers of ultra-gourmet 3 oz. canned cat food.

Exhibit 4.4 Thirty-Second TV Commercial Visually Depicting Amore's Mailing 1 Creative Material

The Art of Bringing Professionalism to List Brokerage

The Kleid Company

Rose Harper, Chairman Emeritus, The Kleid Company, Inc.

*R*ose Harper *began her career at The Kleid Company as controller. Harper has served as chairman of the board of the Direct Marketing Association (DMA) and was treasurer for four years. She was the first woman to serve in either capacity. Harper was inducted into the DMA Hall of Fame in 1985—the first woman to be so honored. She has lectured extensively, and is the author of* Mailing List Strategies: A Guide to Direct Mail Success, *now in its fifth printing. She currently serves as a consultant to The Kleid Company.*

I still vividly remember the day I joined Mailings Inc. The day was July 16, 1950 (of course, I was a kid then).

When Lewis Kleid interviewed me for the position of controller for Mailings Inc., it was difficult for me to understand what business the company was in. But it didn't scare me. I assured myself that a debit is a debit. I could take care of the "books." And starting from square one would give me the opportunity to learn.

Mailings Inc. was founded in 1936 by Lewis Kleid. Initially, the business emphasis was on creative. However, when I joined the company, it was a successful lettershop. Its most important client was the Book-of-the-Month Club. In 1947, the company recognized the growing trend of direct marketing (mail order was the most frequently used descriptor then) and established a list brokerage division.

Lewis and I complemented each other and made a good management team. Lewis was creative and an excellent writer, and I provided the financial background.

After mastering the debits and credits for Mailings Inc., I decided it was time to understand what business the company was in. The best way to learn was by walking around the premises on 45th Street in New York City.

The largest space was devoted to the lettershop services. The "plant" employed 50 to 60 people, depending on the season, who stuffed envelopes with promotional material being used for the direct-mail solicitations. These workers were paid on a piece-work basis. Calculating the weekly pay for each employee was a chore, to say the least, but also a learning experience. It was certainly not the high-tech, high-touch age. At that point, the lettershop produced a high percentage of our total sales and profits.

From my accounting involvement, it was evident that the list brokerage unit was on a visible growth path. In addition to Book-of-the-Month Club, our first account, our sales efforts proved successful in attracting other accounts.

Some of our contacts at that time included Old American Insurance, Milwaukee Dustless Brush Company, Atlantic Advertising, Around-the-World Shoppers Club, Sackheim and Scherman Advertising Agency, *Harvard Business Review*, American Heritage Publishing Company, The Kiplinger Washington Editors, and Time Inc. Interviews were conducted with these clients: It was an excellent learning experience and good public relations for the company. Even though target marketing was not the terminology used in those days, the diverse products and services of these mailers required targeted lists.

In 1952, Larry Chait, then with Time Inc., had a brilliant list concept, *Newly Promoted Executives*. We were one of the companies assigned to participate in developing and promoting the list in its initial stages. This was our introduction into the list-compiling business.

How We Dealt with the Different Parts

It was essential to structure a business plan that would provide the essentials for managing the diverse, but interrelated, aspects of the three segments of our business.

The decision was to create three business units:

- Mailings Inc. would remain in the lettershop business.

- The compiling business would be established as a new business, Research Projects, Inc.

- For list brokerage activity, the Lewis Kleid Company was established as a separate company. The list management business unit was part of the Lewis Kleid Company.

This stratagem turned out to be good operational planning. It led to our next major move, building the list business.

Lists: The Media in Direct Mail

In the early 1950s, there was a small universe of list availability. List owners were very reluctant and had fears about entering their lists on the list rental market. The fears were related to how list rental would affect their own business and that their lists might be copied by the user.

The National Council of Mailing List Brokers took on this issue cooperatively. Its members were Archer Mailing List Service, George R. Bryant Co., Walter Drey, Guild Company, Lewis Kleid Co., Willa Maddern, Mosely Mail Order List Service, Names Unlimited, D.L. Natwick, James E. True Associates, and G.H. Younger. A few years later, it included about 60 brokers.

These companies were the pioneers in convincing list owners to offer their lists on the rental market. They convinced list owners that there was no such thing as a captive audience. I remember calling a prominent company to try to convince them that list rental generated revenue that went right down to the bottom line and would not affect their core business. My contact said, "If you weren't so nice I would kick you right out of my office." I replied, "I'm happy that you're so nice."

It took a lot of effort to convince list owners to put their lists on the rental market. It was essential to address their concerns by developing a process that would assure list owners that their lists would never be out of their control. The next step was to suggest that the list owner work with a list manager. This was quickly accepted as an effective cost-savings approach related to personnel time and overhead. Owners also recognized that list managers would have extensive contact with direct-mail users and brokers. They could bring in the sales, the list rental orders.

The deciding factor, of course, was the profit potential for the list owner and the list manager. There was no doubt that direct-mail marketing was becoming an important part of the advertising concept. Lewis' interviews with prominent direct marketers confirmed the rapid strides that were being made in direct mail. As more and more companies were using this option, it was obviously essential to

- Increase list availability and concentrate on direct mail (which was becoming more complex)

- Increase the educational opportunities in direct marketing in order to attract qualified personnel

How could we ignore these trends? We didn't. We addressed them in our planning strategies. In the early sixties, I tackled a five-year business plan focusing on how best to deploy both financial and human resources for strategic investments. Mailings Inc. was becoming very capital-intensive. Investments were made in inserting machines, but this was not enough. New technology needed to be investigated. Research Projects also had an essential need for capital to deal with list compilations and maintenance in the "new age."

Situation Analysis

In order to reach a considered decision, it was essential to do a situation analysis. This included asking the managers of each division to submit three-year budgets which would include the equipment essential to grow the companies. In other words, start with the basics and look to the future.

The analysis showed that Mailings Inc. and Research Projects were capital intensive. The Lewis Kleid Company, although it also needed capital infusion, afforded the opportunity to build the company strategically with controllable action steps.

The Decision

Kleid management decided to sell both Mailings Inc. and Research Projects to their respective managers and to stay with the Lewis Kleid Company. These decisions allowed Kleid management to concentrate on list brokerage with the objectives of increasing list availability and becoming the List Experts, the professionals. Professionalism doesn't just happen. It requires knowledge, ethics, and dedication both to the clients we serve and to the standards of our industry. This was my message to the staff, and they responded. We had come a long way. To help promote our image, we ran ads, like the one shown in Exhibit 5.1, reinforcing our positioning as professional list brokers and managers.

In the early sixties, we spent a great deal of time with Ed Mayer. Ed was a prominent direct marketer and proponent of the need for direct-marketing education. He did teach, but he felt that direct-mail marketing education needed to be expanded significantly. As a result of our meetings, the Lewis Kleid Foundation made a $10,000 donation to start the Collegiate Institutes, and the Educational Foundation was born.

The purpose of the Direct Marketing Educational Foundation (DMEF) is to help young people learn about direct marketing and its career opportunities by increasing direct-marketing education at the college and university level. The foundation has a roster of activities which has expanded from college students to professors. Several Collegiate and Professors' Institutes are conducted each year. Also, the *Journal of Direct Marketing* was a major step forward. It is a full-fledged academic journal produced by Northwestern University.

Then Came 1970

Dart Industries had put together direct-marketing–related companies such as Market Compilation and Research Bureau (a compiler and advanced list data processing company) and Western Direct, (a creative shop). Dart wanted to add The Kleid Company to this group. This step would allow the companies to pool resources and offer integrated expertise in direct response. The concept of this cooperative made sense.

Dart approached Lewis Kleid, and he decided to sell because he wanted to retire. The negotiations with Dart were my responsibility and were concluded with a very attractive stock deal for Lewis.

During these negotiations, I learned that Lew Rashmir had led Market Compilation into advanced computer list maintenance techniques. Also, Dart's Operation Research Department was extremely advanced in computer technology and mathematical disciplines. Tony Posgay and Marcel Tyszler were our contacts, and they introduced us to the advances in computer technology and predictive modeling. We installed our first mainframe computer in 1973, which proved to be a plus in our accounting and marketing procedures.

One of our cooperative efforts, which was very successful, was to develop the College Student Market for Time Inc. with Market Compilation and Research Bureau. It turned out to be a productive database with many selection options. This introduction to database applications served us well in the years ahead.

Exhibit 5-1 Positioning Ad for the Lewis Kleid Company

The Advent of 1975

The acquisition era, the era of conglomerates, was now turning into the divestiture era. Dart Industries (which later became Dart-Kraft, a unit of the Philip Morris Companies) decided to divest the direct-marketing–related companies, although it's difficult to understand why. Perhaps it was hard, at that point, to identify and capitalize on the synergism that existed with their other divisions. They put Kleid on the market. In a sense it was neither a shock nor a surprise.

I was flabbergasted and flattered to see the enormous interest generated; we had many suitors. However, my unequivocal decision was a *buy-back.* Why not?

In the five years with Dart, we had developed new concepts that presented exciting opportunities for added-value client services, such as the following:

   The *List Selection Guide,* a database of list usage information by product-market category

   A program (in its early stages) to structure complete mail plans

   A program to develop a complete and continuing list history usage for our clients

So, it was negotiation time. I learned that in negotiations you must know how and when to say no and mean it. My message that I would not join any company that bought Kleid came across. Dart Industries graciously accepted my message and really gave me a good deal that I could take to the bank.

At the end of 1975, we were a private company again.

On Our Own

We were on our own again and wouldn't have access to capital from a parent company, if needed. We had no parent. What we needed was a comprehensive five-year business plan which, as we all know, is probably the most important document you ever can put together for the company.

The management team—Michael Manzari, Arlene Minick, Jeff Kobil, and Richard Vergara—was involved in the planning. In addition, executives in accounting, production, and sales were asked for their input. In total, we had the enthusiastic support of all of our employees.

Planning requires forecasting, which can't always be precise. Common sense must be part of the equation. A good starting point for planning is to recognize that the past is more or less a prologue to the future. There is a rhythmic connection between business cycles, consumer trends, and direct marketing.

Let me also say that any competitive activity requires a high level of considered risk taking and self-confidence.

Positioning was an important part of our plan. We didn't want to make the same mistake that, for example, the railroads made. They didn't realize that they were in the transportation business.

Our thinking went something like this: Kleid is in the advertising business. Kleid is in the list business. Let's position ourselves as list consultants, a list agency. This feeling was emphasized when so many advertising agencies were, at last, recognizing direct response by developing or acquiring direct-response agencies. The growth opportunities were obvious. How could we keep our company growing? Through quality and professionalism, as evidenced by the following points:

- Clients choose list professionals by reliability, which encompasses quality list recommendations and services.

- The key to successful list recommendations is to analyze the characteristics of the lists used (which were responsive) and to develop a profile that identifies prospects as potential customers.

- Among the most influential analytical discriminants are demographics, interests, geographics, psychographics, source, RFM (recency, frequency, monetary), and segment used.

- Systems were, and are still being, developed to provide quality and value-added analytical services to our clients on a consistent basis.

- Our information-based systems made it possible to produce our annual Seasonality Report, which is a Seasonality Trend Index. These reports are highly acclaimed and receive extensive press coverage. The primary objective is to bring together information on a month-to-month and category basis to track seasonal patterns. A sample of one such report is shown in Exhibit 5.2.

These advanced strategies, among others, kept our company visible, professional, and successful. Our staff grew from 40 to 70, and sales kept pace.

Saatchi & Saatchi Public Limited Company

It is interesting to note that we never actually pursued a take-over or a buy-out. Yet, in 1970, there was Dart Industries, and in 1984, Saatchi approached us about acquiring The Kleid Company.

Exhibit 5-2 Sample Kleid Company Seasonality Report

Volume XX, No.1   April 1993

Seasonality Study / Update #17

In studying the data used to construct this study, we did note that list order size displayed the influence of three significant factors:

(1) Impact of the recession that prevailed throughout the year—with a trickle-up movement in the last quarter.

(2) Cost-containment efforts by companies which led to the implementation of strategic mail plans based on strict response analysis and modeling techniques.

(3) The efficiency of target marketing. Effective market segmentation does provide the opportunity to mail on a more frequent basis.

These factors could have influenced seasonality to a degree, but not dramatically. The same evaluation process techniques were used. The determining factor is the total quantity for each category.

We still advise that mailers conduct their own seasonality study on a consistent basis. Where more than one product is involved, the study should be conducted for each product. Our experience shows that there is a distinguishable variance by product.

There is a realization that the technology, communications, and lifestyle changes will affect direct marketing. It represents a significant challenge.

Direct mail is measurable. Direct mail is a powerful medium. It's quite impressive to see that we are harnessing this power to our advantage. The more we study, the more we learn.

C. R. Harper/Chairman and CEO

Exhibit 5-2 (Continued)

Categories	1990–1991 Three Top Months	1991–1992 Three Top Months	1992–1993 Three Top Months
Business/finance	December	December	December
	June	September	September
	January	August	February
Cultural reading	December	December	December
	November	November	October
	June	January	June
General reading	December	December	June
	June	June	November
	May	August	January
Self-improvement	December	December	January
	March	May	March
	May	August	December
Health	June	December	December
	December	June	September
	July	August	Apr/June/July
Home interest	June	December	December
	December	June	September
	January	January	June
Parents and children	January	December	December
	June	June	September
	Sept/Dec	September	April
Hobbies/related subjects	December	June	December
	June	December	June
	September	September	September
Entertainment	December	December	December
	June	September	February
	January	August	September
Educational, technical, professional	December	August	August
	October	December	December
	July	June	March
Fund raising	November	November	November
	October	September	September
	January	February	October

Exhibit 5-2 (Continued)

Prepared by: the Kleid Company, Inc.

Seasonality Study
Category: Business Finance
Monthly % of Total Mailings

Month	1988–1989	1989–1990	1990–1991	1991–1992	1992–1993	Five-Year Average
Mar	7.4%	10.1%	6.3%	8.8%	9.4%	8.4%
Apr	6.0	7.1	6.4	7.0	4.2	6.1
May	9.4	12.7	9.2	6.3	5.9	8.7
June	6.4	5.6	10.6	8.3	4.5	7.1
July	5.9	6.8	9.4	10.0	8.1	8.0
Aug	7.5	5.7	7.0	10.6	5.6	7.3
Sept	10.2	8.4	8.9	11.1	10.4	9.8
Oct	6.4	7.5	6.0	5.8	9.0	6.9
Nov	6.0	5.2	3.4	4.3	7.5	5.3
Dec	20.7	14.8	15.6	14.0	17.3	16.5
Jan	10.1	9.9	10.1	7.9	7.8	9.2
Feb	4.0	6.2	7.1	5.9	10.3	6.7
	100.0%	100.0%	100.0%	100.0%	100.0%	100.0%

Comments on 1992–1993: December still won't give up the lead. September and February were about tied for second place.

We were flattered and somewhat reluctant, but challenged. There were obvious advantages: Saatchi was a conglomerate of ad agencies, direct-response agencies, and service organizations. They owned Saatchi & Saatchi Compton Worldwide, McCaffrey & McCall, Yankelovich, and Computer Marketing Services. With the Fortune 1,000+ discovering direct marketing as a viable advertising avenue, this marriage appeared to have specific advantages.

The diverse client list of the Saatchi units would give The Kleid Company the opportunity to expand its client base and to teach, where necessary, the fundamentals and advantages of direct marketing. Kleid would also be able to promote the advantages of a marketing database to clients, particularly since Computer Marketing Services provided this service. We envisioned that this cooperative effort would afford the opportunity to emphasize to clients the obvious benefits of a marketing database. This would not only impact on product development for the client, but also on the creation of general advertising.

Even in 1984, we recognized the opportunities that would accrue to Kleid by capitalizing on the interest demonstrated by the Fortune 1,000+ in exploring direct marketing. And, of course, we could take advantage of the opportunities offered in the global markets.

The conclusion was that Saatchi & Saatchi and Kleid came to an agreement in January 1985. Saatchi & Saatchi purchased Kleid stock at an attractive price. We certainly were excited about the future.

A very interesting challenge and learning experience evolved. We were involved in Saatchi & Saatchi's business planning processes for expansion—and in meetings with prospective clients interested in direct response. It certainly seemed to fit the "picture" of the future in advertising.

After only three years, for reasons difficult to define, we were offered a buy-back opportunity in 1988. We accepted. We're private again.

In Conclusion

Our experiences with take-overs and buy-backs was exciting and sometimes, of course, frustrating. However, the experiences offered insights into market expansion and technology. In direct mail, telemarketing, and alternate media (such as card decks, package and billing inserts, and coventures), *lists* are the media. Lists are certainly an integral part of direct response along with creative, offers, and packaging.

With the enormous availability of lists (100,000 plus), experience and computerized marketing support systems are critical. There is no easy way to select the appropriate lists for a direct-response program. List consultants and list agencies are the answer. Kleid will continue its stratagem of being list leaders.

So, perhaps, direct-response agencies and/or general-advertising agencies might still look for acquisition of list agencies. But until the buzz word "synergism" used in take-over situations is identified and understood, it just doesn't work.

From my own point of view—no more sales of our company or buy-backs. But who can tell? My credo has always been *never say never.*

Bob Stone's
Commentary

Back in the 1940s and 1950s, there were a handful of mailing list brokers. They were trailblazers. Their challenge, as Rose Harper points out, was to convince list owners that it was safe to rent their lists to noncompetitors. List brokers argued that there was no such a thing as a captive audience.

One by one, list owners agreed—many with trepidation—to address their envelopes or self mailers from rented lists. Others, who still feared their customers' names might be "stolen," agreed to rent the names only if they did the entire mailing. Today, the concerns of the past are practically a nonissue.

The list brokers of the 1940s and 1950s were all small business people in the true sense. With a few exceptions, business acumen was not their outstanding trait. Against this background, Rose Harper became the catalyst who brought professionalism to list brokerage. Much can be learned from the strategies she employed to achieve the sterling reputation The Kleid Company enjoys to this day.

- It is better to complement another person than to parallel their talents.

- A prime key to growing a business is to develop a business plan that will give you a route to follow.

- When an industry faces a common problem, it is better to move against the problem collectively rather than individually.

- Growth becomes stagnant unless you increase your product line.

- Participate in educational programs for your industry and learn from the experiences of more qualified personnel.

- Through situation analysis, identify the primary sources of profit for your business. Eliminate divisions that are too capital intensive or unprofitable.

- Give serious consideration to merging with or selling

to another company when the other company has strengths that you do not possess.

Forecasting is an essential, but imprecise planning tool. A good starting point is to consider the past as a prologue of sorts for the future.

It is essential that you clearly identify what business you are in. Don't limit your scope to the product(s) you sell: Position yourself as a player in the businesses you serve.

The key factor in the ultimate success or failure of a business merger or sale is "synergism."

How a Family Business Grew to
Annual Sales of $100.4 Million
Current/Looart Press

Lester B. (Dusty) Loo, Former Board Chairman and CEO, Looart Press, Inc.

"Dusty" Loo, upon graduation from college in 1961, went to work in his family's business—Current. Starting early in his career, Loo set a course for becoming both an industry statesman and a civic leader. His dedication to direct marketing led to his appointment as chairman of the Direct Marketing Association in 1980. Loo is currently chairman of High Valley Group, Inc., a private investment group.

"You know, they're paying ridiculous amounts for companies these days," one of our board members, Jerry Hardy, said. This was somewhat of an aside after one of our board meetings.

The Ten-Year Plan

To my brother Gary and me, this was not just a random comment. Three years previously, we had put together what we called our 10-year plan. The goal was to place our company in a position to be sold within a 10-year period. Selling only three years into the plan seemed a bit premature, but there were certain windows of opportunity that had to be explored.

The reasoning behind this strategy had several facets, the most important being that we had made a decision not to pass the company on to the next generation. Now, of course, we will never know what our children would have done with it, but we had seen examples of what happened to other closely-held companies when passed to cousins or further afield. The companies were ruined or the families developed so much animosity that they were ruined. Also, our children were at least four years or more from being old enough to even join the company, and we were of such a size that it would take a lot of time and seasoning to bring any of them up to managerial levels.

Secondly, if we were going to sell Current, we wanted to do it while we were young enough to enjoy the fruits of our labor. David Rothschild once said at a Young Presidents' Organization meeting I attended, "You're either rich or you own a company." There's some advantage to being rich.

Our specific goal was to sell the company for $100 million dollars or more, and Jerry Hardy thought this feasible. So off to New York we went with our story to visit the merger-and-acquisitions divisions of five previously selected Wall Street firms that had good reputations. Three of these firms thought our price was easily attainable. The other two did not.

One of the principals of a firm that didn't think we could achieve our goal was an old high-school buddy who just couldn't bring himself to believe that we could be that successful. Of the three believers, we picked Lazard Freres as our investment banker. We liked the people involved, Jerry had worked with them before and was comfortable with their methodology, and they had a great name as one of the most respected investment banking houses in the world.

Preparing for the Sale

Picking an investment house was easy compared to the work that followed. This was the spring of 1986. We had to insure that the money and the company changed hands prior to December 31 of that year because 1987 was the year the tax laws on capital gains income took a dramatic shift for the worse. They popped from 20 percent to 28 percent, a huge 40-percent increase. We definitely had a time constraint.

The next step was to put together a confidential memorandum, or offering prospectus, and to compile a list of approximately 10 or more companies of sufficient size and reason for possible interest in Current. Most of these companies were in the direct-marketing business. Three were in the "social expression" business, and a couple were outside long shots.

Conducting a Controlled Auction

Lazard Freres' strategy for selling a company was called a "controlled auction." To be a player in the auction, a company must commit to a bid of over $100 million dollars, and there was a fixed deadline for this bid. Several companies responded and began their due diligence. They visited our offices and factories and received a comprehensive briefing from top management. Through all this, we were able to keep our plan confidential from all but our five vice presidents.

We eliminated all but two companies from those who showed sincere interest. These two were relative giants in direct marketing. One was Avon and the other was American Can Company, which was soon to change its name to Primerica. The controlled auction was on in earnest!

The Current story really begins with Looart Press. It ends there, too, since Looart was the holding company that owned Current, Inc. at the time of its sale.

The History of Looart

Looart was founded by Orin Loo in 1947, one year after he moved to Colorado Springs with his family. Prior to moving to Colorado Springs, Orin was head of the lithography department at Hallmark Cards in Kansas City. He had begun his career at Hallmark as an artist 10 years earlier, so he was blessed with the right skills and had the proper training in all aspects of the greeting-card business.

The end of World War II was a time of great mobility in the United States, and the fledgling Loo family was no exception. Kansas City, prior to wide-spread air conditioning, was almost unbearable in the summer, according to Orin, particularly with Colorado Springs so close (600 miles) and a job offer waiting. In 1946, the family became Coloradans, and, in 1947, after the offered job didn't live up to expectations, Looart was born in the garage behind the family home.

The early years were rough going as it is with most startups. The company survived by doing commercial printing but managed in the first years to publish a small album of personalized Christmas cards which were sold by retail card shops in the region. I might be stretching the truth to say that the company flourished over the next three years, but it did grow and moved out of the garage into a "real" industrial building.

The Christmas card album became larger with more designs and was carried by prestigious stores nationwide. As this was happening, other products were added to Looart's proprietary line. One of these was postcard-size heavy stock with a very nice rose illustration in the upper left-hand corner. This card was dubbed "Post-A-Note."

Looart's Entry into Mail Order

Due to a number of factors, the greatest of which was a need for money, Miriam Loo decided on a foray into mail order. With the rose Post-A-Note as a product, Methodist ministers as a mailing list, and a $1,500 grubstake from her father, a second business was born in the Loo family home. This time the basement was used as a headquarters in place of the garage.

Orin Loo designed a black-and-white flyer with illustrations, shown in Exhibit 6.1, on how the Methodist churchwomen could buy a box of 40 of these cards for 55 cents, sell them for $1.00, and, of course, keep the additional 45 cents for themselves to do whatever good works they wished. Along with the flyer was a full box of notes as a sample.

Due to a small degree of guilt for having been sent such a generous sample, and the fact that the cards were truly a bargain and a great way to make money, the mailing to the churchwomen had a 27-percent response, an almost un-heard-of percentage for those days. The offer also gave the buyer a choice of de-ferring payment until the goods were received and then paying the amount due plus postage, or enclosing a check along with the order and having the postage paid by the company. This little gambit found Miriam with 85 percent of the or-

Exhibit 6-1 Looart's First Mail-Order Flyer

ders prepaid. Current was manufacturing with the customers' money—truly an ideal situation.

Current remained in the basement for 10 years. The company certainly was not static, but it didn't grow much either. The simple post-a-note design was expanded to five or six, and a recipe card, shown in Exhibit 6.2, was added around 1959. The recipe card design featured an old potbellied stove with the caption, "What's Cookin," followed by lines like a notebook on the face of the card. This card proved to be so popular, it stayed in the line for 20 years.

The mailing lists were also expanded to include other clubs and organizations and additional women's church groups. Invariably these lists came from annuals and club rosters. Mailing-list brokers were unheard of by the company's management. Current wasn't on the cutting edge of anything. It was a "seat of the pants," wonderful business.

If Current remained small, it also remained very profitable. It provided the needed additional money for the Loos to educate their children and enjoy a fairly comfortable life. In 1960, Current did a gross volume of around $45,000 and had a net profit of around $20,000. For 1960, this was a true wonder from a business in the basement.

My Entry into Mail Order

I was one of the Loos educated (hopefully) by money from Current. I graduated from the University of Kansas in January 1961 and immediately went to work for Current in the basement. I had worked in the basement the summer before and had taken advertising courses and two direct-marketing courses in college. The university must have been one of the few to offer direct-marketing courses at that time. Our textbooks were by Hodgson, Yeck, and, of course, Bob Stone. These men were my gurus.

First on my agenda was to move the operation out of the basement, and second was to apply my newfound knowledge of mail order, as direct marketing was then known. The first was easy. We found an old house in an even older part of town and moved the business into it by late spring of 1961. There were two full-time and three part-time employees. I was, of course, full time. The others mostly counted and boxed cards.

Through school and outside reading, I was able to somewhat hold my own in the mail-order promotion of our products, but the rest of the business was a befuddlement.

To compensate for this lack of knowledge, we hired our first consulting firm, James M. Kittleman and Associates, from Chicago. Joe Skerpan of Kittleman's firm came out to Colorado Springs, looked over our very small business,

Exhibit 6-2 Current's Popular Recipe Card from 1959

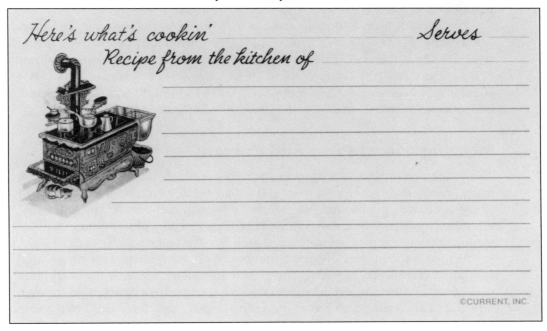

and wrote a scathing document basically saying that we didn't know our hind end from third base. Then he told us how to fix this deplorable situation.

Joe was so right. We completely revamped our finance, manufacturing, and shipping areas into departments that worked very well. We were grossing about $300,000 at the time, so I guess he caught us before fatal mistakes could be made.

Our Use of Consultants

Our first experience with consultants was so pleasurable from a knowledge-gained standpoint that the judicious use of outside help became a part of our management philosophy. Kittleman's firm was used many more times for management and management structures. We've used salary-and-benefits, space-planning, fulfillment, and merchandising consultants. Just about every area of the business was touched in one way or another.

Another much less expensive method of gaining knowledge is through industry trade associations. Early on, I joined the DMA and found it to be an unbelievable source of ideas. One good idea can literally be worth millions. I also became a member of the American Management Association (AMA), which is a very good way to keep track of management philosophy and general business practices and tactics.

The growth from $300,000 gross in 1964 to $800,000 gross in 1967 was not exactly a cakewalk, but it wasn't fraught with major problems. Current was growing at the rate of about 50 percent a year. When you start from a base of practically zero, the compounding effect takes several years before any reasonable size is obtained. To go from $100,000 to $150,000 is no great stretch, but to grow from $50 million to $75 million takes considerable effort.

Merging Looart Press and Current

The year Current hit $800,000 was the year my brother Gary and I decided it made great sense to merge Current and Looart Press, which he was working for at the time. We approached our parents who still had controlling stock and after discussion, cajoling, and schmoozing, they agreed. I must admit there was trepidation on our part too, but it did look like we had a bull by the tail.

Although the merger created a number of opportunities, it mainly created an almost completely vertically integrated company in which the marketing was driven by Current and the manufacturing (from artist's conception through finished printed product) was supplied by Looart. Also, Gary and I had a genuine desire to work together. In 1967, I became president of Looart Press, Gary was vice president, and our parents became members of the Board and relatively passive onlookers. It is highly unusual for company founders to truly give up the purse strings and the power and pass them to their children. I guess we had unusual parents.

Here we were, at ages 29 and 26, with a corporation doing $1.5 million in sales. Where did we go from there? The precepts of professional management always intrigued us, but we knew we didn't have the background to be professional in all areas.

Hiring Professional Managers

We began a planned effort of hiring professional managers from much larger companies, people who didn't have to break new ground with each year's sales increase. In short, people who hopefully knew what they were doing.

We started hiring to our major weakness, which was the area of finance, and we kept going through marketing, manufacturing, material control, human resources, data processing, and so on. Not all of these people stayed with us. Some were caught by the Peter Principal and were replaced. However, by the fall of 1986, we had assembled a team of vice presidents and directors who had literally made Gary and me redundant in the day-to-day management of the company.

You may well ask how Current could accomplish the move from the basement to $800,000 in sales with a product so inexpensive as a greeting card.

The Magic of Tiered Pricing

There are many answers to this question, but the one that looms far over any other is what we called "tiered pricing," which was basically volume discounts. We began with a very simple formula. If a person ordered less than six boxes of our product, the price was our full retail of $1 per box. If more than six boxes were ordered, we would only charge 55 cents per box. In the very early sixties, we only had two products, Post-a-Notes and recipe cards, and they were priced the same. It was easy to force a higher average order, but it wasn't a very high average.

As time went on and new products with different prices were added to the line, the volume discount remained attached to the number of products offered and not the total dollar volume. Our pricing on new products was rising dramatically.

We tried numerous pricing tiers over the course of many years with the goal of getting a larger and larger average order. We used three-tiered pricing as a mainstay, experimenting with various numbers of products per tier. Our highest volume generator was pegging the third or lowest-priced tier at over 18 products. In 1986, we were generating over $50 per order. For such a bargain product, that was almost a miracle.

Current began by selling its products as church fundraisers and branched out to other organizations who could use fundraising products. Schools, 4H groups, and Campfire Girls all became Current customers, but along the way something else happened that was very serendipitous. We found that our products were appealing more and more to people who wanted a great bargain.

Expanding Our Product Line

Beginning with the Post-a-Note and recipe cards, we moved to a small piece of stationery we called a "Just-a-Note." It was mailed like a postcard, but it was folded in three parts like a letter and sealed with a round, gold, pressure-sensitive sticker. The outside was illustrated in a variety of motifs and styles. This one item was an incredible hit, and we were able to double our sales from

$150,000 to over $300,000. Obviously the value of a new and better product was a lesson well learned.

Next, we put Christmas and birthday cards in the line. These were generally sold in packs of 10 to 12 with a variety of designs. Of course, the price per pack was higher than 55 cents, but each individual card at the lowest-volume price was about 18 cents. This compared very favorably with the retail market where cards of comparable quality were 53 cents or more. We were becoming more of a full-line card shop through a catalog and American women were beginning to notice our prices and our quality.

Expanding Markets

We thought that our buyers were organizations wanting to earn a few extra bucks, and we positioned all our sales material that way. "Earn extra money for your group" was the basic theme of a letter that went with the catalog, and that theme was heavily promoted throughout. We were slow to notice the arrival of what became the biggest market of all. We found that military wives, schoolteachers, secretaries in large corporations, or any pool of several women were becoming what we called "group buyers." These women would pool their orders to meet or exceed the product number breaking point with one person designated as the receiver and distributor of the order.

You can see how this snuck up on us. We didn't realize that five or six people were sharing the orders. Once we found out what was happening, our strategy changed. We no longer talked exclusively to "you and your group." We started pulling customer's friends into the act. "Your group or your friend" was a whole new pitch, not only to whom we could mail but how we planned our merchandising.

We now could use lists of women mail-order buyers, which was a huge universe stressing the "friends" part, without forgetting the groups that were still a major piece of our business. Our merchandise changed as we realized we were becoming more of a mail-order card shop for individuals and less of a place to buy a lot of a single product for fundraising.

Post-a-Notes and Just-a-Notes were fading out. Recipe cards were still strong and continued to be so, but we found we could continue our growth in the mainstream.

In 1968, sales were $1,840,000; in 1969, $3,320,000; and in 1970, the next milestone, over $5 million gross revenue. Not all of this came from Current. Slightly over $1 million was contributed by the Looart Press side of our business. The Christmas cards were now supplemented by wedding invitations that were also sold through albums and by posters of ski areas, surfing beaches, and foreign ports. We also purchased another mail-order company, American Stationery, in Peru, Indiana, in 1970.

With each new product category we added to the line, we found our sales increasing significantly. Many of these categories stand out in my mind, but the one that really rises over the others was the valentine product line.

We had an internal debate going for a few years as to whether or not to start a valentine program. The "pro" side obviously argued the merits of increased volume, profitability, and so on. The "con" side questioned whether we could fill orders in time when they came from a catalog mailed after January 1 and had to be in the customers' hands several days prior to February 14. The "pro" side eventually won, and we introduced the valentine line in the mid-1970s.

Historically, the largest dollar volume day in Current's year happened approximately three weeks after the valentine mailing. Based on our experience with valentines during the late 1970s, we introduced many other event-oriented products for Easter, back-to-school, Halloween, and Thanksgiving.

Also, in 1973, Current had its first month of over $1 million in sales. Remember it was only a few years previously that we had celebrated our first *year* of over $1 million.

For many years, the Current mailing piece consisted of an envelope, a 5½" × 8" catalog stitched along the shorter side, a letter signed by Miriam B. Loo, and an order blank with a return envelope. A sample of the catalog listings is shown in Exhibit 6.3. As Current grew and the number of products expanded, so did the order blank. Every item listed in the catalog was also listed on the order blank.

Most companies have 10 lines or so for the customer to list their order. With one line for each product (fully described), we felt we were providing additional impetus to order more items. I'm sure that was the case, too, since we tried many tests around this concept. The fact that it worked was great, but the order blank began to look more and more like an IRS long form.

Concentrating On the Driving Force

We added calendars, recipe books, Mother's Day cards, and other products. All helped Current to grow. During this period, however, the Looart portion of the business was not keeping up. We were concentrating a lot of time and energy in the retail business, and Looart was becoming a smaller and smaller amount of our total sales. What to do? The answer was to shut down all operations that were demanding too much time and energy and concentrate on the horse that was leading the parade.

Exhibit 6.3 Sample Page of Listings in Current's Catalog

BE SURE TO READ "STEP 2" ON PAGE A FOR DISCOUNT PRICES!

ORDER CODE	HOW MANY ITEMS?	NAME OF ARTICLE — CATALOG PAGE NO.	1-7 ITEMS	8-15 ITEMS	16 - ITEMS	TOTAL AMOUNT
1414		Stationery (Sweet Pea Border), p. 10	$2.25	$1.70	$1.25	
1416		Stationery (Yellow Roses), p. 10	2.25	1.70	1.25	
1513		Stationery Gift Set (Daffodil Days), p. 11	4.50	3.40	2.50	
1516		Kitchen Blossoms Gift Set, p. 11	3.25	2.45	1.80	
1566		Rainbow Flight Stationery Set, p. 11	5.00	4.00	3.00	
1567		Iris Blossoms Stationery Set, p. 10	3.50	2.65	2.00	
1568		Fancy Folds (Butterfly Fancy), p. 11	3.50	2.65	2.00	
1603		Gift Enclosures (Sunny Circles), p. 13	1.50	1.15	.85	
1621		Yarn (Yellow), p. 13	1.15	.85	.65	
1622		Yarn (Green), p. 13	1.15	.85	.65	
1623		Yarn (White), p. 13	1.15	.85	.65	
1624		Yarn (Blue), p. 13	1.15	.85	.65	
1625		Yarn (Red), p. 13	1.15	.85	.65	
1690		Gift Wrap (Newborn Joys), p. 12	1.30	1.00	.75	
1699		Gift Wrap (Birthday Wishes), p. 12	1.30	1.00	.75	
1703		Gift Wrap (Anniversary Bouquet), p. 12	1.30	1.00	.75	
1704		Gift Wrap (Congratulations!), p. 12	1.30	1.00	.75	
1714		Gift Wrap (Bridal Blossoms), p. 12	1.30	1.00	.75	
1715		Gift Wrap (Pixie Play), p. 12	1.30	1.00	.75	
1717		Every Occasion Gift Wrap Collection, p. 12	7.25	5.45	4.00	
1721		Reversible Gift Wrap (Fancy Fruit), p. 12	1.50	1.15	.85	
1806		Placemats (Tree Blossom Settings), p. 21	6.00	4.80	3.60	
1855		Clipboard & Memo Pad, p. 18	5.00	4.00	3.00	
1856		Memo Pad (Garden Glow), p. 18	1.30	1.00	.75	
1866		Large Memo Minder (Pencil Partner), p. 18	3.50	2.65	2.00	
1891		Message Board (Quick Reminders), p. 18	2.75	2.05	1.55	
1892		Message Board (Monthly Reminders), p. 18	5.00	3.75	2.75	
2005		Recipe Card Assortment (Kitchen Stitchery), p. 20	1.50	1.15	.85	
2006		Double Recipe Card Assortment, p. 20	1.50	1.15	.85	
2047		Recipe Cards (Flower Pitcher), p. 20	1.50	1.15	.85	
2048		Double Recipe Cards (Herb Garden), p. 20	1.50	1.15	.85	
2081		Recipe Savers, p. 20	1.30	1.00	.75	

PAGE B
TOTAL ITEMS

TRANSFER PAGE B TOTALS
TO ORDER SUMMARY ON LAST PAGE

PAGE B
TOTAL AMOUNT

It was absolutely amazing what talent was unleashed by that discussion. The art department, which had spent most of its time on Christmas cards, moved on to design cards for Current which got better and more diversified; we became very proud of the products we were presenting. Actually, new ground was broken in the greeting-card field with highly realistic animals, birds, and flowers printed on recycled paper. As someone else said, "Copying is the greatest form of flattery." I think it's true. Several of the major greeting-card companies began following in our footsteps.

Breaking Out of a Sales Plateau

In the mid-seventies, Current began to experience a flattening in sales. We were doing about $25 million in sales and profits were fair, but we just seemed to be on hold.

Gary and I were in the Hamptons with our three top executives planning our strategies for the next year. In a private moment, the two of us decided that something drastic was needed. We had to break out of the mold or else. The way to do this was a dramatic increase in stock keeping units (SKUs) and a whole new catalog. We increased the size of the catalog to a full 8½" × 11", as shown in Exhibit 6.4, and doubled the number of products.

We knew these changes would have an affect on our sales, but we thought we were ready. Our board was concerned and cautioned us on the many problems we could have.

We sailed bravely on, comfortable with our planning and not heeding saner minds who thought that increasing our product line over a few more years might be a wiser course.

There was no question that from a gross sales standpoint our strategy was a complete success. Our gross volume ballooned from $25 million to approximately $50 million, but other things happened too.

Our inventory levels were too low. Our ability to process orders was taxed to a point where we were just stacking trays of unopened order envelopes, and the phones were ringing off the hook. We were receiving thousands and thousands of calls each day from disgruntled customers. The phone company told us that we had backed up the long-distance system to Omaha (whatever that meant). It was a true nightmare.

There was one thing we probably did right during that horrible fall of 1979: We refunded over $7 million to customers who did not receive their orders in time for Christmas, and we did everything else in our power to assuage their well-placed anger. We wrote letters, made calls, and sent free gifts and coupons, hoping they would give us another chance.

Exhibit 6.4 Front Cover of Current's Enlarged Catalog

Fortunately, they did. Our customers forgave our lack of good judgment but not overnight. It probably took about three years for the effect of the nightmare to wear off.

Much was learned during that fall. Most importantly, we learned that we really could be a much larger company and, quite frankly, that overrode all the other negatives. We learned that our inventory as a percentage of expected sales had to be much higher. We became more sophisticated in testing each product's percent of total sales and, through earlier mailings, trying to predict with greater accuracy the total volume for each season. Our order processing was changed to accommodate a much higher number of orders. Lastly, because of the increased number of products we had in the line, we successfully broke the not-invented-here (NIH) syndromes, which had a pervading influence in our marketing and art departments. Gary and I knew that a design of whole products bought from outside sources could make our catalog seem much more diverse and attract more sales. From then on, we added many entire design themes developed by outside talent. Suzy's Zoo and the comic strip "Cathy" were two of the design themes that were very successful.

Our board had told us to watch out and we thought we knew more than they did. How we could be so dumb continues to amaze me even now. We must have been wandering in a cloud of debris.

Adding Outside Expertise

We formed our board in 1967 at the suggestion of a management study done by Kittleman and Associates. The objective was to gain some outside expertise for very little money. It worked.

Our first board consisted of the Loo family, Miriam and Orin, Gary and me. The outside directors were the previously mentioned Jim Kittleman, Bill Kirn, the vice president of the bank we used, and a former executive with American Home Products.

The common wisdom states that you should not put your banker, your attorney, or your accountant on your corporate board. I think common wisdom is right, but both Bill Kirn and Bill Cantwell, an attorney, served us well for many years. Cantwell was an estate attorney and didn't handle any company business. Dan Killips was our other board member in 1967. He was an attorney and investment advisor, but, more important, he was a vice prsident of Looart Press in the very early years. Dan came to Colorado Springs for health reasons in the early fifties and stayed with Looart as an investor and officer until 1958. Dan knew all the players well.

Over the years, the makeup of our board changed. Many times we wanted board members with specific knowledge of such areas as computers or marketing. Sometimes we wanted board members for overall business acumen.

Every time new board members were recruited, it was with the understanding that they could be relieved of their duties by the majority shareholders who, by that time, were Gary and me. We'd come through a restructuring of the company and had converted our parents' common stock to preferred.

A few times Gary and I actually exercised that prerogative. We tried to make the board as personal as possible with planned social events. We felt the better they knew us, the better they could understand the company and its culture.

By 1986, the cast had changed completely with the exception of Bill Cantwell and the Loo family. We found that it was fairly easy to attract very high-powered people who could contribute greatly to our growth and professionalism. We recruited these people in various ways, including headhunters. I'd also been chairman of the DMA in 1981, which gave me an entree to the best and the brightest in the business. Our board in 1986, before the conclusion of the sale that caused it to disband, included some very good people.

Other than Jerry Hardy, a direct marketing Hall of Famer, past publisher of *Life* magazine, founder of Time-Life Books, and past president of the Dreyfuss Fund; we had Dave Heneberry, former managing director of Tatham-Laird and Kudner in New York and past president of RCA Direct Marketing; Tom Hodson, formerly chief operating officer of Banctexas, Inc.; and Bill Moxley, past president of Citicorp Diners Club.

Along the way, some of our other board members were Royal Freund, past president of Revell Toys; George Arneson, consultant and past president of Vendo Corp.; Brack Duker, controller for Atlantic Richfield Corp. (ARCO); and Sid McKnight, president of Montgomery Ward. Sid was also a director of Wal-Mart at the time and urged us to buy stock in this up-and-coming company. That was one more missed opportunity due to a lack of significant cash. It was a privilege to have these people on our board and they were great, loyal contributors to Current.

In 1985, we had a piece of luck that is still resounding through the halls of Current. Randy Reynolds, late of Rocky Mountain Banknote, talked with Gary about the possibility of printing bank checks for the trade. Printing checks to sell through banks was not very appealing, but the idea of marketing personal checks to Current customers seemed to have some merit. It was discussed among the officers and was met with a unanimous "Go for it."

There were some very positive aspects to the check business. It was a designed product, and design was one of our major strengths. Correspondingly, but most important, once a person ordered checks from us, the reorder blank was automatically there to use. The chances of keeping a customer in checks for a lifetime was high.

Convincing our customers that they could buy checks from Current and not the bank raised a question mark, but we believed this could be overcome. Randy Reynolds became the manager of the check department, and the production was placed with a company in Texas who dropshipped the finished products. Our pricing was such that we were severely undercutting banks who thought they were entitled to grossly inflated profit margins because the customers didn't know better. I'd always felt that banks weren't very smart to begin with, and this just confirmed my suspicions. It soon became apparent that we had a real winner, so we geared up to produce in house.

This was the situation in October 1986, the end of the first quarter of Current's 1987 fiscal year.

Twenty-Five Years of Learning

We had learned a lot over the last 25 years: the necessity of goal setting, the importance of risk, the power of people as customers or employees. Our board, our officers, all our people had made the whole thing work.

That fall (1986), Current had over 1,400 employees housed in over 600,000 square feet of space in Colorado Springs. We also had four retail stores and a factory outlet. We were probably the fourth-largest social expression company in the business after Hallmark, American Greetings, and Gibson Greeting Cards.

Everything was in order, and Current was enjoying an extremely high 20-percent houselist response. We were using a multiple regression analysis (called DMAS) on our lists which allowed us to truly pinpoint areas of opportunity. This was done with a very large-scale Honeywell DPS 88/81 and was accessed by over 200 terminals, all communicating through Ethernet.

The Culmination

At the end of our June 30, 1986, fiscal year, Current had a gross volume of $102.4 million and the coming year looked a lot better.

The last day of the controlled auction brought all the major players to the offices of Lazard Freres in Rockefeller Center in New York. The merger-and-acquisition people from Avon and American Can, my brother with our chief financial officer, Tom Kelly, from Current, and Arnold Spangler and Don Petrie from Lazard Freres completed the cast.

Unfortunately, I had to be in Las Vegas for the DMA convention, which seemed an appropriate place to be during the biggest gamble of my life. I was in touch by telephone, but there's really nothing like being there. Bids were opened and discussed, and the players were escalating the bids. Finally a winner emerged, American Can Company by a nose. The winning bid was $115 million in cash plus additional concessions which probably totalled about $120 million.

That afternoon, when the smoke had cleared, Bill Johnson and I got together in the MGM Grand for a few drinks. Bill was the president of Fingerhut, also owned by American Can, and Current's management would report to him. Coincidentally, Bill and I were fraternity brothers at the University of Kansas in the late 1950s.

Dewey Ballentine of New York acted as attorneys for American Can, and we used Sherman and Howard of Denver. The sales part over, the nuts and bolts came next, and what a chore that was. I have the utmost respect for the attorneys and financial people in this transaction. They seemed to work around the clock, and there were a few times when I know they did.

Gary and I went to New York in late December to sign piles and piles of documents for the transfer of the business. On December 31, 1986, a check for $115 million was passed to our attorneys, and Gary and I were out of a job.

The story of Current is still unfolding and if any story deserves a few comments in lieu of a sequel, this one does.

During 1987, Primerica, as it was then known, decided to get out of the direct-marketing business. Current was on the block along with Fingerhut and some smaller direct-marketing subsidiaries. Exactly one year later, December 31, 1987, Current was sold to the Deluxe Corporation in Minneapolis for a reported $180 million.

Also in 1987, Avon got tired of direct marketing and started shedding their divisions. I wonder what sort of bids we'd have had if we had tried to take Current to the market in 1987.

Today, Current is the second-largest private employer in Colorado Springs after the giant MCI. It employs over 3,000 people. The check business is a major portion of its sales, and, with Jon Medved as president, I'm sure all bodes well for the future.

Gary, Tom Kelly, and I formed High Valley Group, Inc., an investment company that busily tries to find ways to unintentionally lose money.

In 1961, I read a motivational book by Joseph Cossman, who sold ant farms by mail. The book was called *How I Made $1,000,000 in Mail Orders.* Maybe now is the time for a new one, *How to Make $100,000,000 in Mail Order.*

Bob Stone's
Commentary

The Looart/Current story might be chronicled as the consummate "Horatio Alger Story," "The Ultimate Family Business" or "The Power of Entrepreneurship." In a way, it is all of these.

In another way, the Looart/Current story may be referred to as a classic example of niche marketing at its finest. It's incredible, in a way, that the Loo brothers succeeded in taking a common commodity—cards—and building a $100 million business. Three strategies might be identified as the basic reasons for their success:

1. Quality cards at low prices

2. Catering to specific niches in the marketplace

3. Selling cards by the box

But Current employed many strategies in addition to the three basics. Let us record those strategies.

☐ If you want to sell your company, set a minimum price and a fixed deadline.

☐ If you want to get cash with orders, devise an incentive for prepayment.

☐ Compensate for a lack of knowledge by hiring professional consultants.

☐ Compound your knowledge through membership in industry trade associations.

☐ Hire professional managers who fill in the voids of your major weaknesses.

☐ Use tiered pricing to increase the average order size.

☐ If you are dedicated to niche marketing, continually explore other niche groups in an effort to expand your customer base.

☐ Company growth is directly related to product line extension.

☐ Listing all your products on your order form provides additional impetus to order more items.

Have the courage to disband operations that demand too much time and energy for a small return. Apply that time and energy to the operations that drive the business.

The more choices you give in a catalog, the better your chances to make a sale.

Customer loyalty is vital. Therefore, when you fail to deliver on time, send prompt refunds, gifts, or discount coupons.

Improve the decision-making process of your top people by adding outside people to your board of directors who will complement your expertise.

Tom Nickel and Friends from Day One

Baldwin Cooke Company

Bill Baker, Copywriter, friend of Tom Nickel

*T*om Nickel, *former chairman of the board of Baldwin Cooke Company, began his career selling road atlases for Rand McNally. It was with the idea that such products could be sold to companies by mail, as gift items for valued customers, that Nickel started the Baldwin Cooke Company.*

Bill Baker came to work at Baldwin Cooke Company after getting his start in catalog and mail-order copywriting. He wrote Baldwin Cooke's first direct-response copy, and he insists there are whole paragraphs of that same copy being used today. After leaving Baldwin Cooke to work in general advertising for 27 years, Baker had the good sense to return to the company.

Right away you ask yourself, what in the world does the story of Baldwin Cooke have to do with me? Put directly, what's in it for me?

Well, if you are one of those rare birds who may start your own direct-response business, you may gain some insight into just how it is done. If you are running a business, the same is true. If you are working for someone, it might just help you make a judgment about the kind of job your boss is doing and, consequently, how secure your job may be.

In any case, it is a story of a business that began on a kitchen table and became a multimillion-dollar corporation. One word of caution: You will find no arcane formulas and very little business-school language in this chapter. This is a simple story. Because almost everything Tom Nickel did seems simple. That is, it seems simple once it is done, after the fact.

The paradox, of course, is that in direct response, as in so many of the things we humans do together, it quickly becomes very hard to keep things simple. The rewards of crisp, clear, simple thought and action, as the Baldwin Cooke story demonstrates, can be magnificent.

The Funny Little Street Where It All Began

The story begins in 1956. Tom Nickel was on his way to becoming a superstar salesman for Rand McNally. Come to think of it, maybe he already was. And I was the most junior of junior copywriters working for one of, as David Ogilvy described them, "those wicked old mail-order men of Chicago," Paul Grant, who was indeed a giant back in those days when direct response was called mail order.

As it happened, Tom and I both lived in apartments on a funny little street called Reba Place in south Evanston, Illinois, and we both had toddler-aged first sons (Tommy and Billy, of course). And in that summer of 1956, in the sometimes cool, sometimes quite warm dusk, the two of us would push our young heirs around several blocks of the neighborhood in strollers.

Eisenhower was up for re-election, Sears was America's largest retailer, and, as ever, the Chicago Cubs were losing more games than they won. But whatever else was going on in south Evanston, or anywhere in the world, as we walked the kids back toward home, somehow the conversation always came back to the same subject.

"I know the Rand McNally Road Atlas can be sold by mail," Tom would say. "I know it. The only question is, how? How do you sell it?"

Tom, as it happened, had read a copy of a direct-mail course Paul Grant had written and sold under the title, *How to be a Mail Order Millionaire*. The difference was that unlike about 99.99 percent of all the people who bought that course, Tom was going to do something about actually becoming a mail-order millionaire.

He was going to do something about it because that's what entrepreneurs do about ideas. They don't just talk, they do. And Tom was an Entrepreneur with a capital, boldface "E." Because of this, Tom would not be put off by someone's promise "to think about it." The simple thing to do, really the only thing to do, was to get Tom to answer his own question.

"What makes you so sure you can sell the Road Atlas by mail," I asked Tom more than once. The answer was always pretty much the same.

"Because I can sell it face to face. If I could make 20,000, 50,000, 100,000 sales calls, I wouldn't need direct mail. But I can't. So I do."

A Simple Idea Takes Shape

It is a simple idea. Direct mail is what you do when you can't send a good salesperson. So a direct-mail package should be like a personal sales call. What you should do with a direct-mail package is what a really good salesperson would do face to face. Because that works face to face, works in the mail. Could that be true? Could putting together a direct-response package really be that simple?

Paul Grant always thought so. Master of the 8- or 10-page, or even longer, sales letter, Paul always wrote to one person. No matter how many letters went out, he always wrote to one person, somehow he knew, someone with a problem, a hope, or a dream. What he wrote about was how that problem could be solved or how that dream could come true.

More often than not, he used the same selling arguments his client's most productive sales representative used; the gutsy, this is going to make a difference to you, do-it-now, person-to-person kind of selling used by the street merchants at the open air market on Maxwell Street in Chicago.

Listening to Tom's pitch for the atlas, the same points came across over and over again. He didn't spend much time talking about the accuracy of the maps or the quality of the printing. When you are talking maps, the name Rand McNally makes quite a promise all by itself. It did then; it does now.

What Tom did bear down on was the promise that the atlas would be kept and used, that it was a gift that would be appreciated. As proof of that, when he couldn't close a sale on the first call, he left the prospect a sample, confident that it would be used and appreciated. Then, when Tom made his follow-up call, the prospect usually found himself or herself agreeing that the atlas was a useful gift.

From Face-to-Face to Direct-Response Strategy

You might call it a two-step selling strategy: step one, get a sample in the prospect's hands; step two, make use of the prospect's own experience with the product to prove your case in the follow-up. Just about that simply (or so it seems now), Tom's face-to-face selling strategy was translated into a two-step direct-mail sale. The first step was a letter and catalog sheet offering to send a sample to qualified prospects; the second was a series of follow-up letters on the merits of the atlas as a gift and a special price offer for immediate action.

The insight that put the muscle in the selling proposition followed directly from the recognition that the atlas was not being sold as an atlas to an end user, but rather to someone who was giving that atlas as a gift. What that gift-giver wanted was the assurance that the chosen gift would indeed be used and appreciated.

Even so, the two-step, free-sample strategy seemed more than a bit risky because it could end up giving away a ton-and-a-half or so of free samples before ringing up the first dollar in sales. To mitigate that risk, the qualifying letter offering the sample was written, not to maximize return, but rather to gain a measure of commitment.

Through the rest of the summer, Tom stewed with the idea, fussed at it, and wondered if there wasn't another way. But when it came time to pull the trigger, he never flinched. He believed. Tom Nickel made decisions.

And there were plenty of decisions to make. The name of the company, for example. Baldwin was chosen because the name was vaguely associated with railroad locomotives (strength, reliability, and all that good stuff). He chose Cooke with an "e" because it sounded faintly English and Dickensian (Christmas and so on).

Baldwin Cooke Goes into the Mail

Along the way, Tom had lined up two investors, Marv Burack (who would later join Baldwin Cooke as chief financial officer) and Bob Sternberg (who was in the advertising specialty business). The copy got written, the catalog sheet got printed, and 5,000 letters went into the mail just after Labor Day. And the response was good.

The day the first reply came in, Tom asked about the follow-up letters. What follow-up letters? They hadn't been written yet. But they were, at least the first one, that night. Through the rest of September and all through the fall, Tom could go to sleep at night to the happy sound of the lady in the apartment below his, sitting at her kitchen table, typing away into the late-night hours, typing those individual follow-up letters one by one.

But the real excitement came the day the first actual order came. Tom was exultant. For many years, he opened all the Baldwin Cooke mail himself. It was the part of the day he liked best. (If you ever grow weary of caressing order blanks and checks, it's time for you to leave the direct-response business. Tom never did.)

The Baldwin Cooke (Tom Nickel) Way

The first selling season for Baldwin Cooke was a precursor of the way Tom would steer the growth of the company for the next 29 years. In that startup summer, two of the special qualities that made Tom Nickel a successful entrepreneur and a natural direct-response wizard were especially demonstrated.

First of all, he never made a decision until he possessed every bit of information he could assemble. He never tired of thinking and talking about his business. He would read any book, seek out any source, attend any seminar, consult any individual to squeeze out facts and ideas for his business.

Like Leo Burnett, he knew that an idea did not choose its parent. It could come from anyone or anywhere. He had the ability to listen to every source, to every person in an open, nonjudgmental way. Then, like Leo Burnett and some other great ones I have known, he had the ability to make a clean, sure-footed decision, to take the risk himself. At decision time, he was willing to bet on his own well-considered judgments. He followed this process of assembling information, sorting through opinions, and courageous decision making in every business matter he considered.

Secondly, Tom led by asking for, squeezing, and teasing the very best out of every person with whom he came in contact. Oh yes, there is much talk about teamwork in business. Tom didn't just talk about it. He practiced it because he believed in the idea that all of us together were smarter than any one of us. In Tom's world at Baldwin Cooke, the end result mattered; individual contributions were just not a subject that got much attention.

From the first day, working with a small but very diverse group of individuals, Tom so persisted in his emphasis on teamwork that to this day, no one in that group can be quite sure of just exactly who did what. Tom never made an issue out of who did what; what mattered was the vitality and growth of Baldwin Cooke.

The Second Year: Good News and Bad News

All in all, the first year had gone well. The mailing was a success and made a tidy profit, and the Baldwin Cooke Company was on its way.

Or was it? In the second selling season, 1957, the Baldwin Cooke mailing was quadrupled, and, if anything, the first-time response to the atlas was even stronger. But the first-year customers, the people who bought the Atlas in 1956, didn't want to give the same gift a second time; not that gift, anyway. Those first-year customers wanted something new.

To this day, the Baldwin Cooke Company sells Rand McNally Road Atlases, and more than one kind. Now that service stations charge for maps, it's an even more desirable gift. It's just not one you want to give every year. Maybe every third or fourth year, but not every year.

True, starting small, there was an immense universe of first-time direct-response customers out there for the atlas. But repeat business was going to be a problem. That possibility did not satisfy Tom. He wanted a business like the soap business or the beer business. If you are selling soap, you don't want to sell someone one bar of soap; you want to sell that person bars and bars and bars of soap for years and years and years.

The more Tom thought about it, the more he wanted his business to run on the same premise as a profitable magazine. Magazines invest money to acquire a customer, a subscriber. They are willing to go into the hole to make that first sale. They give special price concessions, offer the magazine at prices below the cost of publication and delivery, even after advertising revenues, to sign up first-time subscribers. They then take their profit by getting those first-time subscribers to resubscribe again and again for years and years.

Another simple idea that can and does pay off for any business with significant benefits. Consider the implications. When you come to think of your customers not just as customers but as "subscribers," as people you hope to be doing business with for years, the mathematics of building a customer base, of course, change. So do your ideas about the quality of products offered and the way those subscribers should be serviced.

It's that simple. (There's that word again.) Once a business starts thinking about customers as people it hopes to be doing business with for years, its perspective broadens and the time frame by which it plans and budgets lengthens. That was the point of view Tom Nickel argued for back in the early sixties, and put in place at Baldwin Cooke.

Right about that same time a number of Japanese automobile companies came to the United States with essentially the same strategy and gave Detroit some thumps it is just starting to recover from today.

Birth of the Executive Planner

What kind of product could be like a magazine, could be sold, resubscribed to, if you please, year after year. As the planning for the third year of Baldwin Cooke went forward, Tom began the search for a product like soap, soft drinks, beer, or breakfast cereals, a consumable product that could be sold over and over again to a satisfied customer.

The particular specific for Baldwin Cooke would be that it should be a product for which the consumption cycle would wind down sometime toward the end of the calendar year, the time of year for business gift-giving.

What would you say to a useful, desk-top, week-by-week planning tool for business people? You like that idea? Good, you're beginning to think like Tom Nickel. Again, after the fact, it seems obvious: If you want to sell something for business gift-giving, something that is given at the end of the year, what could beat a product that changes with the calendar? But it's not just a calendar, it's a weekly planner that works hard all year long and needs to be renewed every January.

Tom had that knack, the knack of seeing the obvious just a little bit before everybody else did, before it indeed became obvious. And that is how the Baldwin Cooke Executive Planner came to be.

The Executive Planner was introduced in the 1961 season with a strategy and execution similar to that used for the atlas; a prospecting letter to place samples in the hands of qualified prospects and a series of conversion letters to follow up that sample placement.

How Things Happened

What made the Executive Planner a success? The weekly planning format was, and continues to be, the most popular format. A cover was designed to reflect simple quality. (Yes, desk diaries, like other books, are often judged by their covers.) That cover kept the Executive Planner out on desktops where the person who had given the book could see it and take that as proof that it was being used. And the name, the Executive Planner, seemed to add something.

But the real truth is, things happened at Baldwin Cooke because Tom Nickel made things happen. For example, in 1961, the same year the Executive Planner was introduced, Tom happened to attend a meeting of what was then the Chicago Direct Marketing Club. There he heard Bob Stone speak at a seminar.

Bob Stone's experience with Tom was much like mine, much like that of nearly everyone Tom met who might possibly have something to give to the benefit of Tom's business. After Bob's speech, Tom came forward, introduced himself, and asked a few questions.

Then there was a phone call from Tom. And then the phone calls became more frequent. Bob remembers that it wasn't unusual for Tom to call four or more times in a given day. And the subject was always some aspect of the Baldwin Cooke business.

Tom could do that. He could get your attention, hold your attention, demand your attention, and yet, never seem to wear out his welcome. Bob Stone doesn't know exactly how he did it. No one who worked with Tom knew. He just did it.

Stunning Idea: The Dollar Offer Letter

After perhaps a year and a half of meetings at direct-response–oriented events and regular telephone calls, Tom asked Bob Stone to review the entire Baldwin Cooke business in the spring of 1963.

As one result of that review, Stone came up with a startling idea for a new prospecting letter, offering a sample of the Executive Planner and requiring the prospect to send in a dollar with the reply card, as shown in Exhibit 7.1. The benefits were obvious. If a prospect sent in a dollar, that prospect would almost certainly be more committed; and the dollars collected would help pay the cost of the mailing. The hope was that this would happen without lowering the response significantly.

The startling outcome was that the dollar offer indeed generated some revenue. More than that, on many lists, it actually increased response. Apparently the idea of a sample offered for a dollar was more valuable and more attractive than something offered for free. Or it's possible that the prospect felt less guilty about paying a dollar for a sample then jumping on a free ride by asking for one free. Like so many things in direct response, no one knows for certain. What is certain is that the dollar offer expanded the number of lists that could be profitably mailed.

Direct-Response Mathematics

The subject of list analysis is fundamental to direct response, and it was an area of which Tom Nickel had an intuitive and mathematical command. For example, in the mid-sixties, he observed that large orders accounted for the essential difference between profitable and unprofitable lists. And he sensed that

Exhibit 7.1 Baldwin Cooke's Dollar Offer Letter

A remarkable offer for
people who give business
gifts to their customers,
clients, employees.

You can have a sample
copy of this $15.95 desk
diary for just $1.00!

It's handsome. It's useful. You'll
like to use it yourself. And you'll see
for yourself why it makes such an excellent gift.

Thirteen full months. See a week at a time on 56 two-page
spreads. Pages are 6 1/2" wide by 8 3/4" high. Plenty of space
to write in for each day. In the back -- twenty pages for advance
planning, expense record keeping, and miscellaneous helpful
information. And a removable telephone/address book.

It all comes in a luxurious padded vinyl cover that can be
imprinted with the name of the person you give it to.

Inside the front cover you can imprint your company's name and
address, or any 4-line message, as a permanent reminder of your
thoughtfulness.

We'd like to send you a sample of the Baldwin Cooke Executive
Planner for just $1.00!

Look it over. Think about using it as a business gift from your
company. And that's that. No other obligation.

Whether you place an order or not, the sample copy of the 1988
Executive Planner is yours to keep and use.

To receive your copy by return mail, simply place $1.00 in the
enclosed return envelope and mail. No postage is necessary. Why
not do it right now?

Thank you.

James E. Dunaway

James E. Dunaway
Vice President

P.S.   You can order the Baldwin Cooke Executive Planner for
        gifts for just $9.95 each when you order five or more.
        Full details will be sent with your sample.

Baldwin Cooke Company 2401 Waukegan Road, Deerfield, Illinois 60015 for Baldwin Cooke the occurrence of large orders was a random event. Extended studies confirmed this, and when these large random orders were removed from the analysis, virtually every list was unprofitable.

This unsettling reality would lead a pessimist or the average observer to conclude that the growth of Baldwin Cooke was dependent on random events, that occasional large order every now and then. Ordinary minds might, and in fact did, suggest that Baldwin Cooke cut back on the size of the annual mailing. But Tom was not a pessimist or average. And he certainly was not ordinary.

Having identified the true cost of acquiring a customer, Tom set about determining how that cost could be recovered. With a minimum of data he built a matrix based on projections of how long a customer could be retained and how much that customer's order might grow in size over the lifetime of the relationship.

He then reasoned that it would be proper to consider the fair price to pay to acquire a customer to be the gross margin—revenue less cost of goods sold—generated by that account over a forecast number of years, less the cost of the first-year mailing and subsequent mailings, less a reasonable profit. This discipline, coupled with a present value analysis, has come to be known as the lifetime value concept, and most direct-response managers use it today. But Tom put it together back in the mid-sixties and essentially bet the Baldwin Cooke future on its validity. It was a bet he won big.

Take Care of Your Customers and They'll Take Care of You

Some very important things follow from an understanding of the lifetime value of a customer, things that have to do with product quality and reliability, but most of all, things that have to do with the way you serve your customers.

Knowing the value of a customer, knowing what it cost to acquire one, Tom Nickel made certain each and every customer was well served.

For example, when Lyndon Johnson's guns *and* butter budget deficits led to persistent inflation in the late sixties and seventies, rising costs pushed up the price of the Executive Planner. Baldwin Cooke was faced with the choice of cutting quality or losing the business of price-sensitive customers. This dilemma was resolved by maintaining the quality of the Executive Planner raising the price modestly, and introducing a new scaled-down version of a desk diary with a lower cost structure under the banner of a new and separate subsidiary company, The U.S. Diary Company. The result: Customers had a choice and got what they wanted, and Baldwin Cooke prospered.

In a like way, the Baldwin Cooke catalog (pictured in Exhibit 7.2) was oriented, like the catalogs of most direct-response companies, to the company's customer base, but with a difference. It came to be seen, in a sense, not so much as a builder of revenue, but rather as a way to conduct a 'dialog' with customers, as a way to suggest new ideas to customers, and as a way for customers to tell Baldwin Cooke what they thought of those ideas. Perhaps this is a subtle difference. The paradox is that by conducting this dialog with its customers, Baldwin Cooke did increase revenues.

This same attitude toward customers prevailed in the use of the telephone. It started with the idea of calling the telephone effort, not telephone sales, but telephone service. Telephone-service people were trained to think of themselves not as salespeople, but as customer "helpers." They were coached to take "No, not right now" for an answer graciously.

Results were measured, not by the returns from one wave of calling, but rather from results for the entire selling season. In the final analysis, repeat sales to customers were measured not as the result of mailings, catalogs, or telephone calls, but as the result of a program of total service and as a measure of that customer's value to the company.

Again, paradoxically, this emphasis away from dollars toward service, worked for the telephone program as it did for the catalog. After the introduction of the telephone campaign, repeat sales, in terms of percent of customer retention, and size of orders increased.

And the rest, as they say, is history. The Baldwin Cooke Executive Planner became the best-selling desk diary in the business-gift category. A number of people took a shot at taking the business away from Baldwin Cooke. They couldn't do it. Whatever resources they had, they didn't have the ability to imagine the future the way Tom Nickel did.

Sadly, Tom left this world in March 1985 when he was in his early sixties, left too soon, left at a time when his love (and love is the right word) for the direct-response business was undiminished, and his vision of the future was still clear.

And yet, because starting back on a funny little street in south Evanston nearly 40 years ago, and over the years in between, Tom did so many things right, the Baldwin Cooke Company continues to grow and prosper; its employees continue to know security and good rewards; and the Baldwin Cooke Executive Planner continues to appear on more and more desktops and in more and more briefcases every year.

I think Tom would say that's a happy ending. I hope so.

Exhbit 7-2 Sample of the Annual Baldwin Cooke Catalog

Bob Stone's
Commentary

For years one of the most popular columns in *Reader's Digest* was "My Most Unforgettable Character." Of the hundreds of entrepreneurs I have met and known over the decades, Tom Nickel shall always remain my most unforgettable character.

Tom was a man who was driven. His thirst for knowledge was unquenchable. His loyalty to his associates was legend. He was generous, almost to a fault.

Tom Nickel was a man's man. Whenever Tom's batteries needed recharging he'd head off to a remote fishing village in Canada, casting out each day from his cabin that he built with his own hands. Upon his return, he'd hit the ground running.

Bill Baker, a talented writer, has captured the man, his talent, his strategies, and his unique ability to bring out the best in every life he touched.

Thinking strategically was a way of life for Tom Nickel. Let us review his strategies, as identified by Bill Baker.

☐ If you can sell a product face to face, chances are you can sell it by mail.

☐ The best way to sell a product is to put it in prospects' hands so they can experience the benefits and thereby sell themselves.

☐ If you are offering free samples, don't try to maximize response. Instead, try to gain a measure of commitment.

☐ Look at the orders you receive so you get a feel for who is buying your product.

☐ You will make better decisions if they are based on every bit of information you can assemble.

☐ Avoid pride of authorship like the plague: Be open to other people's ideas at all times. After considering all ideas, make your decision and take the responsibility for the actions.

The perspective of your business broadens when you think of doing business with your customers for years, rather than once or infrequently.

Consumable products are the best candidates for repeat business year after year.

If you ask for a modest amount for a sample, the prospect is more likely to be committed than if you offer to send a free sample.

If you know the lifetime value of a customer, then you know how much you can afford to invest to acquire each new customer.

If your product(s) are in the "top-of-the-line" category, the best way to compete with lower-quality, lower-price competition is to develop similar products at similar prices and sell them under a different company name.

Catalogs can serve not only as revenue builders but as dialog vehicles, a way to suggest new ideas to customers and let them tell you what they think of those ideas.

The trick to telemarketing is to serve the customer in the mode of telephone service rather than telephone sales. Such low-key approaches cement relationships and increase sales.

CHAPTER

8

The "Overnight" Success
Quill

Jack Miller, President, Quill Corporation

Jack Miller started his own office supply business in 1956 with a $2,000 loan and a phone in his father's chicken store. Working with his two brothers, Harvey and Arnold, Miller transformed his business into a $400 million dollar corporation. In 1991, he received the first Lifetime Achievement Award from the Direct Marketing Association. In 1993, he was honored as the Direct Marketer of the Year.

June 1, 1956, a new business was born. With a phone in Dad's chicken store, $2,000 borrowed from my father-in-law, and a few catalogs from a wholesaler, I started Quill Office Supply Company.

Today, Quill Corporation is a $400 million company and is still growing. With over 700,000 customers nation-wide and in Canada, five distribution centers, an office furniture division, and over 1,000 employees (as well as being totally debt free), Quill is one of the leading office-products distributors in the country.

In between were 37 years of hard work, fun, challenges, and constantly evolving strategies, including strategies that had to be drastically changed in the past seven years as the deep discount superstores invaded the industry.

But let's go back to that first day of June in 1956 when I was 27, married two years, the proud owner of a home with a staggering $15,000 mortgage, and ready to take on the world.

My Early Years in Business

After graduating from the University of Illinois with a degree in advertising, I had spent the better part of a year at a few different jobs. One was working for my father for a short while after graduation. Ever since, I've felt that scraping chicken droppings from the pans under the chicken cages is a great way to put the world in perspective for a recent college graduate.

After that and another job or two, I went to work for an uncle who owned a specialty food manufacturing company. I was with them for five years, travelling the country by car, often being on the road three to six weeks at a time. I called on food distributors from Minnesota to Florida, New York to California, and I often worked with their salesmen calling on restaurants, hospitals, diners, wherever food was served.

It was the greatest learning experience I could have had, a "bird's-eye" view of how distribution worked. Selling to and working with hundreds of distributors gave me an insight that was invaluable when I started by own distribution company.

Four years into the job, I got married, but the constant travel made my times at home seem like weekend dates. So after a year of that, I took an offer from a local businessman to run a small ($75,000) division of his sample case business. My division sold briefcases made by other companies to business firms around the country by catalog. And so I became exposed to the mail-order business. I produced the catalog and also spent a good bit of time "on the street" selling to businesses in the Chicago area. I was to own 25 percent of the company, paid for out of profits.

But after a year, the fellow who owned the sample case business and 75 percent of my division decided to sell the business and move to California. I had no say in it, and I didn't want to stay with the people he sold to. So I began looking for a job. Fortunately, I didn't get any offers I liked, even managing to fail the psychological test at one company.

I Decide to Become an Entrepreneur

So I began thinking about starting my own business. But what kind of business to start was the first question. Well, I reasoned, during the year with the brief-case firm, I had personally sold to a number of business firms in the Chicago area, so maybe I had some kind of a base with that. But I knew I couldn't make a living selling just briefcases in the Chicago area and I didn't have the money to go into the mail-order business, even if I had thought about it. But every company, I reasoned, also buys office supplies. So why not sell briefcases where I could and add office supplies?

I found a company that had just gone into the wholesale end of the office supply business to sell to dealers for resale. They were willing to waive their rule that a customer had to be a stocking dealer if I would put up a $300 deposit. And they were willing to sell me a supply of catalogs on which I could rubber stamp my name.

And so I started. I didn't have the vaguest idea how big the office products industry was, what the competition was like, or what I could offer in price or service that would be any different than anyone else. One of the people at the wholesaler tried to talk me out of it. "There are over 100 dealers in Chicago," he said. "You don't have a chance." Almost 30 years later, I took great pleasure in giving him a tour of our brand new 160,000-square-foot headquarters on 36 acres of land.

So, on that first day in June 1956, I was ready to start. With the wholesaler's catalog under my arm, I started knocking on doors. My pricing policy was simple. If it looked like a small company, I would give them 10 percent off the list price. If it was a medium-sized company, it was 15 percent off, and for a large company, 20 percent off. A few years later, it had become too confusing to remember who was getting what discount so we changed it to a straight 15 percent off for everyone.

That was using the "Keep it simple, stupid" strategy, and we have tried to follow that strategy ever since. Right from the beginning, I tried to do things in such a way that someone else could take over the job without having to be a brain surgeon. It has worked well for us.

In any event, I called on every friend I had. My father-in-law and his brother were in the food brokerage business, and they got me every account they could. My dad did what he could.

That first month in business, I sold $960.00 worth of merchandise and made about $35.00 profit. Today, we do that much business every 25 seconds.

I was calling on businesses all over Chicago, making 20 to 25 calls a day, almost all of it cold canvassing. It's a good thing I had a thick skin because the "nos" were much more frequent than the "yeses." But one by one, I did get yeses, and my roster of customers and number of orders slowly grew.

To give the best possible service, whatever I sold in one day I would call in to the wholesaler the next morning, pick up the merchandise that afternoon, and rush back to Dad's chicken store to pack the orders. Then I would pile them into the trunk of my car and rush to the United Parcel depot to get them on the 6:30 p.m. truck for delivery the following day.

So if someone ordered something on Monday, I would ship it on Tuesday, and they would have it on Wednesday. Today, any order that comes in by 6:00 p.m. gets shipped the same day and is delivered the following day in most places across the United States. And, by the way, our prices also are a lot better than 15 percent off list. Today, they range from 30 percent to more than 70 percent off of list.

Having graduated from the school of advertising and having handled some of the promotion work at my uncle's firm plus mail order at the briefcase company, I guess it was sort of natural that in that first year, I made my first mailing. As illustrated in Exhibit 8.1, it was a mimeographed penny postal card sent to 156 people I had called on. There were five items on sale.

I followed that up with additional mailings, single-page, black-and-white mailings. For illustrations, I cut pictures out of the wholesaler's catalog and for type, I used a typewriter. For display prices and headlines, I just hand printed the copy. In a few of those mailings, we enclosed samples, such as rubber bands, strips of adding machine tape, or whatever. Crude as they were, the mailings worked well enough to encourage me to keep on doing it.

Something was working because by the end of the first year, I was doing enough volume to be able to draw a little money out of the business. By the way, one of the things we had counted on was my wife Audrey's salary. By the time I started the business, we had been married for two years and she hadn't become pregnant so we figured she would be working for a while longer. But three months after I started, she became pregnant. Oh well, so much for planning.

During that first year, I had been talking to my younger brother, Harvey, about joining me in the business. He had gotten out of the Navy a few years ear-

Exhibit 8.1 Early Mimeographed Quill Postcard Mailing

lier, was married, had one child, and was working behind the service counter at a wholesale electrical supply company. Harvey joined me in September 1957, and we decided to each draw about $100 a week out of the business, which meant we would lose money unless we got more business.

Also, we now needed an "office." For that first year or so, I had set up a folding table and chair in an empty bedroom at home, and Audrey was typing my invoices for me.

Fortunately, Audrey's Uncle Herb had a two-flat about four blocks from Dad's chicken store. Years before, he had converted from coal to oil, so he had an unused coal bin with about a ton-and-a-half of coal in it, a perfect size for an office, and the rent was going to be "right."

So one weekend, Harvey and I shoveled that coal up out of the coal bin and hauled it to the dump. We then used left-over paint from home to paint the coal bin. Since Harvey had a son and by then I had a daughter, and the left over paint was from their bedrooms, we ended up with a blue and pink office, complete with two kitchen tables for desks. The phones were extensions from Dad's chicken store, so when we were out selling he or Uncle Abe could still answer them for us.

While in that basement office, we even hired our first employee, a part-time person to type invoices and keep the books. There were many days when she had to find her way through the hanging laundry to get to the office.

From the sales territory viewpoint, we kept it simple with Harvey covering the North Side of Chicago while I covered the South Side. Business kept growing. We began to stock a few items in that basement, using old ham boxes nailed together for shelving. It wasn't long before we outgrew the basement; rented a 900-square-foot store a few blocks away; and set up an office area, a small warehouse area, and a packing and shipping area. We also hired a part-time bookkeeper, as well as a full-time person to handle the phone orders.

During this time, our mailings got a little bigger, evolving into 8- and 12-page flyers. I would still work on them at night, clipping illustrations from the wholesaler's catalog and typing the copy. I was getting a little better at that. And we were renting some prospect names in addition to using the names of people we had called on.

As we continued and expanded the mailings, we began to find ourselves staying in more and more to handle the increased number of phone calls. And it wasn't long before we would only go out to call on someone if they asked us to. It wasn't too long after that when we decided that we wouldn't go out and make calls at all.

We Go into Mail Order Full Time

Much to our amazement, five years after I had started, we found ourselves in the mail-order business. We soon moved again, this time to Dad's old chicken store, converting the big garage area where he used to keep the live chickens into a warehouse and the store area into offices. Dad had gone out of the retail business and was acting as a broker, so he didn't have to handle any product and just needed desk space. Now he had a desk in *our* office and we answered the phones for *his* office when he was out. By then we had about five employees.

Our sale flyers had grown to 24, 32, and 48 pages. But we were still using the wholesaler's big full-line, 300-plus–page catalog which we sent to every account once a year. But that forced us to buy a lot of product through the wholesaler rather than selling product we were stocking and buying at a lower cost. We decided to produce our own catalog so we could direct customer orders into product lines that we showed and that we bought direct and at a better discount.

To accommodate an expanded inventory, we rented the building next door and broke through the walls to connect the two buildings. I set up an office in the new building and locked myself away there with an assistant to produce the catalog. By then, of course, we were using typesetters and glossy photographs in our flyers. For the catalog, we decided to also use an art studio. Harvey was busy running the business while I selected items, wrote copy, did rough mock-ups, and worked with the art studio.

Finally, in 1963, seven years after I had started, we produced our first "full-line" catalog, four-color cover and all. It was a beauty. The art work and printing were great. And there were 96 pages filled with merchandise. We mailed it out and waited in great anticipation for the flood of orders to start rolling in.

Well, the orders didn't start "rolling in." Day after day, week after week, we kept waiting for that massive wave of orders. But, business just continued growing at about the pace it had been before. We really began to get nervous because we had needed to borrow money to help pay for the extra building, to fill it with inventory, and to produce the catalog.

I think the total amount we borrowed was about $15,000. Petty cash money from today's perspective, but the national debt from our perspective then. And we had committed to pay off that loan at the rate of $2,000 every three months.

Having that additional rent and the loan to pay off, we were getting a little desperate when business didn't "explode" as we had expected it to. Harvey,

Dad, my father-in-law, and I had a meeting one evening at Harvey's apartment to talk about the situation. There was talk about giving up on mail order and going back on the street selling. But I refused to do that, and we decided to live or die with mail order.

And then I did one of the dumbest things I had ever done. Thinking that the catalog was a failure, I began to cannibalize the art work from the catalog, using it to produce flyer pages. No sooner had I done that then the catalog began to have the hoped-for effect on our business and volume started growing at a faster pace. But by then it was too late. The catalog art work was totally destroyed and it would be several years before we once again produced a full-line catalog.

We learned a lesson then that I have never forgotten. Everything takes longer than you expect it to. It was true then, and it has proven to be true throughout the years. I suspect that oftentimes, folks who don't realize this truism give up right on the eve of success.

In a few more years, we outgrew our space and bought a 27,000-square-foot building a few blocks away. Now we were really in business, with a substantial building, a loading dock, real honest-to-goodness offices, and everything. Dad, who was a partner in the building, had an office there, and in his spare time he used to handle the addressograph plates, which is how we maintained our customer list in those days.

By then our pricing strategy had evolved to where we were showing everyday discounted prices in our catalog, and our flyers showed most items at those prices with 10 or 15 items on special sale.

Our mailing strategy was simple, uncomplicated. We bought 100,000 prospect names on gummed labels, with an original and three copies. We then mailed to 10,000 prospects a week for 10 weeks, waited a few weeks, and then used the carbon copies to repeat the process three more times during the year.

To do this, we produced a new flyer once every three months, and we used that same flyer to mail to our customers once every three months. During this time, we went back to a full-line catalog.

Our basic selling strategy remained the same. Discount prices, now as much as 30 percent to 40 percent off on many items, plus very fast service (we often shipped orders the day we received them, but usually no later than the following day). Business kept growing, and, by 1973, we were out of space and once again had to move.

This time we bought land in a far Northern suburb and built a modern one-story, high-ceilinged building. It was, and still is, beautiful. We still own that building, renting it out to another firm. Unfortunately, Dad died before we built it. He would have been bursting with pride.

It was also at that time that our brother Arnold joined the firm. That would have made Dad very happy also. Arnold was a certified public accountant, with his own practice in California. At the time, we were doing $3.5 million in volume, and we made Arnold an equity offer. When he joined us, that really completed our management team, with Harvey in operations, Arnold in finance, and me in marketing.

It was also about this time that we changed our mailing strategy. And we hit the jackpot with the changed strategy. Here's what happened.

The year was 1974. Inflation was running rampant at the rate of 11 percent per year. Price increases were coming so fast from vendors we couldn't ever be up to date.

Well, we were stuck. By then we had gone to semiannual catalogs for our customers, but were still mailing quarterly sale flyers to both prospects and customers. With this rapid inflation, we felt there was no way we could guarantee prices for the three-month life of the flyers, much less the six-month life of the catalogs.

The "solution" we came up with was that in our 1973 Fall and Winter catalog, we told our customers, "Sorry, but due to the inflationary market, we can no longer guarantee prices for the six-month duration of this catalog."

Then, in January of 1974, we began mailing our customers every month instead of once every three months, and we guaranteed the prices for that month only. This strategy achieved what we wanted. We maintained our profit margins, and I can't remember a single complaint about the price changes. Customers were used to price increases by the time we started doing this. I guess a wild and continuing inflation dulls one's sense of outrage at constantly increasing prices.

But a surprising (to us at the time) and unintended consequence of this strategy was that our volume began to shoot up. For two years running we had 60 percent and 65 percent sales increases. And for a number of years after that we continued with high-volume increases in the 20-percent plus range. The law of unintended consequences—it's amazing and it's always in action. In any event, we felt as if we had discovered a great new law of direct marketing. Mail your customers more often!

We had more than we could handle for a few years, so we didn't exploit that new law more fully until the early 1980s.

We developed tabloids, similar to our monthly flyers but printed on a larger (11½" × 14") page size. We followed this up with "multimailers," envelopes filled with one or two pages of special offers. We had "one-ons" and then specialty books, books focusing on just one area of the business, such as filing.

It wasn't very long before we were burying our customers with mailings. Every customer, defined as anyone who had bought from us in the last 24 months, from the largest to the smallest, began receiving four, five, and sometimes six mailings a month.

Our volume continued to increase nicely, but so did the complaints about getting too much mail. I can just picture some small one- or two-person office that ordered office supplies once every few months receiving all that mail from us. But sales were continuing to increase, and those were the days of high margins, the kind of margins that covered a lot of sloppiness for many businesses.

We were also getting complaints about our confusing pricing policies. Every mailing had a number of items on sale, and since we were mailing so often, the mailings were spaced out during the month with different ending dates. Sometimes we would even have the same item on sale at two different prices, one sale just ending and another just starting, but with an overlap of a week or two. In addition, we had a policy that customers would only get the sale price if they ordered from the sale media, using the special item sale number.

As I look back on it now, I can't believe what a stupid, confusing, customer-antagonistic policy we had. Some in the mail-order business still follow such a policy.

How Superstores Changed Our Business

In any event, for us, this whole crazy policy began to crumble starting in 1987 when the office supply superstores crashed into our nice, quiet, nonaggressive industry: first Staples, then Office Depot, then a whole host of others.

The folks who ran these companies came from other discount retailing industries: food, hardware, and others. And they came with a mentality that said, "Low, low everyday prices, including loss leaders, backed by a rapid expansion of stores and massive advertising."

At first, none of us in the office products industry could believe they would make it. "They couldn't exist on those margins," we said. But they did. In the early years, they hemorrhaged money. Losses were staggering. "Their venture capitalist backers wouldn't stand for this. They have to raise prices or go out of business," many of us thought.

They did neither. They went public and raised all kinds of additional capital. A company showing continuing and massive losses going public and actually getting people to buy stock?

We couldn't believe it. But we should have. We should even have bought stock ourselves and lots of it. Because they were here to stay. They have become successful, capturing over 15 percent of the market and still growing rapidly.

We continued to grow, but at a much smaller rate. After watching them for three years, we were finally convinced we had to do something if we planned to continue to be a player.

So in February 1990, midway through our 1989–1990 fiscal year, we cut our prices across the board by 18 percent, cutting our gross profit margin overnight from 43 percent down to 34 percent. Since then, we have lowered prices even more.

We also changed our pricing policy. We went from the "game" where our customers had to look through every mailing piece, find the lowest price, and use the special sale item number to a "lowest price in effect" policy. In other words, no matter what media the customer ordered from, even if they just used the reorder number on the product without using any media, they got the lowest price then in effect. If an item was on sale in any media, they got that sale price.

We didn't make a nickel for the rest of that fiscal year. Our profits for the year were cut in half. (Ah, the joys of being a privately owned company. We didn't hear a single complaint from any irate stockholders.)

Then we got busy cutting costs. From the smallest to the biggest savings, we looked for them all. A new, longer life, lower wattage light bulb in exit signs saved us $12,000 a year. We also added a few more carton sizes so we could fit the box to the contents better and use less fill. As a result, we went from buying three trailer loads of "peanuts" a day down to just one, a savings of over $200,000 a year. With an investment of about $1 million, we installed a complete desktop publishing system, generating close to $3 million in savings a year.

And there were hundreds of other savings we found, all of which we could have done earlier but didn't until we were forced to by tough, unrelenting competition.

Discovering Database Marketing

Most importantly, we began to examine our mailing strategy. We couldn't afford all the waste that was going on with our multitude of mailings. With four, five, and six mailings going out every month, we were showing some of the same merchandise in at least two or three of them all the time. The incremental business was great, and our merchandisers were scared stiff of giving it up. But at what cost was it "great?"

At that time, we were mailing everything to everyone indiscriminately. "Gosh, what were all those seminars we sat through on database marketing about?" we began to wonder. We sure as heck weren't doing a lot with the information we had. But our suddenly reduced margins and highly impacted bottom line was like getting hit over the head with a two-by-four. It really focused our attention.

So, we began to look at our mailing strategy. One of the first things we did was to cut out "multimailers" with all those loose sheets of paper (an example of which is shown in Exhibit 8.2). Many of our customers hated them and weren't shy about letting us know.

When we started to look at how we could cut our advertising costs, that was the first piece we looked at. We cut it out, and, lo and behold, our sales continued to increase. We even got some comments from customers, thanking us.

We looked at other mailing pieces. How could we change them, make them more unique? Who should be receiving them? We used to mail one special promotion to over 400,000 customers several times a year. After studying the results and the costs, we cut the mailing down to 37,000 (now back up a bit to 75,000 including prospects), and our volume on those items continued to grow.

Database target marketing began to take on new meaning for us at Quill. Now we are ardent, practicing proponents of it. As precisely as possible, based on the current state of our own database and our studies, we are targeting our mailings more and more carefully.

Customer Service

But we didn't feel that pricing and cost savings alone were enough to make us a winner. We also focused more than ever on customer service. We had always worked hard to give good customer service, but now we felt it was a critical element for success.

Our everyday low pricing and lowest price in effect policies were a good start toward better customer service. We followed this up with more training than ever for our people, with an improved and expanded catalog (see Exhibit 8.3), and with a new shipping policy. Previously, we promised to ship all stock orders in 8 to 24 hours. In November 1991, we changed that to, "Any stock order placed by 4:00 p.m. will be shipped the same day." When our competitors followed us quickly on that, just to keep them moving, we changed it to, "Any stock order in by 6:00 p.m. will be shipped the same day."

We're working on a number of other areas where we can improve service to our customers. But low prices and great service are just the "price of admission" in today's marketplace. Now we have to find better ways to go to market, better ways to sell product, even better ways to service our customers. We need to find the differentiating "edge" that will assure our success in the

Exhibit 8.2 Typical Multimailer Insert

Exhibit 8.3 Cover of Present-Day Catalog for Quill Products

Front cover of present-day 475-page catalog, featuring thousands of items.

years ahead. And "the bar" keeps going up and up. But we are determined to be a leader in pushing it up.

Our Journey to the Supreme Court

No story about Quill would be complete without a few words about our Supreme Court case in which we beat the State of North Dakota on the use tax issue.

Over the years, my belief in the integrity of our various government bodies at the federal, state, and local levels had been declining. But in the past few years, as I have seen what the state governments have been doing on the use tax issue, it has really taken a nose dive.

The background on this issue is that in 1967, the Supreme Court ruled in the Bellas Hess case that the states could not force out-of-state companies to collect sales tax for them unless these companies had a definite nexus (presence) in the taxing state.

To try to capture these taxes, the states changed the definition of "sales tax" to also include the concept of "use," so that anyone who bought a product from out of state would pay a use tax equal to the sales tax. They then tried to get their citizens to voluntarily submit the use tax due on such purchases but, by and large were unable to do so.

In recent years, the states have been strapped for cash and in their desperate attempt to raise more money, they began to change their laws to try to redefine "nexus." In my opinion, in doing so, they knew they were doing something that was contrary to the laws of the land and to the ruling of the U.S. Supreme Court. But they did it anyhow, and then they went after out-of-state companies to try to force them to collect. They used all types of threats.

North Dakota officials came after us, trying to get us to collect their taxes for them. We refused, citing the Bellas Hess case, but they went ahead and sued us. We went to trial in the North Dakota district court and won. Prosecutors appealed to their supreme court where we once again went to trial. We lost that case, so we appealed to the U.S. Supreme Court.

In June 1992, we won the case in the U.S. Supreme Court. The court said that if North Dakota wanted to force out-of-state companies to collect sales tax for them, they would have to get the U.S. Congress to change the laws. The states will no doubt try to do that. But, in the meantime, many of them are still sending out threatening letters, using misleading information to try to scare companies into voluntarily acting as their tax collectors.

Just one of the problems with us being a tax collector for the states is that there are over 7,000 taxing districts in the country. There are thousands of different rates which are changing constantly, and many different rules on what is taxable. In one state, all food is taxable; in another, only some foods; in still another, no food. Different types of clothing are taxable or not taxable in different states, and so on.

Just think of 50 different state auditors coming in to audit the books. Every company that sells across state lines would have to have a separate department just to deal with them all. And keeping current on all the complex and constantly changing tax rules would be a major job, even with computers.

But the states don't want to, or somehow find it impossible to, work together to resolve these issues. They just want the money no matter what they have to do to get it.

North Dakota hit on Quill. It took us over 35 months, with my brother Arnold and several more of our people spending a great deal of time on the case. It cost us over $1 million. (Just imagine if they had hit on a smaller company, one that couldn't afford either the time or the money. What kind of justice could that company have gotten?)

In any event, after we won, we sued North Dakota for the right to go to court to set legal fees (triple our costs, which came to about $3 million). This went directly to the state supreme court. And after a long delay of about 11 months following the trial, the North Dakota supreme court came down with a decision denying our claim.

So, we once again began the route to the U.S. Supreme Court. It cost us additional legal fees, but we were determined to see justice done. It wasn't. The U.S. Supreme Court turned down our appeal to collect legal fees.

The Free Marketplace Works

Such is the story of Quill, "The Overnight Success." Today, as a result of tougher competition, we are a much leaner, much more focused company. We are continuing to grow and we have regained our bottom-line profits. Our gross margins have continued to shrink and, under the constant pressure of the competitive free marketplace, will probably continue to do so in the future. So the customer is the winner. Lower prices, the same or better quality items and better customer service. Competition and our free marketplace do indeed work wonders.

Bob Stone's
Commentary

The centerpiece of the Quill story is Jack Miller, a modern-day Horatio Alger. A visionary with all the traits of a successful entrepreneur, he's gutsy and firm of purpose, a risk taker, and a marketer first, last, and always. Jack is decisive, turns on a dime, and views every challenge as an opportunity. He understands, more than most, that there are two ways to make money: increase sales or cut costs. Quill does both.

Jack, like so many successful executives, assumes two responsibilities; one to his company and one to his industry. He is a frequent lecturer at universities and trade meetings across the country. An acknowledged statesman, he assumes leadership for vital industry causes, generously contributing time and money.

What Jack and his two brothers have accomplished earns the accolade, "only in America." Now let us review the strategies that have made Quill so successful.

- Prior work experiences can serve you in good stead should you decide to start your own business.

- When it comes to a pricing policy, the best strategy is to *keep it simple.*

- You will be more profitable if you create your own product line and buy direct.

- Since everything takes longer than you expect it to, be careful lest you give up too soon.

- Customers will accept price increases more readily when other products and services they buy are likewise being increased in price.

- If another channel of distribution (retail stores in Quill's case) is beating you on price, meet fire with fire and reduce your prices.

- The best way to make up for reduced income due to

price slashing is to slash costs.

- You can mail less and make more money if you develop a database that enables you to target mailings to those who are most likely to buy.

- The faster you ship, the more likely customers will

buy from you again. Uncompromising service is the key.

- If you believe you are being wronged by governments (or anyone) have the courage and determination to fight.

CHAPTER

9

Converting Conviction to Cash
National Demographics & Lifestyles

Jock Bickert, Chief Executive Officer, Looking Glass, Inc.

Jock Bickert is the chief executive officer for Looking Glass, Inc., a firm that provides client companies and organizations with real-time customer feedback about how customers regard their products and services. Within 24 hours, clients can learn which of their customers have had positive or negative experiences with their company, and how customers respond to new products, product enhancements, or promotions. Bickert founded National Demographics & Lifestyles in 1975.

In 1988, the Harvard Business School published the first of two case histories on National Demographics & Lifestyles (NDL). Had it not been for the rigor and candor with which those cases were prepared and my subsequent appearances at business school classes in which those cases were debated, I would now be tempted to ascribe NDL's success to brilliant strategic foresight alone. These constraints, however, have forced me to acknowledge the role of chance and good fortune in the process. This account will therefore attempt to credit NDL's success to the interplay of strategic acumen and plain dumb luck.

Birth of a Zealot

In 1970, along with two compatriots from the University of Denver's Research Institute, I formed BBC (then Bickert, Browne, Coddington and Associates), a firm destined to become a leading market and economic research organization in the Rocky Mountain area.

In those days, aside from running the survey research function, I was the dabbler in the company, chasing after new ideas amid great clouds of pipe smoke. One conundrum recurred in meeting after meeting with research clients: how to communicate more effectively with consumer groups sharing known characteristics.

Upon receiving survey reports cross-tabulated by endless endographic categories (such as sex, age, income, marital status), clients would invariably ask something like: "Well, what media can we use to advertise to our affluent, middle-aged, married couples?" After rejecting television, radio, and newspapers as inefficient, someone would plaintively ask, "Wouldn't it be wonderful if we could send a mailer to those people?" But, of course, there was no list of such prospects (a database was a much too futuristic concept in those days).

A BBC consultant named Peter Lenz and I would periodically ponder the problem to no avail. (Peter Lenz was a statistical and programming genius who wore a ponytail, granny glasses, and bib overalls, and who, as we stood in line at LaGuardia, with a straight face described himself to curious New Yorkers as "just another businessman.") Peter introduced me to the concept of cluster analysis and how it could be used to group objects and people in terms of their commonalities. As a former clinical psychologist, I was always intrigued by ways of categorizing people in order to make some sense of their behavior.

In 1972, we got an opportunity to put our speculations to work. With a grant from Scripps-Howard Newspapers, Peter and I developed a geodemographic cluster system of Colorado census tracts, with 13 neighborhood types to which we internally assigned irreverent names, such as Little Old Ladies in

Tennis Shoes. As far as I can tell, that system antedated PRIZM, VISION, ClusterPlus, and all the other current geodemographic systems.

But we failed to take the crucial applications leap, to apply the system to geographically encoded, compiled name and address lists, which would allow users to access those market segments. The process did, however, reinforce my interest in market segmentation. If only there were a way to build a proprietary database outside the restrictions to individual information that the U.S. Census imposed.

At about the same time, I was introduced to Common Cause, then a fledgling public-interest nonprofit organization headed by John Gardner, former Secretary of the Department of Health, Education, and Welfare under John Kennedy. Common Cause, with less than 50,000 members at the time, had a stated intent to launch a massive direct-mail effort to secure 2 million new members.

I proposed that Common Cause develop a database using a questionnaire in the initial prospect mailing to secure individuals' demographics, their interest in various issues (environmental concerns, taxation, bureaucratic reform, and so on), their talents (writing, public speaking, organizing), and their personal access to the political structure and to the media (acquaintance with a congressperson, a governor, a television anchor). Such a database would have allowed Common Cause to orchestrate its emerging membership to achieve the maximum political clout. John Gardner, however, had a different perspective: To him, a computerized database was "impersonal and mechanistic," and he quickly dismissed the proposal. As I left their headquarters in Washington, I observed nearly 100 volunteers hand-addressing "Dear Friend" membership solicitations. So much for a personalized, nonmechanistic approach!

Finally, I located by "dataBeta" site: The Junior League, a woman's volunteer organization. The president of the Denver chapter immediately saw the benefits of building a database of volunteers that catalogued their skills, interests, and access to the political, business, and media structures. I developed a questionnaire that was administered and updated annually, and we quickly built a member database.

When a project coordinator needed appropriate volunteer skills, she specified the characteristics to the computer and immediately obtained a list of individuals who fulfilled those specs. The database was a great success, and I became a zealous believer in the potential of database targeting.

Strategy 1: Stand by Your Plan

Now I wanted to apply the concept to a large consumer population. Discussions with some right-brained computer jocks convinced me that product warranty cards represented a promising medium. After all, when consumers wished to register a product warranty they were required to return a form. Why not include a questionnaire in that process?

My partners at BBC, however, satisfied with the traditional direction of our very profitable research company, did not share my ardor for a new venture into uncharted database waters. Consequently, I sold my share in BBC in early 1975 and moved to a 280-square-foot, two-room office in a bohemian area of Denver.

The new company's basic business proposition was quite simple: We would ask durable-goods manufacturers to insert in all their products a questionnaire attached to the warranty registration card. That questionnaire would consist of three sections: (1) product and purchase-related questions that would be proprietary to the manufacturer; (2) demographic questions asking the purchaser's age, income, marital status, and so on; and (3) a lifestyle inventory of activities, hobbies, and interests. Purchasers would be offered an incentive to return the questionnaire to us.

We would enter the data and provide the manufacturers with information about their buyers. We would then accumulate the demographic and lifestyle information from all clients' cards and build a massive database from which we would rent segmented lists to direct mailers. It was the latter activity that would provide the company's main revenue source.

We figured that every individual on the database would have roughly 45 selection opportunities (37 lifestyle and 8 demographic factors). In other words, the same individual could be included on a list that called for upper-income women, as well as on one that required middle-aged joggers. That multidimensional list selection potential produced some rather astounding theoretical "turn rates" and, consequently, some eye-popping revenue potential. Although it turned out that we overestimated the turn rate by a factor of four, that variable still produced the kind of leverage that made NDL attractive to investors.

With the assistance of my close friend, Bruce Ducker, I spent much of that summer fleshing out the NDL concept and developing a rudimentary business plan. That same year, the passage of the Magnusson-Moss Act eliminated the consumer's obligation to return any form in order to register a warranty and spelled the death of the "warranty questionnaire" notion. No longer could we link questionnaire return to the warranty registration. The misnomer, "warranty card database," however, remains NDL's curse and legacy.

Meanwhile, Bruce and I toyed with many corporate names for the new venture, especially those that played off the names of existing banking organizations (in those days, "databank" was the common parlance for today's database). Fortunately, we mutually rejected DataBank of America and First National DataBank. We finally settled on National Demographics Limited (NDL) because, although the initial questionnaire contained 37 lifestyle activities, the marketplace emphasis was on demographic data. We also speculated that prospective clients might subconsciously associate National Demographics with *National Geographic* (a magazine that was to play a more substantive role in NDL's later development) and attribute to our totally unknown company far greater stability and credibility than we deserved. Indeed, on several early sales calls, prospects actually commented, "Oh yes, I've heard of your company." Who says that perception isn't nearly as important as reality?

Finally, on October 31, 1975, NDL was launched with an initial capitalization of $2,250, $500 of which came from my meager resources and $250 from my friend Ducker. That amount was to be supplemented by income from the new company's research and consulting activities. Armed with a four-figure bank account, a tiny office, and a half-time secretary, NDL was off the launch pad. The only thing missing? Clients! The search for prospects had to be limited to Colorado, because the travel and entertainment budget accommodated no more than the cruising range of a 1971 convertible, a Whopper and fries, and a motel room.

Strategy 2: Get the Money and Run

Within six months, the database stood at 7,000 households, 92 percent of which contained 20-year-old skiers. At that size, it represented only an annoying liability with no offsetting revenue. Fortunately, the research and consulting business was thriving and NDL was profitable, but it was now becoming apparent that, if it was to implement the database concept, NDL had to expand its sales capabilities and raise capital.

I had a series of meetings with a close friend, Rob Johnson, who was then marketing for a large Dallas-based residential developer. Rob was intrigued with the NDL concept and agreed to join the company for an equity stake. His first task was to write a private placement memorandum to raise $476,000 in equity capital, in our estimation a more than sufficient amount to bring NDL to profitability within a year.

Hats in hand, we went out to peddle the concept to wealthy, local investors. Of course, no one understood what we were talking about. Until I presented the idea to Lucien Wulsin. At that time, Lucien was chairman of the board of Baldwin-United Corporation, a $2 billion conglomerate that owned power companies, banks, insurance companies, savings and loans, a data processing firm, and Baldwin Piano Company.

Lucien saw NDL as a useful piece in the corporate puzzle, providing marketing information to subsidiaries as well as becoming a large client of their service bureau. Baldwin-United's president, Morley Thompson, questioned the investment, but in the end Lucien prevailed, and in January 1978, Baldwin-United became an 80-percent shareholder in NDL.

Boy, did that $476,000 burn a fast hole in our pockets. We quickly moved into new quarters and added much-needed sales and account service staff. The expenses escalated, particularly data-entry costs, as we began to add high-volume card clients like Minolta and Panasonic, with database records in the hundreds of thousands.

Strategy 3: Control Cost

Those costs from outside data-entry suppliers were especially galling in view of their accompanying high error rates. We learned that Neodata in Boulder was operating a successful data-entry operation in Ireland, and we looked into that option, as well as others in Jamaica and western Canada. As the possibility of doing data entry outside the United States became more intriguing, I developed a checklist of the criteria necessary for a successful foreign operation: stable government, English-speaking workers, high literacy rate, strong work ethic, and low wage scale.

One night I was leafing through back issues of *National Geographic* magazine when I chanced on a feature story about Barbados, an island whose lure for me had dated back to early Harry Belafonte records. A sidebar story on Barbados revealed the following characteristics: a 400-year unbroken history of British occupation and influence, an anomaly in the Caribbean where nearly every island had undergone periodic and frequent occupations by the English, French, Spanish, Portuguese, and Dutch; the second-highest literacy rate in the world, with mandatory public education through age 16; a lower wage scale than that of the United States; and a large, motivated work force. Eureka! My list of key criteria!

Not much later, during an NDL board meeting, Lucien Wulsin asked me what we were doing about the growing data-entry problem. I replied that we were investigating Ireland, Jamaica, and western Canada, and then timidly added Barbados, whereupon Lucien revealed that Baldwin-United owned the power and light company in Barbados and, that if we were serious about the island as a location, it would benefit Baldwin politically.

Two weeks later I was in Barbados for a 17-interview-in-three-days schedule. The island even surpassed its press clippings, and we made the decision to establish a subsidiary data-entry operation there—a company that today, with its nearly 300 employees, is one of the 10 largest private employers on the island. That extremely cost-efficient data-entry facility now stands as one of NDL's core competencies.

Back at the ranch, however, expenditures continued to mount, and by mid-1978, we realized that the well would run dry many months before NDL attained profitability. We broached the bad news to Baldwin-United and received even worse news in return: Morley Thompson refused to sink another penny into the oddball member of their conglomerate.

Although we were successful in signing up durable-goods clients, the database was growing more slowly than anticipated due to the unforeseen lag time between contractual agreement and receipt of the first questionnaire. And at a total database size of less than 50,000, the ability to rent highly segmented lists was nonexistent, resulting in no immediate revenue potential.

Faced with the chilling realization that Christmas 1978 was unlikely to see turkey on the table, Rob Johnson and I entered the province of big money—the financial canyons of New York, Chicago, Boston, and Washington—where we attempted to elicit some interest in our database company from a group of venture capitalists accustomed to backing high-tech companies with tangible products. Selling the concept of database marketing was painful, and we learned to accept rejection as easily as Rodney Dangerfield.

I was at the end of a New York trip consisting of dreary meetings with disinterested venture capitalists when the phone in my hotel room rang. It was John Kidde, a Princeton friend, seeking a favor. He had a small stake in a Connecticut research company and wondered if I could journey to Glastonbury the next day, look the company over, and give him my opinion regarding its future potential. Possibly, but how on earth does one get to Glastonbury? Simple, said Kidde. A friend of his, Jerry Hardy, was leaving in a limousine from the GM Building the next day and, if I was interested, I should be there at 8 a.m. All I could promise Kidde was a definite maybe.

Next morning, as I waited half-heartedly in the checkout line at the Sheraton-Russell Hotel, I picked up snatches of a mild dispute between the cashier and the gentleman immediately ahead of me. Something about the man's publisher's responsibility for the room bill. Obviously an author.

He looked familiar and, as I watched him circle the quaint, book-lined lobby five minutes later it came to me. That's James Michener! I walked over and introduced myself as a Coloradan who'd recently enjoyed reading *Centennial*. Michener appeared faintly pleased at the recognition and asked if I'd care to join him for breakfast.

The invitation posed more of a dilemma than it should have: Share a three-hour limousine ride with a stranger to evaluate a company in which I had no interest or go one-on-one over breakfast with one of America's story-telling giants? It should have been no contest: Michener by 30 lengths. But an inner voice intruded, and instead I hurried to the GM Building for my date with Jerry Hardy.

The limousine ride could have been scripted by the tooth fairy. The "unknown" Jerry Hardy turned out to be a former publisher of *Life* magazine, the founder of Time-Life Books, and a future member of the DMA Hall of Fame. He interrogated me for three hours about NDL, and at the journey's conclusion opined that we had an opportunity to revolutionize the direct-marketing industry.

He offered to open any doors he could in support, and less than a week later recommended me to a venture capitalist friend of his, Tom Claflin. Claflin invested, he and Hardy joined the NDL board, and, true to his word, Hardy made us a part of his extensive direct-marketing industry network. But James Michener never called with a raincheck.

It's tempting to categorize that incident as "luck," and probably at that time it was. But it's since become an integral part of a personal strategy to "follow my nose," occasionally at the expense of the much more rational alternative.

Strategy 4: Put on the Gloves and Fight for It

Less than a month after I met Jerry Hardy, NDL mounted its first exhibit at the DMA Fall Conference. By now we had given our list product a name, calling it The Lifestyle Selector® (TLS) to differentiate it from other direct-marketing companies that had made demographics their hallmark.

Although we were ill prepared for a product launch of TLS due to insufficient database size and the absence of stringent testing, Rob and I were urged by an anxious board of directors to answer the one remaining question regarding the NDL concept: Would a database constructed from questionnaires packed in consumer durables produce lists of mail-responsive individuals?

Our little band of five NDL representatives (one an ex-Playboy Club housemother), supported by our new two-man list management firm, List House East/West, arrived at the exhibit area of the Washington Hilton with high hopes. Prospective mailers and brokers, their interest piqued by the wealth of available selections on the database, visited the NDL booth in droves.

Every several hours, Jerry Hardy would arrive with a curious prospect in tow. "Ben," he admonished the president of Columbia House, "I want you to listen to these people. They've got the most exciting innovation since the zip code." And Ben (or Rose or Doug or Joyce) would listen intently while we wove our promise of trillions of potential list selection combinations. Then Ben (or Rose or Doug or Joyce) would break the spell: "This is fascinating! How many names do you have in this new database?" "Fifty-six thousand," we answered meekly, knowing that one of our esoteric selection examples of sex, age, marital status, foreign travel, and squash (squash?) would yield a list of maybe five people. "Be sure to call us when you get to a million," Ben (and Rose and Doug and Joyce) would giggle as they swiftly walked away.

Nevertheless, TLS was launched. Rob and I spent every other week in New York or Chicago calling on durable-goods database prospects and skeptical list brokers. We switched list managers, moving to Woodruff-Stevens, then the giant in the industry. Woodruff-Stevens provided us with key list contacts and initiated us into that subsegment of the greater direct-marketing community.

But the concept of TLS was too novel and sophisticated for an industry accustomed at that time to data-poor compiled lists or one-dimensional response lists. Tests were slow coming in and, more often than not, our selection recommendations were based on no information about our clients' customers. In retrospect, it's no surprise that our lists produced only listless performance.

So while the database (and its attendant data-entry costs) was growing, revenue sputtered. A year later, we were again running short of capital. Tom Claflin was exhorting his network of venture capitalists to invest, especially Bill Egan of Burr, Egan & Deleage, but the desultory list performance made many potential investors wary.

In the meantime, we met the head of a then highly respected (now defunct) Wall Street investment banking firm who, along with a company specializing in management training courses, appeared very interested in making a major investment. After reviewing the offering prospectus, they invited us to New York to entertain an offer. Rob, Bruce Ducker, and I headed east with high hopes.

Following an hour of lubrication with cocktails at an Upper Eastside apartment, we adjourned to the austere Metropolitan Club. After two hours of trivial conversation and several fine Bordeaux, we began to squirm. Where was the offer? Finally, the lead man produced a single sheet of paper and handed it to me with the admonition that he had a train to catch in 20 minutes and would appreciate an immediate answer.

I looked at the offer sheet in horror. They proposed only a modest infusion of cash, for which they would receive all of the shares in the company, leaving management with no equity position. It was a classic "rape and pillage" operation. We decided to stall for time and stated that we had to take it to our board and that we'd reply in a week.

Actually, we were trying to figure out how we would get our highly confidential business plan back once we turned them down. In dismay, Bob, Bruce, and I retreated to the Oak Room at the Plaza where, like the bewildered French generals in World War I, we reviewed our meager alternatives over cognac. At 3:00 a.m., we decided to continue the fight.

Several days later, a good friend called to inform me that he had been offered the presidency of NDL by the lead "shark," who had confided to him that he planned to replace all of the existing NDL management and move the company to New York. The next day, Rob and I flew to New York, and at precisely 4:00 p.m. we staged separate, simultaneous commando raids on the two offices of the purchasing syndicate.

We presented the formal refusal of their offer and demanded an immediate return of our business plan. Although they tried to stall, we refused to leave until the plans were in our hands. Eventually they relented and reluctantly handed them over.

When Rob and I rendezvoused uptown an hour later, we grinned at one another and high-fived. The raid had been successful. We still had our company and our integrity, but no money. Butch and Sundance were surrounded by hordes of banditos, and their ammunition was running low. But the calvary, in the guise of the venture capitalist, Bill Egan, came riding to the rescue. The investment consortium, led by Egan's venture capital firm, invested over $1 million, and again NDL was momentarily saved.

Strategy 5: Keep Looking for New Ways to Squeeze the Orange

Egan's decision to invest was intriguing. Holding to the tenets of business school appraisal, before investing he surveyed 20 leading figures in the direct-marketing industry. What did they think of this revolutionary concept? Could a combination of demographic and lifestyle selections perform well enough to merit mailers' consideration? "No way!" seventeen of the 20 replied. Egan, however, listened to his gut, not the research, and invested. So much for conventional market research!

A year later, however, in January 1982, another financial crisis—which was to be the last—occurred. Month after month revenues had failed to exceed expenses. After a number of agonizing appraisals, Rob Johnson and I concluded that three major additions to the company were needed: (1) an in-house data processing center, (2) our own TLS sales staff, and (3) three more chiefs in addition to Pete Kelley, head of data processing, and Jack Scheu, who headed NDL's research and development (R&D). We needed a senior list sales manager, a chief financial officer, and someone to head our sales and service efforts with durable-goods manufacturers.

The most critical area was lagging list sales. After promising the list industry that we could deliver superior list performance, we had continually failed to meet expectations, particularly among catalog mailers. (In fact, one of my most embarrassing moments occurred when, as I was taking two prospective clients to dinner at the 1981 DMA Fall Conference, I was accosted by a furious list broker who represented six catalogs and who interrupted our conversation to shout in my face, "Bickert, your list stinks!"

The reason for our dismal list performance was obvious: We had no idea what any mailer's market looked like and, consequently, were unable to make valid recommendations. Coming from a market-research background, I had assumed that most large mailers would at least know their market's demographic profiles. How wrong I was! In meeting after meeting, we encountered mailers who debated among one another about the true characteristics of their house file:

Fred: "Their age? Oh, we appeal to the mature market."

NDL: "And how do you define that?"

Fred: "Anyone over 30."

Ed: "No, Fred. It's probably over 50."

And the debate would begin. Income estimates would vary by as much as $25,000, and, unless the mailer served an obvious vertical market (such as golfers or foreign travelers), no one had a clue as to lifestyle characteristics. So we'd eventually agree on the likely selection criteria, pull a three- or four-variable list, and wait for the inevitable thud to occur. (Our lowest point came when a mailer ordered a test of 1,500, after which his broker called in wonderment to tell me that, in 15 years in the business, it was the first time he'd ever received a zero response to a mailing.)

Enter Bob Cuniffe, a data processing consultant with List Maintenance Corporation, who one evening over dinner suggested the mechanism of a file overlay in order to obtain mailers' market profiles. His suggested methodology, like many great breakthroughs, was elegant in its simplicity.

We would ask mailers to send up copies of their house files, after which we would run a merge-purge against the NDL database. We would then treat that match sample as a quasisurvey and, by profiling that sample by the variables in the NDL file, we would know the demographic and lifestyle characteristics of the master's file.

With Cuniffe's help we ran overlays on 12 mailers' house files at our data processing facility, Baldwin Deco. The overlays led to six successful tests and all of us, with the exception of our chief of data processing, Pete Kelley, were ecstatic.

His trim Van Dyke beard turned gray when he received the one month's data processing bill for $70,000. It was the prototypical good news/bad news situation. We had discovered the initial key to better list performance, but the mechanism for producing the life-saving overlays was devouring cash at an alarming rate. The only solution was to purchase our own computer.

That simple process of using an overlay procedure to produce customer profiles was the first in a long line of NDL's R&D projects aimed at enhancing list performance. Those first profiles were strictly univariate (that is, distributions of single characteristics), but subsequent generations of the product led to multivariate analyses and from there to sophisticated response modeling techniques. Those enhancements not only markedly improved the responsiveness of the list, but also served as newsworthy opportunities for us to contact clients and prospects.

Our R&D efforts were not limited to TLS. We had initially envisioned using the database as a source of marketing information once it had attained a sufficient size. We likened the database to an orange being squeezed. The mailing list represented the delicious, freshly-squeezed juice, but plenty of usable pulp remained beyond that.

We teamed with Standard Rate & Data Service (SRDS) to produce *The Lifestyle Market Analyst,* an annual publication that profiles 212 metropolitan areas by demographic and lifestyle characteristics. Other information products, such as Scout®, a syndicated marketing intelligence service, and Cohorts™, a household-level market segmentation system, arose out of NDL's in-house R&D function.

Strategy 6: Surround Yourself with People Smarter than You

Aside from those initial performance problems, our penetration of the list industry was agonizingly slow. Woodruff-Stevens had represented us very well, but the complex Boolean selection process and esoteric analyses required hands-on daily interaction between sales and analysis. We needed our own dedicated sales force in order to achieve faster industry penetration.

That also meant a top-flight sales manager. And if we were to add sufficient durable-goods manufacturers to grow the database, we had to dedicate one person to the twin tasks of selling and serving those clients; Rob and I were juggling too many other balls to do that as well. Finally, we needed a financial pro, someone who could institute disciplined cost controls.

Those three requirements threatened to break the bank again, so reluctantly we went back to our venture capitalists. After excruciating deliberation they backed all three requests, but with the cryptic admonition that it was the last time they'd support *this management team* until profitability was achieved.

We moved quickly. We hired a creative chief financial officer, Karl Friedmann. We brought Mitch Barnes from Young & Rubicam to take responsibility for building the database. And we added a world-class list manager, Tony White. We now had the senior management team we needed to accomplish our mission.

At the same time, we laid the foundation for a strong *future* management team by hiring outstanding young people, all characterized by intelligence, resourcefulness, and wit. We also initiated a special recognition program for high achievers. The award was based on an incident reported by a magazine writer who, in a story on the unappreciated intellectual prowess of professional athletes, recalled an interview with Ken Stabler, the then quarterback of the Oakland Raiders. At the interview's conclusion, the writer read Stabler the following quote by the author Jack London:

> I would rather be ashes than dust. I would rather that my spark should burn out in a brilliant blaze than it should be stifled by dry rot. I would rather be a superb meteor than a sleepy, permanent planet.

The writer then asked Stabler what he thought London was saying. After a moment's thought Stabler replied: "Throw deep!" In 1984, NDL established the "Throw Deep" award to recognize those employees who, through ingenuity, initiative, and extra time and effort, developed a product or process that produced a major enhancement to NDL's business. (The small, abstract, wooden quarterback that represented the award was much more valuable and more treasured than the $500 check that accompanied it.)

Those middle years were truly euphoric. In 1984, we surpassed 1983's revenues by 58 percent and 1983's profits by 310 percent. We were on a roll, and everyone sensed it.

Strategy 7: Don't Forget to Play

During the early 1980s, NDL's physical environment was constantly in flux. The Baldwin-United financing in 1977 had allowed us to expand beyond our original office-and-a-half into more elegant quarters, but we were chopped into seven little enclaves on different floors in different buildings. We felt the need to pull the company together physically. The bullish financial performance of 1983 finally allowed us the luxury of consolidating our space, and in

May 1984, we moved to NDL's current building. Finally, we were one unified group—with a new set of unanticipated problems.

Many of us were surprised to discover that the long-awaited move, rather than automatically eliciting an upsurge in team spirit and cooperation, instead produced just the opposite, bickering between what had been seven separate subcultures.

For the first time we had to address the need to formally shape an integrated company culture that encompassed all of the implicit, unwritten values that had somewhat haphazardly evolved over seven years. We realized that we now had to *work* to maintain something that had been *play* in the past.

We began by forming what started out as an ad hoc employee group, initially dubbed the Committee on Morale and Personnel Practices but that, after one meeting, became known as the Happy Committee. From the Happy Committee platform, our bookkeeper initiated a relationship with a downtown nursing home, whereby NDL employees volunteered their noon hours to chat with lonely residents. We held a crazy garage sale/auction to benefit Children's Hospital and encouraged employee contributions for needy families at Christmas.

At the same time, the Happy Committee sponsored spontaneous parties, promoted the formal observance of NDL's corporate birthday on Halloween, initiated an employee fitness program where participants received gift certificates for meeting self-established fitness objectives, and initiated a weekly Leisure Day when the rest of corporate America was still adhering to the severe dress code popularized by IBM. The stature of the Happy Committee grew to the point that employees were begging to become members, necessitating a company-wide election in which candidates campaigned with banners, slogans, and speeches.

Strategy 8: Exploit Your Natural Charm

At the Aspen International Design Conference, I met Wally Olins, a British design guru, who urged CEOs to incorporate their office environments in their formal marketing process. Our new "high-tech/high-touch" office environment lent itself to such an approach, and soon we were encouraging existing and potential clients to visit us, especially on Leisure Day when they could "kick back."

We got our first opportunity in early 1985, when the DMA held its spring conference in Colorado Springs. We invited clients and friends to visit our offices on the way to the Springs. They were met at the airport by our English systems analyst, dressed in blue chauffeur's livery and driving a borrowed London taxi. They were then royally feted at the office, after which they met with members of the account staff. The occasion led to the signing of two of NDL's largest clients.

Several nights later at the DMA conference, NDL gave its first blockbuster DMA party, renting the Broadmoor Ice Arena for a Cajun music concert. Thus began the NDL/DMA tradition for creative, exciting parties that culminated at the San Francisco Aquarium and the Computer Museum in Boston.

The DMA played a major role in NDL's success from the very beginning. Early on, we determined that we could best showcase new products and enhancements by exhibiting at conferences. Those conferences also provided excellent networking opportunities. We were heavily involved in speakers' programs. We supported the Educational Foundation, not only because it was an effective means of spreading the word about direct marketing, but also because it offered a cornucopia of young talented individuals, many of whom we hired.

Strategy 9: Carpe Diem Like Crazy

Nineteen eighty-three also saw NDL make its first international move. Our original 1977 business plan had noted the potential for international expansion, but had assigned it a low immediate priority. British direct marketers were entranced by this new medium called database marketing, and, after several whirlwind exploratory trips, Rob and I were convinced that the U.K. direct-marketing industry was indeed primed for the concept.

The lack of a magazine subscription mechanism had stunted the growth of consumer mailing lists in the U.K. British newsstand agents had for years successfully kept magazine publishers from selling subscriptions directly, the original cornerstone of the American list industry in the 1930s.

Brokers and mailers begged us to come over, a heady situation following our years of rejection by the American list industry. We quickly secured board approval to proceed, and, in 1984, Rob and I began the process of identifying and wooing potential British investors.

Our initial efforts seemed to attract every scoundrel in the U.K. The owner of one marginally ethical company accosted me at a DMA conference with a merger proposition and demanded that I write him a check for $400,000 on the spot because I was obviously "a rich American bloke." (He had never ridden in my rusted-out 1971 Volkswagen.) Another shady operator tried to bluff us into giving up TLS rights for nothing or "get shut out of the country."

Our first London lawyer turned out be the front man for the Adnan Kashoggi's Iranian arms shipment. When last seen on "60 Minutes," our lawyer was being led out of a motel in the Bahamas handcuffed to federal agents.

By 1985, we had raised a large portion of the necessary funds from our U.S. venture capitalists, and we opened a London office in September 1985. Tony Coad was hired as managing director, and by the end of the year we had our first 10 durable-goods clients, a good start on what was to become the largest database of individual households in the U.K.

Strategy 10: Keep Your Dancing Shoes Polished Because You Never Know When You'll be Invited to the Ball

The mid-1980s were also years of financial consolidation. The news of NDL's financial growth reached the East Coast, and soon two groups began to make inquiries: companies seized with the acquisition "feeding frenzy" of those times, and investment bankers wishing to play a role in arranging an acquisition. We became the "darling" of the latter group, as Karl Friedmann adroitly maneuvered NDL's financial position.

Quarterly financial reports were distributed to key investment bankers. We made major presentations at the many information industry seminars held by those firms in New York, Chicago, and San Francisco. In many ways, we were behaving like a public company, romancing potential acquirers with exciting financial performance and the mystique of having been the database marketing pioneer, and in Denver of all places.

The big fish began to circle. Throughout 1985 and 1986, three major American and British firms launched serious efforts to purchase us. At each overture, our response was the same: "The company's not for sale. But we'd be derelict in our duty to shareholders not to listen to what you have in mind." Then the mating dance would begin, eventually culminating in an offer, always smaller than we wished.

Periodically, the investment bankers would attempt to prod us toward an initial public offering (IPO), exclaiming that "the window of opportunity is open and it may shut at any moment." Although neither Rob nor I wanted to take the company public (a process that friends like Bill Howe at Metromail had warned us consumed up to 40 percent of management's time merely making goodwill presentations to institutional investors), we felt obligated to discuss that option at NDL board meetings. Then the "window of opportunity" slammed shut on October 19, 1987, when the stockmarket took its most precipitous plunge since 1929. Any consideration of an IPO died.

In early December, we met with a large publishing company to discuss a possible joint venture. As the meeting drew to a close, the senior vice president requested that we stay on briefly after the day's agenda had been completed. When the door closed, he asked with a straight face, "I know your company's not for sale, but would you entertain an offer of $X million?" He named a figure three times larger than any offer we had received from our earlier suitors.

I managed to stifle a whoop of glee and acknowledged with an equally straight face that, although NDL was certainly not for sale, I had an obligation to report the company's interest to our investment group. Hurrying from the room, Rob and I immediately contacted the NDL board, and, at a board meeting several weeks later, we made the decision to engage a friendly investment banking firm, Alex Brown, to prepare an offering memorandum and to present it to the 16 companies that we felt might top the publisher's figure.

From that point on, events moved swiftly. We established a "hurdle" price, that is, the figure any acquirer would have to be ready to offer before we would meet with them formally, and most of the potential suitors dropped out. The publisher that had triggered the process refused to go above half their opening offer, stating that their initial figure had been preliminary and less than serious. Their "capricious" number of $X million, however, became the goal of all NDL investors.

By June, the list of suitors had dwindled to the three major list compilers: R.L. Polk & Co., Metromail, and Donnelley Marketing. Both Metromail and Donnelley were attractive in terms of the synergies they offered, as well as the comfortable relationships we enjoyed with their respective CEOs, Jim McQuaid and John Cleary. We had had a long relationship with Polk, dating back to some 1978 overtures when we had unsuccessfully approached them about investing in NDL. We also felt that the greatest chance of maintaining NDL's operational integrity rested in merging with Polk. The board agreed: If Polk met our desired price, NDL was theirs.

Polk agreed to the price and after July 28, 1988, Rob and I could truly say, "Sorry, the company's not for sale." Like most long-anticipated events in life, the actual signing of documents was anticlimactic. As I drove back to the office alone, I mused, "Is this all there is?" Somewhat flat, I walked to my office through a hallway deserted at the lunch hour. But there in my office were Jack Scheu, Karl Friedmann, and Jo Moniak, our vice prsident of marketing, all dressed in cycling attire. "Let's go for a bike ride!" they shouted. And four whooping cyclists rode up the Platte River trail.

That moment, and the later emotional distribution of the sale proceeds to the 62 employee shareholders, will remain with me forever. The journey of nearly 13 years had ended. We had fulfilled the expectations of those trusting investors who could have deserted at many points of disillusioning early performance but didn't. And we had retained the company's operational integrity. It was a sweet combination of good fortune, resourcefulness, and, the strategic acumen of Rob Johnson and the other members of the senior management team and a supportive board of directors.

Reviewing the Strategic Balance Sheet

1. We decided to use product registration cards to build a large consumer database of households with known, not inputted, characteristics. Eighteen years later that methodology still forms the cornerstone of the company's database development activities.

2. We raised equity capital to support the database development rather than attempting to "bootstrap" the endeavor. Although we diluted our financial stake in the company, we learned the lesson that many entrepreneurs overlook: It's better to have a small share of something very large than a large share of nothing.

3. To control our largest cost item, data entry, we started a wholly owned subsidiary in Barbados. It was worth all of the ribbing we took about the necessity of visiting the facility several times every winter.

4. We retained the integrity of the company and were willing to fight for it. There were many occasions when it would have been much easier to turn the operation over to someone else.

5. We built an in-house data processing facility, thus not only reducing costs, but also assuring high-quality list production. The file overlay capability grew in complexity over time, and NDL's current modeling sophistication would have been cost prohibitive in an external bureau environment.

    We also invested heavily in R&D as a means of continually attempting to optimize database use; R&D has been the mechanism not only for improved list performance, but also in the development of analysis tools for database clients and of new information products.

6. We hired the very best people and let them run. Some people mistakenly assume that the success of a database marketing company rests on its technological sophistication. It's people who make the difference, and at every turn we tried to attract the very best.

7. We worked at having fun. Business and financial pressures often militate against providing an environment where employees enjoy spending their workday. We recognized that in order to maintain that type of

environment we had to establish formal mechanisms that would transmit and reinforce that aspect of the corporate culture.

8. We used an attractive, energetic work environment as a tool in our marketing bag. We discovered that many clients expected a high-tech company where computers would dominate the landscape. Instead, we showcased our most important asset, our people.

    We also made full use of the DMA: its conferences, its networking facilities, and the opportunities it afforded us to showcase the company. From the beginning, we used the speaker's platform to tell our story to the industry. We made key contacts at the conferences. And we tried to develop a reputation for giving unusual, creative parties that were relevant to our products and services.

9. We took advantage of market momentum. The decision to establish a British affiliate was made on the basis of not only our growing acceptance in the United States, but also the realization that the British direct-marketing community was looking to the United States for new ideas. We anticipated ready acceptance by U.K. direct marketers, and we got it.

10. We kept our financial condition fit and attractive. We not only kept costs under tight control, but we were also cognizant of the balance sheet. In so doing, we earned the respect of the investment banking community and established a situation where they pursued us rather than vice versa. When the time came to sell the company, the suitors were plentiful.

Every once in a while we just got lucky.

Bob Stone's
Commentary

Jock Bickert is a visionary with a capital "V." He fits the *American Heritage Dictionary* definition to a tee: **vi-sion-ar-y** 1) Characterized by vision or foresight, 2) Having the nature of fantasies or dreams.

Jock fits a second definition equally well: **en-tre-pre-neur** A person who organizes, operates, and assumes the risks for business ventures, especially an impresario.

The NDL success story is the end result of what happens when an entrepreneur is willing to put his or her career on the line to make a dream come true. Jock Bickert's dream was a precept shared by many—*the more you know about the characteristics of a consumer, the more effectively you can communicate.* The difference between Bickert and the others was that he turned the precept into reality.

Jock would be the first to acknowledge that he wasn't an instant success. Few entrepreneurs are. He had a number of false starts, suffered from growing pains, was impeded by a lack of cash. It just wasn't easy. But, in the end it was the strategies he employed, many out of sheer necessity, that made the dream come true. Jock has closed his chapter with a concise review of the strategies that made NDL successful. Let us now translate his major strategies into general statements that can be applied to practically any organization.

- ☐ If your partners don't buy into your precept, it is best to abandon your relationship and partner with others of like minds.

- ☐ Control costs or costs will control you.

- ☐ When your position is most forlorn, you have two alternatives: quit or fight. Fight is better.

- ☐ If a marketeer can't give you an accurate customer profile then, in order to provide a list of best prospects, you must first create an accurate customer profile for the marketer.

- The best way to recognize and motivate future management is with a meaningful award program.

- If your goal is to have happy employees, you've got to devise ways to have some fun.

- If your headquarters conveys a positive statement of what you do, make every effort to get prime prospects to tour the premises.

- When you entertain, entertain royally. Such a strategy has a lasting effect.

- If you wish to be acquired, romance those capable of acquiring you.

- In order to bring serious suitors to the fore, it is wise to establish a "hurdle price," a figure the suitor must be ready to meet.

The Ultimate
American Success Story
Lillian Vernon

Lillian Vernon, Chairman of the Board
and Chief Executive Officer,
Lillian Vernon Corporation
As told by David C. Hochberg,
Vice President/Public Affairs

Lillian Vernon is the founder and chief executive officer of Lillian Vernon Corporation, a specialty catalog company that markets gift, household, gardening, decorative, and children's products. She started her company in 1951 with $2,000 of wedding-gift money. Over the last four decades, the company has experienced exceptional growth, with revenues for the 1994 fiscal year exceeding $196 million.

Lillian Vernon Corporation is a 44-year-old specialty catalog company that markets gift, household, gardening, decorative, Christmas, and children's products. As one of the largest specialty catalogers in the United States, the company mailed 141 million catalogs in 20 editions and received 4.4 million customer orders last year. Headquartered in New Rochelle, New York, with a 486,000-square-foot national distribution center in Virginia Beach, Virginia, it employs over 2,000 people during its peak season. The company has grown significantly through the past four decades, rising from $1 million in annual sales in 1970 to over $196 million in 1994.

Lillian Vernon, who is the founder and chief executive officer of the company, is considered a pioneer in the direct-marketing industry. As a woman in a field dominated by men, the significance of her achievements ranks with those of mail-order pioneers Richard Sears and A. Montgomery Ward.

She started in 1951 as a pregnant, 24-year-old woman seeking a way to earn a few extra dollars while staying home to care for her new baby. Although she possessed little formal training, she began on her kitchen table by doing a small direct-response ad for a magazine.

Forty-four years later, she mails out 141 million catalogs offering over 2,000 products and generating $196 million in sales. The following is her story.

The Beginning, 1951–1970

Lillian hardly had her sights set on a multimillion-dollar direct-mail empire when she launched her business in 1951. In fact, as a pregnant 24-year-old housewife she had a considerably more moderate goal: earning $50 a week. She was motivated by the fact that she needed the money. "I married a man who worked in his family business, a small retail shop, and there wasn't enough money to support a family," she said. "The mail-order business was a job that I could run at home; so I wouldn't have to leave my baby. I started at my kitchen table."

Entrepreneurship seemed a natural to her. Her parents, Herman and Erna Menasche, had brought 10-year-old Lillian, along with her brother, to the United States when they fled Germany to escape the Nazis in 1937. Her father had been a successful merchant in Leipzig, the center of the German clothing industry. In America, he applied his knowledge of women's wear, working for a dress salesman, salvaging zippers for the garment industry during World War II, and then working in leather goods.

Herman Menasche's adaptability made a lasting impression on young Lillian. "I so admired the fact that if he couldn't sell zippers anymore, he found something else in short supply and got into that," she remembers. "It's a quali-

Exhibit 10.1

The ad that launched the Lillian Vernon Corporation
appeared in the September, 1951 issue of Seventeen Magazine.

ty I admire in people today—the ability to turn on a dime and to do what has to be done. He was my role model. There weren't any female role models like the ones young women have today."

Using $2,000 in wedding-gift money as her startup capital, Lillian began marketing a purse and matching belt of her own design. The price was $5.58; her special offer was free monogramming. "Be the first to sport that personalized look on your bag and belt," said her small, black-and-white ad in the September issue of *Seventeen* magazine.

Her $495 advertising investment paid off. Thirty-two thousand dollars in orders poured in, and the business was launched. Lillian knew she was really on to something, so she put all the profits back into her business, taking out more ads and buying more handbags and belts. A few years later, she decided to expand her product line and run a magazine ad for a personalized bookmark retailing for $1.00. Again, she offered what the customer needed and wanted, and the ad brought in $40,000 in orders.

Three years later, in 1954, Vernon Specialties (named after Mount Vernon, New York, where she lived) launched its first catalog: Sixteen pages in black and white that offered combs, collar pins, and cuff links to the 125,000 customers who had responded to her ads. Two years later, Sam Hochberg, Lillian's husband, left his family business to join her in the expanding mail-order business.

With each new product introduction, Lillian's business grew. By the mid-1950s, she employed a dozen people. Where did she get the money to bankroll each expansion? From her own cash reserves. "In those days," she explains, "you got paid first and sent out merchandise later. Of course it's different now, with the use of credit cards. We had a good cash flow."

Despite her incredible success, creditors considered her a bad risk in those days. "Women had no financial credibility then. Unfortunately, they still have much the same problem. We were doing well, but suppliers still demanded the money up front. The banks wouldn't even talk to me," she says. "I owned some AT&T stock at the time, and I constantly had to use it as collateral for loans."

In 1956, Vernon Specialties outgrew Lillian's apartment and took over a storefront to use as a warehouse, renting a building next door for the monogramming operation and a store across the street for the shipping department. With greater space and a proven success, the company soon engaged in the manufacturing of custom-designed products for other companies, including Max Factor, Elizabeth Arden, Avon, and Revlon.

Several years later, with their two sons in school, Sam Hochberg, thinking that mail order was too risky, concentrated his efforts on the manufacturing end of the business. In 1969, after their marriage ended in divorce, Sam kept the manufacturing business and Lillian kept the mail-order operation, which reached $1 million in sales in 1970.

Building and Growing, 1970–1987

By 1970, Lillian, with her sons both in college, devoted all her efforts to running her company. Her strategy was to fill her catalogs with exclusive merchandise that she felt her loyal customers could not live without. Her mission was to select these products and display them on the pages of her digest-size, black-and-white catalog, while communicating their benefits in catalog copy with her own personal touch. People loved the concept! For them, it was like having their own country store in their living rooms.

Her touch was honed before the explosive growth in direct mail. When Lillian entered the business, voluminous wish books, like those from Sears and Montgomery Ward, filled the needs of the country's growing middle class. Smaller, specialty catalogs, like Lillian's, were harder to find. Her competitive advantage was that she personally chose all of the products that went into her catalog, so the customer did not have to. Today, the industry still respects her phenomenal talent for selecting merchandise. One industry insider has commented, "She has a special knack of understanding who her customers are and what they want. She's got a magic touch." Lillian has said that she evaluates merchandise from a personal perspective. "I always have someone specific in mind when I choose a product."

During the early 1970s, she saw that her selection of domestically sourced products could not meet the growing demands of her customers. She was determined to find the best products from around the world for them. In 1972, she began to travel extensively, mostly to Europe, and, in the early 1980s, she was one of the first merchants to do business in China.

In 1983, she opened her own buying offices in Florence, Italy, and Hong Kong. She won't sell products that have been overexposed. If she sees something in a department store, she doesn't want it in her catalog unless something is done to make it a Lillian Vernon exclusive. For example, in 1984, she sold the popular French jelly jar glass, but instead of its hallmark orange caps, she had the color changed to white.

As Lillian's buying power escalated both domestically and overseas, she developed high standards for the products she accepted. She would only buy products that she would proudly use in her own home. She also had tremendous respect for her customers' taste levels and was very careful never to underestimate them. This rule still applies today and affects the purchases made by all the buyers in her merchandising department.

Lillian is fond of saying that the key to her success is offering "unique, affordable, personalized products of high value" to women like herself. Her merchandise selection is a result of market research, demographic surveys, and her gut instinct. "It's really my golden gut," she says. "You can do so much research, and in the meantime your competitors could come out with something and make a lot of money. Our research is: We like it, we think there's a need for it, and we put it in the catalog. We either lead the parade and have a winner while everyone else is still researching it, or we've lost a little money by testing it in the catalog."

As the business grew, so did the careers of her two sons, Fred and David Hochberg. After obtaining a Master's in Business Administration from Columbia Business School, Fred became a director in the marketing department and worked his way up to president and chief operating officer. David, now vice president of public affairs, spends most of his time cultivating his mother's public image.

During the 1970s, when the company was experiencing extraordinary growth, Lillian began to realize the tremendous importance of employee loyalty. She knew that without her key employees, she never would have made it! As a result, she has taken a special interest in developing and fostering her employees' careers. Where other small companies tended to hire their senior management from outside the company, Lillian always felt strongly about promoting from within. She rewarded hard work and dedication and believed in giving all her employees a strong sense of responsibility. As a result, her key executives, some of whom entered the company in administrative roles, have been with her for years, not only benefitting financially, but also acquiring a strong sense of pride in themselves and their work.

Lillian feels that her company was able to get where it is while others have failed because of the high motivation level of her staff. She has always focused heavily on rewarding people for good performance; she has been rewarded by hardworking, dedicated employees.

By 1986, her business achieved over $100 million in sales. Fueling the tremendous growth of mail-order companies were basic changes in the American family, one of which was the increase in the number of working women. Catalogs gave them an easy way to shop without tying up their precious leisure time. The demise of local merchants and the rise of national chain stores in regional malls made consumers more comfortable with the notion of buying from a stranger.

An industry insider once stated, "Now the customer's local merchant isn't a neighbor and friend. Once that bond was broken, direct marketing was a natural." The emergence of nationally accepted credit cards, faster delivery, and toll-free telephone numbers also eased the process of buying by mail. Computerization assisted in the development of better-targeted customer databases.

Taking It Public, 1987

By the end of fiscal year 1987, the company had achieved sales of $115 million. It employed over 1,000 people during its peak season and occupied 275,000 square feet in four facilities in Westchester County, New York. It was at that point that the company had to intentionally slow its growth because of the limited space in its existing distribution facilities. It had "maxed out."

Since Lillian planned a strategy of long-term growth, she knew they would eventually have to make a significant financial investment. The company executives chose a 52-acre site in Virginia Beach to build a 486,000-square-foot, state-of-the-art operations facility. They knew that the additional space provided by the Virginia Beach national distribution center would allow the company to explore development of targeted spinoff catalogs featuring specialty lines of merchandise. With this facility, they would also have the option to acquire other catalog companies that would enhance Lillian Vernon's appeal.

Another investment would be obtaining a more sophisticated computer system for their data processing needs. They knew that in order to remain competitive in the future, their computer systems and distribution facility would have to be the best available. Going public was the most effective way of achieving their objectives.

On August 13, 1987, Lillian Vernon Corporation began trading on the American Stock Exchange, as the only Amex-listed company with a female founder. Operating as a public entity had a significant impact on the way Lillian conducted business. Since the financial results of her company were now public information, she was accountable to many people: the Securities and Exchange Commission, lawyers, accountants, investment bankers, and investors. Going public put the company at a tremendous advantage: it now had the capital to grow.

Growing in a Tough Economy, 1987–1994

A month after Lillian Vernon went public, the economy was jolted by the stock market crash. Soon after, the "Reagan years" were over, as the disposable income of the 1980s vanished. By 1990, the real estate market was in a fast downward spiral, followed by the country's worst savings and loan bank crisis. At the same time, the recession began. More and more companies declared bankruptcy, leading to widespread layoffs through the country. Consumer confidence was at its lowest point in years. Lillian knew that since consumers were thinking differently, they would have to be treated differently, and she would have to implement some creative ideas in order to thrive.

In addition to a volatile economy, the nature of the catalog industry was also changing. Between 1980 and 1987, the industry grew from 1,000 catalogs to nearly 4,000 catalogs. Consumers were being inundated with everything from apparel to housewares, and there was a race among catalogers to see who could capture the customer. Thousands of catalogs bombarded consumers, each claiming they had the best service, best prices, best-quality merchandise, and best guarantee, but many consumers were overwhelmed by the hundreds of catalogs they received. On top of this, the industry was struck by a major blow in 1991 when postal rates were increased nearly 30 percent.

Lillian Vernon Corporation still managed to increase sales and profits every year from 1987 to 1993. The company also achieved response rates up to 4 percent, one of the highest in the industry. Lillian attributes the success of her catalog during these years to good communication with her customers. "This is a business built on trust," she says of direct mail. In an industry in which customers are asked to send money far away, Lillian established an immediate rapport with her customers through her catalogs.

All of her catalogs carry her photograph and introductory message with her first-name signature. Ironically, as enormous department stores and vast suburban malls have depersonalized shopping, Lillian managed to bring back a sense of human contact for the customer. She has personalized that most impersonal of retail operations, direct mail.

During these tough economic times, Lillian's strategy focused on pleasing her loyal consumer base, which never let her down. She knew that keeping customers satisfied would be the key to survival. She was constantly thinking of new ideas to keep them happy, ideas that would be too risky for other catalogers to try. She knew of something they wanted that she could provide, although it would mean more work for her and her staff. She believed that customers wanted to see more new products offered in every catalog. This meant that her staff had to buy merchandise more aggressively and take riskier inventory positions. It also meant increased workloads for the operations staff as well as the creative and marketing departments.

By 1994, each catalog offered over 120 new products. This became a tremendous competitive advantage for the company because products would be seen in the Lillian Vernon catalog before competitors or retail stores had them. In addition, the company was able to get a head start on analyzing new-product performance.

Most decisions Lillian makes are based on long-term performance. Although she is usually the first to introduce new products, her company is cautious in implementing expensive new technology. Her philosophy is, "Let the others be the guinea pigs, and if it works for them, then I'll implement. If it was a bad decision, then they will bear the consequences. I'll be better off in the long term." This theory has worked to the company's advantage on several occasions. For example, waiting two years after the technology was perfected to transfer their extensive inventory files over to a very sophisticated computer system enabled them to make a smooth transition. By the time the company implemented the new system, consultants knew exactly which system would best meet the company's needs. Professionals who were hired for training and consultation on the system already had significant experience.

Another example of her late entrant strategy was the decision not to institute a toll-free number when other major mail-order companies did. In the 1980s and early 1990s, her market research continued to show that the cost of offering an 800 number far outweighed the benefits. By 1993, however, competition was fierce among the major telephone companies, causing them to compete on price. As a result, implementing a toll-free number became extremely cost effective. Lillian Vernon was able to introduce a toll-free number at less than half the cost that other mail-order companies incurred when they introduced theirs.

Plans for the Future, 1995 and Beyond

Today, Lillian, her executives, and her board of directors, are focused on developing new, creative ways to grow the business. The company strategy is geared toward starting new specialty catalogs that target specific customer niches. Lillian has said, "It's just too risky these days to mail catalogs to people who have a very low probability of purchasing the merchandise offerings. Catalog space and mailing costs are just too expensive." With a mailing list in excess of 14.7 million people, the company has the capability to define specific niches in the marketplace, and with years of relationship-building with vendors around the world, the company has the merchandising expertise to buy a broad range of products.

Lillian has been attuned to niche marketing for several years. In 1989, Lillian noticed the large increase in her customers' orders for children's products. This gave her an idea. A year later, the company launched a separate catalog, *Lilly's Kids,* offering children's toys and educational products. At first, this catalog (shown in Exhibit 10.2) was mailed mostly to core buyers, but now it has its own highly profitable house file.

This business has achieved $24 million in sales in three years. A similar launch was made in 1992 with Christmas-related merchandise in a specialty catalog called *Christmas Memories,* pictured in Exhibit 10.3.

In 1993, a separate catalog called *Welcome,* consisting of home decorations, organizer products, and housewares, was developed for people who moved recently. Exhibit 10.4 shows the cover of a *Welcome* catalog. The company consistently researches new, lucrative business ideas and concepts, which are based fundamentally on the purchasing power and demographics of its most valuable asset, its house file.

Exhibit 10.2 *Lilly's Kids* Catalog

COSTUMES
sold on pages 4 and 8

Exhibit 10.3 Lillian Vernon's *Christmas Memories* Catalog

Exhibit 10.4 *Welcome* Specialty Catalog

Although mail order through print media has been her mainstay for 43 years, Lillian does not shy away from experimenting with new ways of doing business. For example, interactive home shopping via television is one area that has captured her attention. In 1993, to test home shopping, she appeared on the QVC shopping network. Because much of the interactive technology is not in place, it is an area that the company will continue to monitor but not emphasize at the current time.

Another exciting line of business for the company is wholesale marketing, selling bulk orders of merchandise to other businesses. This area has been performing well and is being expanded.

Off-price retail is another area to which Lillian has been giving much attention. Because of the company's high name recognition (over 30 million Americans are familiar with the Lillian Vernon name), its six outlet stores in New York and Virginia have performed well. The company will expand this business to profitably dispose of overstocked and discontinued products.

Regardless of the selling vehicle, Lillian Vernon Corporation is still based on the same idea Lillian had 44 years ago: providing unique, quality, personalized products at affordable prices.

Though by today's standards that first *Seventeen* ad seems quaint, it contained several of the elements that still distinguish Lillian Vernon. Free personalization, embossing names or monograms on everything from tote bags to brass door knockers, continues to be a Lillian Vernon tradition. The chatty, but explicitly descriptive, copy still characterizes the company's catalogs today. Lillian never strayed far from this fundamental premise, and as a result, focused all of her company efforts and resources on her one, initial idea. Forty-three years and millions of satisfied customers later, she has earned respect and admiration as one of the leaders in her industry.

Bob Stone's
Commentary

American success stories are punctuated by people of vision who have beaten odds that most people regard as insurmountable. In mail order, the success stories that bring the most enthusiastic accolades are those about people who literally started their businesses on their kitchen tables. Such is the story of Lillian Vernon.

Back in 1951, the chances of a 24-year-old woman succeeding in business would have been regarded as less than zero. The "man's world" of that era regarded female executives with the same disdain cats had for mice. It was in such an atmosphere that Lillian Vernon beat the odds and, in a major way, paved the way for female executives to come.

It's unlikely that Lillian strategized her growth in a formal way. It's more likely that she grew her business based on "gut feeling." Be that as it may, with the luxury of hindsight, we can translate the steps Lillian Vernon took into strategies.

- Whatever your restraints may be, do what you have to do to better your situation.

- Establish a point of difference, such as personalization, to distinguish yourself from your competition.

- Specialize in exclusive products and services in order to grow a unique business.

- Understand completely who your customers are and what they want.

- Consider the world to be your source for new products. Don't limit yourself to your country of origin.

- Use market research and demographic surveys as a guide, but rely on gut feeling as well.

- Great success is not possible without great employee loyalty. Nurture it.

- Understand the basic changes in the American family. Provide an easy way to shop.

- Ease the process of buying by accepting credit cards and toll-free telephone orders. Provide fast delivery.

- Create a database that enables you to target market in a precise manner.

- Invest in a state-of-the-art fulfillment facility capable of handling dynamic growth.

- Consider a stock offering as a major way to finance accelerated growth.

- The companies who survive during tough times are those who build their businesses on trust.

- Introducing a continual flow of new products creates a competitive advantage.

- When it comes to adapting new technology, it's best to let others be the guinea pigs. This avoids unnecessary risks.

- Be forever on the lookout for new market niches.

- Test new media as it comes along, but wait for it to mature before making a firm commitment.

Love, Guilt, and Christmas
Helzberg Diamonds

John Goodman, Vice President of Marketing, Helzberg Diamonds

John Goodman is nationally recognized for his advances in retail direct marketing. His areas of focus are database segmentation and creative execution. He maintains a well-balanced understanding of the applications of database-driven marketing strategies within the retail marketplace. As Vice President of Marketing for Helzberg Diamonds, he is responsible for all advertising, marketing, strategic planning, direct marketing, sales promotion, and credit marketing for this specialty retailer with 150 stores nationwide.

We've all been there: It's two days before Christmas or the afternoon of Valentine's Day and you haven't bought a gift for that special someone. Or maybe it's your wife's birthday or your anniversary that you've forgotten, and you need a gift solution right away. These situations and many like them occurs to millions of American consumers and represent an enormous business opportunity for retailers, particularly those who practice database-driven, direct marketing.

Those gift retailers who have developed a consumer database of previous purchasers have the ability to capitalize on these situations by delivering the most appropriate offer at the most opportune time to solve their customer's gift needs. This chapter identifies several database-driven marketing strategies, all of which have been executed in the real world of today's retail environment.

Unfortunately, most retailers tend to believe that direct marketing is simply another term for mail order. Thus those retailers who shun mail order are likely to overlook other opportunities offered by direct marketing.

Many of the examples given come from my experience in specialty gift retailing; however, all of these strategies can be applied to a wide array of retail businesses. For the sake of clarification, the primary goal of these direct-marketing strategies is to generate store traffic, as opposed to mail-order sales.

Capitalizing on the Gift Business

Gift retailers are thankful (particularly to Hallmark) for the consumer demand brought about by the traditional gift holidays: Mother's Day, Valentine's Day, Father's Day, and, of course, Christmas. There are also many other individual life events that are cause for gift-giving and celebration, including birthdays, graduations, anniversaries, marriages, and, today, remarriages. Generally speaking, people celebrating and shopping for these gift-giving occasions are filled with love, happiness, and, in some cases, guilt.

In order for the gift retailer to capitalize on these gift occasions, it is important to first understand the consumer attitudes involved in these purchasing decisions. In many cases, particularly in the jewelry category, where there is often a large degree of emotion overspilling these purchases along with a void of product knowledge, there exists a huge opportunity for store associates to step in and establish a strong relationship with the customer. If this relationship is successfully fulfilled, the retailer has not only gained the initial sale, but laid the groundwork for all future direct-marketing efforts, which are intended to create repeat sales.

It's important to look at the entire experience of the customer in the store because all subsequent communications are influenced by this initial encounter. This store experience forms the basis for the core direct-marketing strategy, which is to *strengthen* this relationship and further bond the customer to the business.

The objectives of this strategy are to: (1) build customer loyalty and defend market share from competitors attempting to lure customers away; and (2) create repeat purchasing, upselling, and increased store traffic among the existing customer base. A by-product of this type of relationship is the ambassador role customers will play by referring future customers to the business because of their high level of satisfaction.

In addition to capitalizing on gift business brought about from traditional holidays, gift retailers can use the consumer database to develop specific messages to consumers between these major gift occasions in order to create incremental sales and traffic. For example, birthdays are one of the most important occasions for making a gift purchase. The beauty in marketing to this occasion is that there are 12 opportunities a year to present this buying opportunity to the customer base, as opposed to one major holiday weekend.

Based on the information in the database, retailers can send personalized "birthday cards" with an appropriate offer (based on previous purchasing history), which can be directed to high-priority customer segments just prior to their upcoming birthdays. This particular type of direct-marketing program is designed to instigate a self purchase (see Exhibit 11.1), so the creative message must focus on the self-reward aspect of the purchasing decision ("treat yourself, you deserve it").

In addition, by appending birthday information to other household members, a second creative message can be developed aimed at a gift purchase for another member of the customer's household (see Exhibit 11.2). A separate creative approach is designed to capitalize on this buying scenario ("Shhh, birthday coming up? We'll keep your secret").

As well as marketing to specific gift-giving occasions, the previous type of product purchased and the amount previously spent can determine specific creative messages and offers. This has particular application in the department store context where there is a broad merchandise mix and greater opportunities for cross-selling, as opposed to narrower product classifications.

However, there are still many applications for specialty gift retailers in the form of targeting specific merchandise exhibits and trunk showings based on previous products purchased. Also, for specialty retailers using catalogs to drive store traffic, selectively binding specific merchandise signatures into catalogs directed to specific individuals (based on previous purchasing patterns) enables the retailer to present the most tempting array of product mix to the most likely purchasers.

Exhibit 11.1 Package Promoting Self-Purchases

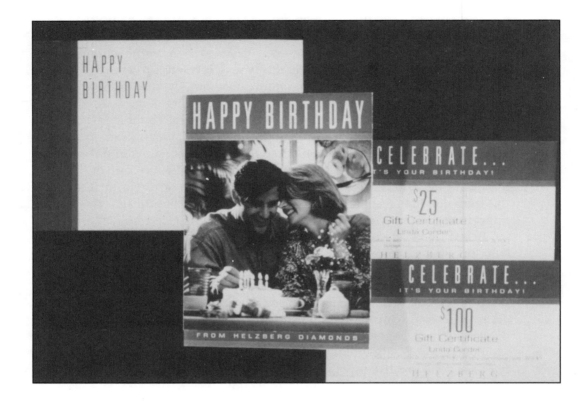

Exhibit 11.2 Package Promoting Gift-Giving

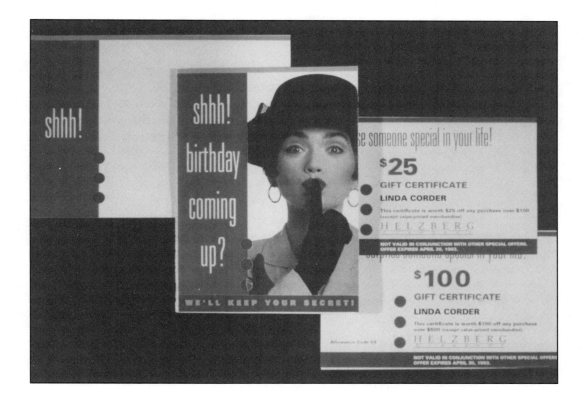

Jewelry Junkies, the Jones' Bass Master, and My Alma Mater

In addition to gift purchases made for loved ones for these holidays or other special occasions, there is a strong trend today toward self-purchasing for reasons of self-reward or self-interest. In many cases, these purchases are made by people who display an exceptionally strong interest or affinity to a product or store and are often the most loyal, productive type of customers. These frequent buyers, commonly referred to as "heavy users," or in the case of the jewelry business, "jewelry junkies," whose purchasing enthusiasm never seems to wane, are represented in all retail classifications.

In my retail marketing experience, I've had the pleasure of building database marketing programs with specialized retailers other than upper-end gift retailers. These include collegiate sporting goods and boating accessories businesses. What I've discovered is, whether it's depth finders, diamonds, or college sweatshirts, the 80/20 rule is always present. The very best customers, the 20 percent who contribute a disproportionate amount of sales, come from people who have a very strong affinity with the product or loyalty to a store.

These people have a strong attraction to the product or store because it allows them an opportunity to express their own personality. These are not just customers who make one large purchase and never return; rather, they are customers who purchase frequently and feel perfectly comfortable dropping by the store just to see the new merchandise arrivals or to learn a little bit more about their "hobby."

This strong affinity with the product or store personnel is very common in many different retail environments. For instance, in the boating accessories business, having the latest bell or whistle for a bass boat is second only to religion on the fisherman's priority list. So when a catalog of the latest bass boating equipment reaches the home of this "heavy user," it is almost a reflex for him to visit the store and find out more about these new products.

A similar allegiance to a product exists in the marketing of college sporting goods apparel, where the customer has an opportunity to express their individuality by wearing their collegiate "badge" on their chest. These products provide college supporters with a chance to show people just what they stand for when it comes to supporting their alma mater.

So jewelry enthusiasts, college fans, and bass fishermen all share a common trait—they are firmly entrenched in a relationship with a particular product or store, and they are willing to pay a lot for this relationship!

The implications for retail direct marketers who can identify these "heavy users" on their customer databases are abundant. Loyalty programs will provide this customer with a vehicle to continue to actively participate in their interest as well as to reward their frequent visits to the store. These customers also should be the first to receive invitations and private announcements about product information, seminars, or exhibits.

Based on the degree of their previous purchases, these customers are ideal targets for gift certificates directing their future purchases toward higher tickets. In short, these customers are the lifeblood of any retail business and should receive more extensive, more expensive direct-marketing communications that will further enhance their purchasing relationship with the store. With a consistent direct-marketing strategy, these customers will continue to contribute disproportionate amounts of sales and profits to the business.

Staying Electronically Ahead of the Relationship

As demonstrated in the previous examples, all we are trying to do with the customer database is to stay electronically ahead of the relationships between the store associates and their customers. By providing the most relevant information to the customer at the most appropriate time, we can significantly influence the probability of that customer returning to the store.

The customer database provides us with the strategic tool to prioritize and segment valuable consumer information captured at the point of sale so we can more profitably and deliberately grow our business.

When retailers leverage this information to their advantage, they can definitely determine who should receive the marketing message, the likelihood of response, traffic, and ultimate purchase. This likelihood is projected in quantifiable terms for *each* customer receiving the communications piece and the specific return on database investment for each segment contacted. The subsequent results can be measured against these projections.

Hook Slides, Sharp Turns, and Customer Databases

Most retailers agree on the many merits of using a consumer database to more efficiently drive a business, particularly gift retailers, who can target a particular purchasing occasion. However, it is still puzzling why so many store retailers are not practicing direct marketing. It could be because of the inherent conflict of trying to develop a long-range strategic marketing tool (consumer database) in the midst of a short-range operating environment (retail).

Retailers operate in an environment of sharp turns, quick changes, and a constant series of hook slides. We arrive each morning reviewing the previous day's sales and gross margin reports along with our first cup of coffee. It is, for the most part, a short-range operating environment where priorities are given to receiving and displaying merchandise, and simply making sure there are enough qualified sales associates on the floor to open the store and service the customer. In effect, retailers are conditioned to view their business from this short-range perspective.

The challenge in the midst of this setting is to develop a long-range strategic marketing tool, the customer database. Two strategies will enable retailers to meet this challenge: (1) Remember what business you truly are in, and focus on it; and (2) let an experienced database resource assist you in setting up your systems, segmenting the data and coaching you on the use of this information while you continue to keep the customer happy and the sales line healthy.

In other words, do what you do best; whether that's selling chocolates, diamonds, or ladies' blouses, focus on your strength. Don't let the database get in the way of accomplishing the business mission. Remember, the database works for you! You don't work for the database.

One other pitfall that retailers often fall into in developing a customer database is trying to gather and assimilate so much information they become paralyzed and are unable to convert it into marketing action. Therefore, it is important to identify the key levers that impact your business and start capturing the data surrounding these levers.

At the same time, separate this data from the information that is not a priority, that is, separate the *need* to know from the *nice* to know. There will be plenty of time after you start up your program to enhance and append additional information to the database. Therefore, the key point is to study and determine what transactional information is most critical to the development of your business and only retain this data.

When developing the retail database, try to capture this data on as many sales transactions as possible, as opposed to the path most retailers have traditionally taken, which is to capture private label charge card sales alone. Collecting all transactions will increase the universe of your customer database and play a pivotal role in the rate of growth of the database itself. Not only will the universe expand, but the quality of noncredit card customers in some segments may very well challenge the productivity of your own charge card groups.

Another real issue that greatly impacts the success or failure of a database program within the retail environment, involves a term not often found in retail dictionaries: patience. Developing a database of high caliber consumer information takes time. This is influenced by the volume of traffic entering your stores, the scope of your business, the seasonal patterns of business and the growth phase of the business itself. However, more important, the success of the database marketing concept is dependent on the long-range commitment of the management within the organization. This commitment must be made from the top down and the conviction to maintain the database from the ground up.

A customer database is like any other long-term investment that takes time to develop, yet when it comes to fruition, you will have discovered a virtual gold mine. Once you have the ability to leverage the purchasing information on the consumer database and convert it to repeat purchasing, you will have created one of the most valuable assets of any retail business.

Acknowledging the importance of the customer database within the retail environment, identifying what information is most critical to capture, and building this key asset over time are all important strategies for developing a successful database marketing program. However, the single most important strategy for developing a database within the fast-paced, day-to-day retail environment is to create ownership of the database among the front lines.

Inform the sales team how this consumer purchasing information is being rechanneled back to them in the form of repeat visits and sales from their best customers. Just tell the stores *why* they are gathering this information and *how* it will be used to their benefit, and you will earn their support. This shouldn't be a very difficult idea to communicate, particularly to the better salespeople who've endorsed the concept of relationship building and "handshake marketing," long before automated databases came into the picture.

If it's put to them in their own language, they will surely comply with the request; however, be careful not to explain the virtues of direct marketing in terms of regression analysis, predictive models, and so on. Discuss it in terms of their personal economic benefits, more sales commissions and bonus checks. The degree of cooperation gained from the front lines depends on whether the business is privately held, a public company, a franchise, or a dealer program, since this impacts your ability to control their compliance. However, the same approach of explaining the benefits of direct marketing in their terms holds true in each of these settings.

Another benefit to the "internal marketing" efforts of the database strategy is building better teamwork between the front lines and the marketing team. This will result in a higher level of awareness of upcoming direct-marketing efforts, and therefore, the front lines will be better prepared to maximize the store traffic and sales resulting from the traffic. We work hard to create the initial sale and get the customer into the store; unfortunately, we all too often hear of the situation where a customer asks an associate about a recent mailing and the associate has no idea what he or she is talking about. With a clear, consistent communications link to the store line, these missed sales opportunities can be minimized and, instead, cross-selling and up-selling opportunities can be emphasized.

There are several other distinct benefits gained from involving the store line in the ownership of the database marketing program. For instance, improving the accuracy and integrity of the information the store associates enter into the database will have a huge impact on the profitability of your future direct-marketing efforts. If the store associate enters inaccurate residential or purchasing data, this will not only create potential waste in your future mailings, but, more importantly, this misdirected mail will be at the expense of a bona fide customer who will not have an opportunity to receive the communications piece. The dollars in wasted advertising is a misfortune, but the incredible amount of business lost by not reaching a qualified, prospective customer is a tragedy.

Where the Right Brain Meets the Left Brain

Gaining the cooperation of the front lines to gather, enter, and execute a database marketing program is an essential management strategy in developing a long-term effort. Retaining this analytical, transactional information serves as a basis for targeting the audience and provides them with the offer that is most relevant to their needs. These are all core elements to a successful direct marketing strategy; however, equally important is taking this analytical information and converting, or "recycling," it into the creative strategy.

The goal of our creative strategy is to create store traffic and sales so we will be first on our customers' mental shopping list. Using these "clues" left behind from previous purchases allows us the opportunity to develop a dialog with our customers and invite or entice them back into the store.

The ability to successfully convert this information with enough creative impact to differentiate you from all other gift retailers in the mailbox is the critical challenge. Again, we are competing against all retailers and mailers, not just against those in our specific category. Therefore, the creativity of the direct-marketing efforts must cut through both the clutter and the competition.

The pinpointing of the audience and the timing in which the message is delivered are key tactical components; yet, the relevance of the message and the creative impact of the piece itself will determine whether or not the communication is opened. The database can be used to feed the creative product in an effort to ensure that the mail does, in fact, get opened.

There are traditional ways of integrating this previous purchasing information into the creative process, such as personalization or referencing of local store locations, local store manager's names, and store phone numbers, as well as specific product or pricing based on unique market situations. Simply dropping these variables into your creative package is not enough to break through the clutter of today's mail. Therefore, the database should be used as a creative resource to help craft the entire creative package, whether it is in the form of copywriting, graphics, or other direct-marketing techniques.

One traditional use of data extracted from the database is the use of personalization. However, the use of personalization can take on an uncommon look or a very "high-touch" quality when executed properly. For instance, when private invitations to a particular event arrive in the form of a hand-addressed, hand-stamped envelope or when close-faced envelopes with typed names and addresses arrive in the mailbox, the true impact of personalization can be maximized.

These types of "private" invitations can be mailed to 100, 100,000, or 1 million customers. One way to execute this labor-intensive technique is to use a variety of nonprofit organizations who can hand-address and hand-stamp these envelopes, so the revenues will be directed to worthwhile causes.

Personalization can also be a very powerful technique when used in an unexpected and carefully executed manner. Personalizing the front cover of a catalog where the customer's last name is a part of the actual headline can be a very effective approach (see Exhibit 11.3). However, be cautious when executing this technique, because if the customer perceives it as a "mass" technique, the hoped-for individuality could actually backfire, and your best, most important customers could be turned off. The consumer's privacy antennae also could go up when they see their name appearing too boldly, so be careful and couch this in a tasteful and appropriate manner.

Using the customer database to help determine the proper incentive or offer to instigate a store visit is a key attribute of the database. These offers can be developed based on the customer's previous purchasing history. Will a free gift do the job instead of a gift certificate? Or should the gift certificate be applied only to certain purchase amounts or certain product classifications? Or perhaps a similar offer can be juxtaposed to the customer in a way that will generate even more creative impact.

For example, in the specialty retail and department store environments, there is a common public perception that store personnel receive substantial discounts on their personal purchases. By tapping into this perception, an offer can be developed based on the employee's discount privilege. This essentially

Exhibit 11.3 Personalized Front Cover of Catalog

offers the same discount a customer would have received with a gift certificate; however, by juxtaposing the offer based on this consumer perception of a better deal, a unique traffic-generating promotion can be developed. The execution of this promotion comes in the form of a mailing to the customer entitling them to their own "employee discount card" (see Exhibit 11.4). This is perceived as a much stronger offer than a typical gift certificate and yields results accordingly.

In addition to these tactics for using the database to feed the creative product, the database also allows retailers other strategic opportunities, such as identifying and marketing to the many different audiences contained within the database. Thus, the ability to reach the many niche markets of today's fragmented marketplace is yet another strategic advantage.

An example of this ability can be demonstrated through a unique point-of-purchase sign program. Using the database to identify the penetration of specific market niches within a designated trade area, we can pinpoint where these audience segments are most prevalent. Then, by using back-lit point-of-purchase signage as our creative medium, we can depict the specific demographic niches in scenes most relevant to their purchasing situation. For example, an anniversary scene depicting a silver-haired couple is used in markets overrepresented by the over-55 age group. A formal military wedding scene is depicted in stores that are highly represented by military customers. Markets overrepresented by Hispanic customers are shown celebrating appropriate festivals.

The point is, the "canvas" for applying transactional purchasing information to your creative efforts can take on many forms, both traditional and nontraditional.

X-Rays and Expectations

The consumer database not only provides essential information to drive the creative strategy, it also provides a vehicle to enhance consumer research efforts. This consumer research can provide a retailer with a snapshot, or "x-ray," of the vital signs of the business. Whether it be x-rays of previous product purchasing patterns, customer demographics, geographic penetration, or customer migration from moderate to heavy use, the database allows the retailer to better understand his or her customers and how these customers impact the business.

These x-rays can result in a wide range of benefits for the retailer: more effective real estate site selection, more accurate prospecting for new customers based on profiles of existing customers, and even determining mass media

Exhibit 11.4 Honorary Helzberg Diamond Employee Discount Card

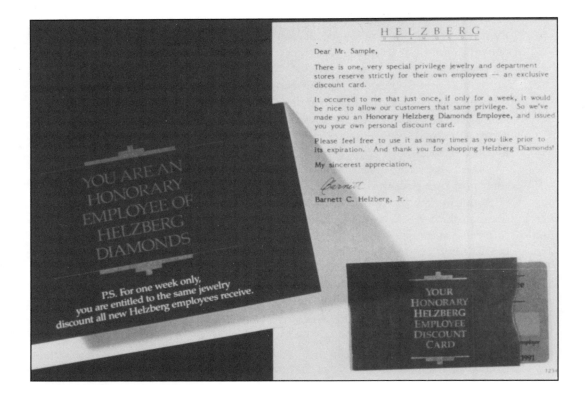

strategy by correlating station ratings with customer penetration in specific zip codes.

As you can see, the customer database is a very versatile marketing tool and can be tapped to provide insight into many strategic decisions involved in successfully building a retail marketing strategy. However, this strength can also be a weakness. To avoid this, retailers must single out the primary benefits and expectations for using the database in order to maximize its full potential.

These primary benefits and expectations must be delineated from the many secondary benefits. In the case of store retailers, the primary mission of the database should be to drive store traffic. Getting the customer back into the store in order to reestablish a relationship is the main objective. Keep in mind, the strategy is simply to get the customer back into the store and create the opportunity for a sale, not the sale itself. Once the customer is exposed to the dynamics of the store setting, then the purchasing decision is in the hands of the customer and the associate.

Conclusion

In summary, if you haven't developed your customer database, begin today. Be resourceful and look around you, there is a wealth of information right under your fingertips.

If you have developed a customer database, look closer at the factors driving the hard data and rechannel it back to your customer in your creative efforts. Ask yourself, what is the customer telling us through this data?

By using nontraditional direct-marketing techniques to leveraging the database information you will be able to cut through the clutter of today's mailbox. Used in the appropriate manner, the database will significantly enhance your response rates, store traffic, and sales.

Also, take advantage of the huge opportunities for involving the store line in your direct-marketing strategies. All too often we go right by the initial purchasing situation, which is the starting point for collecting data in the first place. This "first impression," driven by the level of customer service received, lays the groundwork for all future efforts. Remember, work from the customer transaction backward in developing the communications strategy. Whether it's response rates, traffic flow, or sales productivity, each will be heavily influenced by the degree of satisfaction the customer received in his or her previous visit.

And finally, customer information gathered from previous purchases enables retailers to mold their marketing strategies around what the customer is currently telling them he or she wants most from the business. A key ingredient to successful retail marketing today is to stay flexible and be able to adapt or change your business to meet the current needs of your customers.

Those who understand the needs of their customers best will be capable of serving them best. The vehicle to listen to customers and create a dialog with them is the customer database. In short, today's customer is a moving target, and successful retailers recognize that the consumer database allows them to reach the elusive target while continuing to set their business ahead of the retail pack.

Bob Stone's
Commentary

This chapter by John Goodman is a superb blueprint for all who would make a commitment to retail direct marketing. No retailer can succeed at direct marketing today without database-driven marketing strategies. John shows the way.

Interestingly, while many retail chains have opted for mail-order catalogs, with store traffic as a secondary objective, Helzberg Diamonds uses catalogs and mailers for a sole purpose: *to create store traffic.*

The wisdom of this approach might be clarified by a simple question: Would you be more likely to buy a diamond ring from the printed page, or would you be more likely to buy a diamond ring after putting it on your finger in a Helzberg store, seeing it through a jeweler's glass, and comparing it with other rings available?

As to John Goodman, he, like all the authors in this book, is a giver. He gives freely of his knowledge and experience. Let us now review the database marketing strategies he has contributed.

- The objective of a retail direct-marketing program is to strengthen relationships and further bond customers to your business.

- Gift retailers can use their consumer databases to develop and deliver specific messages to customers between major gift occasions and thereby create incremental traffic and sales.

- A properly maintained database will paint a picture of each individual customer, type of product(s) purchased, and amount(s) previously spent. With this knowledge at hand, you can tailor specific creative messages and offers.

- On average, 80 percent of your business will come from 20 percent of your customer base. Put your best efforts toward your best customers and you will maximize sales and profits.

- Your challenge is to set up a long-range marketing tool, remembering what business you are truly in and focusing on it.

- In order to develop a database that will work for you, let an experienced database resource assist you in setting up your systems, segmenting the data, and coaching you on the use of the information.

- When you develop a database, study and determine what transactional information is most critical to the development of your business. Resist the urge to include "nice to know" information.

- Acquiring usable data requires the complete cooperation of the sales team. Sell the value by citing the history of repeat visits and sales of their best customers.

- Use your data input as a creative resource to help craft the creative message. The specific product offering or the incentive used to initiate a purchase can be developed from the customer's previous purchasing history.

- In order to maximize the full potential of a database the main objective should be to get the customer back into the store in order to reestablish a relationship. The strategy is simply to create the opportunity for a sale, not the sale itself.

CHAPTER

12

A Funny Thing Happened on the Way to the Mimeograph Machine
Raphel Marketing

Murray Raphel, Raphel Marketing, Inc.

Murray Raphel is a speaker, writer, and consultant to major business organizations including retailing, food industry, insurance companies, and financial institutions. He was given the prestigious Montreaux Award for his international contributions in the field of direct marketing. Raphel writes monthly columns on marketing for Direct Marketing *and on supermarket retailing for* Progressive Grocer. *He is the author of* The Great Brain Robbery, The Do-It Yourself Direct Mail Handbook, Mind Your Own Business, Tough Selling for Tough Times, *and* Customerization.

In Papua, New Guinea, there are a small group of talented performers that go from village to village performing plays and entertainment for audiences, not unlike the troupe that visited Hamlet in Elsinore. They continue to ply their wares because of the lack of modern communication linking the small towns. They are called the "Wokabouts" because they literally "walk about" from village to village performing classical routines or, for a payment, making up a skit to advertise a product for sale in the nearest store.

Next time, I'm coming back as a Wokabout.

I feel immensely qualified. I've always been a salesman, selling products, merchandise, and ideas to anyone who would listen to me in print or in person.

At Syracuse University, a double major in drama and journalism meant I had the qualifications to join the folks in Papau to write and perform. Instead, Atlantic City beckoned for my new wife Ruth and I to join her sister and brother-in-law in their little children's store. This step would result in my becoming an "expert" in retail direct mail which led to my life-long goal: helping the small business person stay in business.

Half the new businesses in America fail in the first three years. Eight out of 10 fail in the first 10 years. If there was only some way to keep these folks in business. After all, they are the ones that create the most jobs. After all, nearly 9 out of 10 businesses in America are owned by individual entrepreneurs. One way to keep them in business was to learn how to survive myself.

How I Became An "Expert" in Direct Mail

Penicillin, rubber, photography, x-rays, the telescope, and my beginnings in direct mail happened by accident. Each had someone who wanted to do one thing and wound up doing another far more successfully.

Our 600-square-foot baby shop was called Gordon's (my brother-in-law's last name). Our annual volume of business was about $20,000. That's total business, not salaries.

We expanded by going door to door asking people to join our club: Pay $1 a week and at the end of 10 weeks, you had $11 credit. This was an echo of the Suit Club pioneered by turn-of-the-century immigrants when they arrived on New York City's East Side in the early 1900s. We knocked on about 2,000 doors and found 300 people willing to join, which doubled our annual business.

And then came the thought, "Why not tell our customers that when we come for next week's payment, we'll have something on sale for them?"

We would convey this message with a weekly mimeographed mailing. I typed a stencil listing the specials I would have in my car the following week.

The customer would buy what they wanted and simply increase their weekly payment to $2—$1 for their club, $1 for their bill.

Our business doubled again.

I loved selling and retailing but, most of all, I wanted to write. My early experiments in fiction resulted in a series of rejections. Ruth said the secret was to write about what I knew so why not write an article on how our business increased by sending out the weekly mimeographed letters. I skimmed through *Writer's Digest,* which listed all the published magazines and found one called *The Reporter of Direct Mail Advertising.* They wanted stories on what I was doing, selling through the mail.

The story was sent to then-editor Pete Fischer who called a few days later. "I'm sending you a check for $25 for your story. But the main reason for my call is that I think retail direct mail is the coming thing, and since you're an expert in this field, would you write a monthly column for us?"

Yes! I hung up the phone, turned to Ruth, and asked, "What's retail direct mail?"

The local library had little or no reference to direct mail much less the subcategory of the "coming thing," retail direct mail.

More mailings were sent to our customers. A friend in Philadelphia did direct mailing for his business and that gave us a few columns. A campaign for the Atlantic City Convention Center to generate more conventions was good for another column on "how it worked."

What I discovered was this direct mail thing *did* work. And, for the small business, it was affordable. Advertising space in newspapers or on radio was too expensive, but a simple mimeographed message mailed to a few hundred customers a week was not. I soon realized that direct mail was the direction to take for my personal goal of selling what I could do to help the small business person stay in business. All I had to do was tell the message to other retailers! Not an easy job. Individual retailers are individuals.

Sometimes it seems they were all born in Missouri and then spread across the country because of their "show-me" attitude. They are entrepreneurs, proud of their independence and wary of strangers bringing gifts.

The monthly columns continued, telling the stories of how our retail business grew through the years mainly because of direct mail. Since I was the only one writing about retail direct mail, I became the "expert." Within a short time, several cities invited me to their annual direct-mail conferences.

I served as a panelist to discuss the future of retail direct mail, which was mostly limited to mailings to customers of my store in the upcoming months.

Through trial and error, I was learning what worked and what didn't. Enclosing gift certificates in a mailing brought in more customers. Customers didn't want "coupons" to come from my store. They associated coupons with supermarkets. So we sent them gift certificates. Printing the customer's name on the gift certificates brought in even more customers. I collected retail mailings to find out what others were doing. When I saw a trend, I copied and tried to improve it.

Through the years, I subscribed to retail trade magazines, joined retail organizations, and built a list of contacts throughout the United States of individual stores doing direct mail. We continued our mailings, which helped us grow from the tiny 600-square-foot baby shop to a nearly block-long retail complex of 35 stores, restaurants, and offices—the first pedestrian mall in the state of New Jersey.

One of our most successful direct-mail promotions that has been copied worldwide was the New Year's Day sale.

All retailers have fall and winter sales after Christmas. Most wait a few weeks till after Christmas exchanges so you don't have problems with "What is the *real* price?" In choosing a date, I suggested, "How about New Year's Day?"

The response from my partners was immediate as to why it would fail:

"It's the morning after the night before."

"All the other stores in town are closed."

"Men sit at home on their couches and watch the football games coast to coast all day with beer, pretzels, and potato chips."

They finally agreed to try it. Once. But, since the up-front notice would only go to customers on our mailing list, we would play it safe and backup the sale with a crash promotion the day after on January 2; a full-page newspaper ad and two local radio stations doing "live" interviews all day in our store.

We sent out 5,000 mailings (a sample of which is shown in Exhibit 12.1) to our customers telling them the sale would be held for only three hours on New Year's Day, from noon till 3 p.m. We emphasized that it was *not* advertised to anyone except the regular customers on our mailing list, so they had first choice.

The day of the sale dawned bright and clear. We went to the store around 10 a.m. to straighten up counters and add missing signs. As we approached, we saw a small crowd outside the store. Our first thought was something terrible had happened, a fire or a break-in. But no, they were waiting for the doors to open!

By 11:30, the police were called for crowd control. The store opened at noon and quickly absorbed the maximum 600 people allowed by fire department rules. The doors were locked. Police let people in as others left. We closed around 3:30 p.m. and in that short period of time we did more business than in any other week in our history. What would the next day bring when the store

Exhibit 12.1 Self-Mailer Announcing New Year's Day Sale

Here's YOUR lucky coupons!

EACH ONE HAS YOUR NAME!

- **FREE** dollars (**You** already have won with **your** lucky number!)
- **FREE** merchandise (Bring in **your** certificate for drawing)
- **FREE** New Orleans trip for two (Bring in **your** certificate for drawing)

Here's your lucky number: № 2297

You have already won dollars on New Year's Day. Bring this coupon with your name to Gordon's on New Year's Day. Look for the big signs at the front and rear wrapping counters. Match your lucky number above to the ones posted. You WILL win from $2.00 to $250.00 in merchandise!

Here's your entry for the $1,000 in merchandise

Simply deposit this certificate in the big box on the counter in Gordon's on New Year's Day. twenty one winners will be drawn at the end of the business day.

1st prize $ 250.00 in merchandise	2nd prize $ 100 in merchandise
3rd to 10th: $ 50 in merchandise	11th to 21st: $ 20 in merchandise

Win a trip for two to New Orleans!

This is your entry for the free trip for two to New Orleans. Bring to Gordon's New Year's Day. Winner drawn at end of day. Adults only. Employees of family members of Gordon's not eligible

IMPORTANT: New Orleans weekend trip NOT exchangeable for any other award. Must be used Friday to Sunday. Reservations when confirmed are not changeable. Trip includes round trip air Philadelphia-New Orleans, two nights at hotel. Reservations must be made by Gordon's Alley Travel a minimum of 30 days before departure. Not available during Holidays. Restrictions apply. Must be used on or before July 1, 1989.

the shops in.
Gordon's
gordon's alley, atlantic city, n.j. 08401

Bulk Rate
U.S. Postage
PAID
Permit No. 63
Linwood, N.J. 08221

The
New Year's
Day Sale
In Gordon's
Alley.

See YOUR three personal gift certificates on the back page.

A Special Invitation for...

Address Correction Requested

Exhibit 12.1 (Continued)

Gordon's Alley presents our....

Silver Anniversary

New Year's Day Sale.

January 1, 1989

Noon till 4 PM. A private sale for our customers only. Park free on our big lot on South Pennsylvania avenue next to the firehouse.

Welcome to the 25th silver anniversary of our New Year's Day Sale. This means it must be something special, exciting, different, unusual and fantastic.

Well, read through this brochure and we think we've fulfilled all those adjectives. And more.

(If you haven't looked at the back page of this mailer yet, stop reading right now and take a look.)

You see you have already won free dollars

Your first certificate has your name and lucky number. Bring your certificate and match it to the numbers posted in the store. **You have won from $2.00 to $200.00**

Your second certificate is your entry in the **ONE THOUSAND DOLLAR** clothing sweepstakes. (You can be one of 21 winners!)

Your third certificate is for the drawing for the free weekend trip for two to fun filled New Orleans. Walk through the French Quarter. Have Beignets (French doughnuts) and cafe au lait tot the Cafe de Monde in Jackson Square. See the artists around the square. Enjoy delicious French cuisine. Take a buggy ride through the French Quarter. Walk along the Mississippi. Go to Preservation Hall one evening and hear authentic New Orleans Jazz.

The New Orleans weekend trip is arranged with Gordon's Alley Travel.

If it's New Year's Day...it must be Gordon's Alley!

·The Door Buster Specials·

(Come early for these . . .!)

ELEVEN FALL JACKETS FROM JEFF'S WE SELL TO $100. SALE: $29.99 Assorted men's fall jackets. Button and zip fronts Melton wools, lined dungaree coats, blazer style jackets. They sell from $80 to $100 each. Only eleven! Small to XL. Come early for this one. **SALE: $29.99**

FOUR OUTFITS FROM OUR WOMEN'S SHOP ON SALE FOR $29.99. These sell to $240 each and include dresses and slack/skirt sets.

SEVEN MEN'S SUITS WE SELL FROM $250 TO $450 ON SALE FOR $99. You read it right! Beautiful all wool and wool/silk blended suits from our Men's Shop. From Perry Ellis and Polo University. Sizes 40 to 44 regulars and longs. Slight alteration charges. But be first in line for these!

A POLO SALE IN OUR MEN'S SHOP

The Polo classic knit shirt. The most popular short sleeve knit shirt of them all. Discontinued styles and colors from the fall/winter collection. Interlock and weathered mesh. All sizes medium through x-large but not all colors. This is the $40 and $45 shirt. **While they last. Sale: $29.99**

The Polo classic oxford button down shirt. Once you wear this shirt you will never wear another. In charcoal, pink, blue kry, yellow, raspberry, turquoise, blue/white stripe and pink/white stripe. Sizes 14.5 thru 17.5. Not all colors in all sizes. This is the $52.50 classic shirt in discontinued colors. **While they last. Sale: $29.99**

The Polo ties. Elegant classics and silks and patterns. They sell for $37.50 each. Your choice of your pattern. **On sale: $19.99**

Our classic ties: We carry ONLY natural fabrics. silks, cottons, wools. No rayons. No synthetics. A collection of our $15 to $24 ties. **Sale: $9.99**

Our all-wool dress slacks: Never before on sale this year. A select collection of dress pants we sell for $85 and $90 each sizes 32 to 40 Pleated front. All new. Right from stock. Sizes 32-40　**Sale: $49.99**

The Men's Shop

RALPH LAUREN WOMEN'S BOOT AND SHOE SALE: $79.99.
RALPH LAUREN WOMEN'S SPORTSWEAR ON SALE: $29.99 to $59.99
RALPH LAUREN BETTER SPORTSWEAR ON SALE: $79.99 to $99.99

RALPH LAUREN HALF PRICE HANDBAG SALE
The $29.99 - $59.99 Sportswear Sale: Choose from turtlenecks, rugbys, cotton shirts, cotton pants, denim and chambrays skirts and skirts. WE sell them to $120 each.　**SALE: $29.99-$59.99**
The $79.99 - $99.99 Sportswear Sale: Sweaters & skirts & slacks & blouses. Finely tailored classics. Mostly solids, some plaid. We sell these to $190 EACH. **SALE: $79.99-$99.99**
The Half Price Handbag Sale: Mostly karabu and pigskin leathers in camel,black and brown. Shoulder and clutches designed to never go out of style.　**The Boot and Shoe Sale: $79.99**

The Ralph Lauren Shop

LOOK WHAT'S ON SALE IN OUR WOMEN'S SHOP BY BELLE FRANCE, FLORA KUNG, MAGGY LONDON, SILK CLUB, GENE EWING BIS, PERRY ELLIS, JOAN VASS AND ADRIENNE VITTADINI.
Dresses, jumpsuits, skirt sets: Silks, washable silks, rayons and knits for career and dining. These sell to $250.00 each.　**Sale: $69.99 to $99.99.**
Sportswear for office or weekends: Knit slack sets, sweaters,blouses, skirts & slacks. Originally priced to $175 each. **Sale: $39.99 to $79.99.**
Half Price Sale: Designer coats, jackets and suits by Perry Ellis, Jimmy Houthan and our imported Finnish ski jackets by One Top and Luhta. **SALE. One half the original price!**

The Women's Shop

SOCKS FOR $3.99, SCARVES & GLOVES FOR $7.99, BELTS FOR $19.99.
HANDBAGS ON SALE STARTING AT $39.99. IN OUR ACCESSORY SHOP.
Fringed wool scarves by V. Fraas. Values to $16.00.　　**Sale: $7.99**
Knitted berets, scarves & gloves by Ane. Values to $18　　**Sale: $7.99**
Great selection of fun socks by Hue & E.G. Smith.　　**Sale: $3.99**
Better belt sale: Leathers in brown, black, purple, burgundy. Originally priced to $54. each.　　**Sale: $19.99**
Handbags and fine small leather goods by Franco Godi, Coach, Perry Ellis and Anne Klein. Only once a year and only New Year's Day for these. So hurry for this one.　　**Sale: $39.99 to $69.99**

The Accessory Shop

was open for eight hours with a full-page ad and two radio stations live?

At the end of the second day, the store wound up with less than half the business of New Year's Day! This inspired a story for the now-retitled *Direct Marketing* magazine with the phrase that became my slogan and theme for my national and international direct-mail programs: "Dollar, for dollar, nothing increases your business as much as direct mail."

For 25 consecutive years, this day was the largest single volume day in our history, increasing every year, and maintaining the record established the first time of doing more business in a few hours than we did any other week of the year.

We tried to come up with unusual and different mailers every year. One time we mailed a replica of a theatrical playbill with two "tickets" for admission to the sale with the customer's name printed on each ticket.

The phone rang: "Murray. This is Jane Smith from Chelsea Heights. I just received your mailer for your New Year's Day Sale and the two tickets. I have an aunt and her friend coming in for the weekend and I was wondering—could I have two more tickets?"

"Let me get this straight. You want me to send you two more tickets for two more people to come and spend money in my store. Is that right?"

She said, "Yes."

"Hmmmm, I think I can handle that."

Writing a monthly column led to invitations to speak at direct-mail conferences in cities around the country, which led to the next step of speaking.

How I Became an "Expert" in Speaking

I was at the Boston Direct Mail Conference in 1968 with a panel of other "experts." Some spoke on catalogs, others on financial marketing, and I on my favorite subject, retail direct mail.

After the usual 15-minute talk, I rejoined the panel to hear the next speaker. He came on stage wheeling a shopping cart filled with direct-mail pieces for banks. The title of his talk was "To Market, To Market."

He stepped to the front of the stage, took out one product at a time from his shopping basket and explained how each worked. His pacing, humor, and story-telling were so superb that I laughed loudly at every joke. He took his microphone to me and asked, "Why are you laughing so loudly?"

"Because you're funny," I answered.

"Well, take your chair to the front of the stage so I can see you when you're laughing, and you won't interrupt me."

He helped me move my chair to the front as he continued his talk. After each joke, he would look at me waiting for my laugh.

After the program he introduced himself. "My name is Ray Considine. I work for Dickie Raymond in direct mail, and I'm about to leave and go into the speaking business full time. Would you like any criticism on your talk today?"

"Sure."

"Well," he said, "You talk too fast. You garble a lot of your words. You don't have any pacing in your stories."

"Uh, thanks for your opinion," I mumbled.

"Wait, I'm not through," he said. "But you have a lot of terrific ideas. So here's my plan. I'll teach you how to be a good speaker, and you can share some of your ideas with me, and we'll do seminars together where people in a business get together to listen to experts. And since you're an expert in direct mail…"

Aha! He knew who I was. And he was willing to teach me to be an "expert" in speaking as well. Why not? Ray had me tell stories into a tape recorder, then played it back. He told me where my pacing was wrong; we did it over and retaped. He had me listen to the rephrasing and then repeat it once again.

Throughout the next 10 years, Considine and I shared seminars across the country, but the very first job we did was one of the most interesting. The client was the World Hockey League.

"But Ray, I don't know anything about hockey!"

"Great," he replied, "they need somebody objective."

In preparation, I made an appointment in New York City with Harry Rubicon, promotional director of *Sports Illustrated* magazine.

If you want help in anything, call the top person and, more often than not, they will help you. It's getting past the minions below the leaders that's difficult. If you're looking for a sure-fire, never-miss sentence that will open the door to give you the advice, project, support, and direction you need, here it is: "I have a problem, and I need your help."

Harry heard about me doing this show with no knowledge of hockey. Never saw a game. My experience was in retailing. His answer: "The owners of hockey teams forget they are nothing else but retailers. They have the same customers that shop the five and ten."

"Retailers? Really? Hey, I'm one of them!"

During the day-long seminar owners of teams impressed with our program would ask Considine, "Say—how many hockey games has Murray seen?"

Each time, he'd answer, "You wouldn't believe me if I told you."

And they'd shake their heads in wonderment and reply, "That many?"

What I learned from that experience: Harry Rubicon was right. The business of sports is the same as the business of retailing. The last question of the day was asked me by the owner of a team trying to build his attendance. He said, "You haven't answered the most important question, Raphel."

"Really?" I asked. "What's that?"

"I want to know how to sell 10,000 tickets."

I thought carefully and slowly answered, "One at a time."

He nodded in agreement.

After 10 years of working with Considine, we discovered we were going in different directions. His direction was selling and training-the-trainers. I was more interested in marketing. We split to pursue our individual strengths. To this day we correspond and call regularly to share ideas and advice.

One day I received a phone call from Walter Schmid, creator of the Direct Marketing Symposium in Montreux, Switzerland. Walter came up with the idea for this international meeting in 1969. From the beginning and for many years, this was the only place in Europe where direct marketing practitioners could gather in one place and exchange ideas and make contacts in one place at one time.

Walter had read my columns in *Direct Marketing* and called to meet me in New York City. We had an instant rapport and he invited me to speak at the Symposium in 1977.

That first speech began a relationship with Walter and Montreux that continued for 15 consecutive years.

Since people from more than 30 countries came to Montreux, many heard me speak and invited me to come to their countries to talk on direct marketing. Soon, I was appearing in Stockholm, Oslo, Helsinki, London, Milan—all over Europe.

One day, in Montreux, Eddy Boas from Australia heard me speak and said, "Hey, mate, would you like to come to Australia and have a fair dinkum time?"

Again, a new and lasting friendship to this day and we began speaking at his Pan Pacific Direct Marketing. (Nineteen ninety-four marked our eleventh appearance.)

The talks around the world resulted in more talks and more consulting where I would learn as much about the country or the client as possible to talk on my same basic theme: "Dollar for dollar, nothing returns to you as much as direct mail."

Today, Ruth and I travel more than 200,000 miles a year around the world. Speaking has allowed me to follow my avocation to help small businesses stay in business by using direct mail.

The ultimate honor came when we received the "Montreux Award" in 1989 for our work in spreading the word of direct mail to businesses throughout the world.

The speaking and consulting and writing began to take more time. I was torn between writing and speaking to taking care of the marketing of our retail complex. The coming of casino gambling to Atlantic City meant businesses and populations moving to the suburbs. Staying in business became a challenge, even after a successful 35-year history. How could we not only attract new people but keep our current customers?

Leaving for one of our speaking engagements I sorted out the needed membership cards and noticed, with astonishment, that my wallet contained more than 30 plastic cards—each one offering me a special value or offer in hotels, airlines and major retailers. Why not do this program for Gordon's? After all, Pareto was right. The Italian philosopher who originated the 80/20 rule that 80 percent of your business comes from 20 percent of your customers made us rethink our direct marketing.

Why were we only mailing to our now total list of 15,000 customers several times a year? Why not select our best customers and mail them more often? We would enroll them in a very special club: The Gordon's Gold Card.

We went through our computer printouts of who spent what and set a criteria of membership: you had to spend $1,000 a year in our shops. That gave us 500 members. That meant we had 500 customers doing nearly $2 million dollars in business with us. (Yes, I know that 500 times $1,000 is $500,000, but some of these customers spent $2,000, $3,000, or more in one year).

Needed: A "Welcome to the Gordon's Gold Card Club" letter. Time to review all the Frequent Buyer and Frequent Flyer letters from airlines, hotels, other retailers across the country. I examined each in detail and found certain sentences appeared in *every one of them.* They were finding out which sentences worked best and using it for themselves. I can do that, and put the program together with specific benefits to this specific, elite, prestigious, spends-lots-of-money-with-us group.

The two-page letter to our customers began, "Your association with Gordon's and your annual volume of business with us places you in a unique group which requires and appreciates special recognition."

If that sounds familiar to you, it should. You've read it in half the "club card" promotions mailed to your name. Why? Because it works.

We also enclosed a questionnaire to find out more about the customer.

(Side note: There are 16 radio stations in our area. We spent most of our radio advertising on one station that I liked. And if I liked it everyone liked it, right? Wrong. Nearly 60 percent of our customers wrote they listened to one station, and not mine. We promptly switched our radio dollars to the new station and did more business.)

Also included was a book of gift certificates for 12 free lunches in the Alley Deli, one a month.

This was the postscript: "Because we like happy endings, we've enclosed a $15.00 gift certificate for you to use for anything in our shops." No minimum purchase. Number redeemed, 344; average sale, $55.16.

These customers received a notice of something "special" once every three months, then every two months, then every month. The return (average 25 to 30 percent) remained constant. At the end we sometimes mailed them twice a month with the same return,...plus a $15.00 gift certificate on their birthday *and* their spouse's birthday. No minimum purchase. Average return, 65 percent, average sale, $43.00.

Nearly all of these customers spent much, much more with us after becoming Gold customers than previously.

This promotion positively, absolutely, maintained the bottom line the last three years we operated our shopping center—all because of direct mail!

Our business was sold in 1990 to a business consortium. We kept one building to house our new Raphel Marketing offices. This gave Ruth the freedom to work full time with me. Now we could focus on writing, consulting and speaking to businesses around the world.

Our son Neil joined us as a partner after several careers that included work as a tax attorney and president of a New York commodity firm. He soon developed a publishing business where we offer marketing books and tapes (with an emphasis on direct marketing) to small businesses.

They are written by businesspeople for businesspeople. This lets us tell the story on a much broader scale than my speaking and writing.

By now I was writing a book every couple of years outlining what I learned in retailing and by consulting other businesses. Each book included an emphasis on direct marketing. One, *Tough Selling for Tough Times,* written with Neil, was chosen as an alternative book-of-the-month selection by the Executive Book Club. Another, *The Do-It-Yourself Direct Mail Handbook,* was written in partnership with good friend and writer Ken Erdman, who called one day and said, "You've been writing for years that small businesses ought to do direct mail. But there's no book that tells them in easy-to-understand language how to do it. Let's you and me write a book." We did. It's now in its third printing.

My first book, written with Considine, *The Great Brain Robbery,* has sold nearly 25,000 copies. Not bad when you realize NONE of our books are available in book stores. They are all self-published and marketed through (you guessed it) direct mail. Now William Morrow has decided to publish our newest book, *Up the Loyalty Ladder,* for national distribution in Fall 1995.

The Dream Continues: Direct Marketing in the Independent Supermarket

We continued to pursue our commitment to small businesses which led to work with American Express and U.S. West to give seminars and write direct marketing programs for the independent smaller businesses they both service.

Here's how that began. The year was 1976. It was one of those busy days in our store when Bob Aders came into our shop.

He looked at the photographs on the wall of me with various political celebrities. I was active in politics in those days, being elected head of county government and running several campaigns for local officials.

One of the pictures was of me with Ronald Reagan, whom I had as a speaker at our county Republican organization when he was Governor of California.

Another picture was of me with former President Ford thanking me for my help in his Presidential campaign.

Bob approached the back counter where my sister-in-law Shirley was finishing a sale.

"Is Murray going to the Republican convention in Kansas City?" he asked.

Shirley, assuming he knew me, said, "Yes, he may be a delegate."

"Is he going to vote for Ronald Reagan or Gerald Ford for president?" he asked. (You may remember that was Reagan's first attempt for the nomination. He succeeded four years later. Ford won the nomination, but lost to Jimmy Carter.)

"Ronald Reagan," said Shirley.

"Why?" asked the man.

"Because Ford won't help New York City." At that time New York City was about to declare bankruptcy. The City appealed to the federal government to bail them out and President Ford said "No." The New York Post carried the news with a front page headline: "Ford to New York City: 'Drop Dead!'"

"The President changed his mind. He's going to help New York City" said Bob.

"How do you know?" asked Shirley.

"He told me so," said the man.

"Who told you so?" asked Shirley.

"President Ford."

"Really?" said Shirley, "When did he tell you?"

"Yesterday at breakfast."

Shirley looked at him for a moment, dialed the intercom, and said, "Murray, there's someone here to see you."

Bob Aders was then serving as the number-two man in the labor department. An attorney, he had worked his way up in the Kroger supermarket organization, one of the nation's largest supermarket chains, to become their CEO.

He also represented the food industry during President Nixon's "Phase" campaign to keep food prices as low as possible. His work was so outstanding he was asked to join the Labor department as deputy secretary.

We talked for a while, and he noticed, in my office, a poster advertising *The Great Brain Robbery.*

"What's that all about?" he asked.

I explained it was the marketing/advertising/promotion seminar I did with Considine.

"Would it work for the supermarket industry?"

"Sure," I said. "Marketing is marketing is marketing."

He left. I thought little more about it until a phone call came a few months later. Bob had left government service to become the first president of Food Marketing Institute (FMI), the trade organization that represents U.S. food retailers and wholesalers.

"Mr. Aders wanted to know if you could put on your marketing program for our convention," said Bob's secretary.

"Certainly," I replied, pulling out my fact sheet to list all the information.

Yes, the date was free. Yes, we would direct the program to supermarkets. Yes, the fee was fine.

"And how many people do you expect at the convention," we asked, having done, at that time, seminars for groups that ranged from 50 to 500 so we were ready for anything.

"Oh, about 30,000," she answered.

We gagged, mumbled something about, sending a letter to confirm everything and hung up.

Thirty thousand people? Yes, that was the attendance at the convention. About 3,000 came to hear us that day, and we have continued for 19 years drawing the largest crowds and high audience ratings.

Who was out there saying, "I am an expert in supermarket advertising, marketing, and promotion?"

No one.

So I said it. And proved it by working year-round to discover what was new, exciting, different and, most of all, successful in supermarketing. Reading all the trade publications. Attending seminars. Writing a newsletter aimed at the independents (fulfilling my private goal of keeping the small businessperson in business), writing a book on who-did-what-and-why-and how called, *The Compleat Food Marketing Handbook.*

Soon wholesalers called and asked us to speak to supermarkets they supplied.

And supermarkets called and asked us to review their marketing plans.

This led to a column in the industry's prestigious publication, "Progressive Grocer" that I write with son Neil.

The 1990s brought in the age of "the consumer is king." There was a revolution in the supermarket industry as they sought a plan that recognized their customer as the ultimate long term relationship to keep them in business.

Joe Capo, editor of *Advertising Age,* wrote, "What other business do you know of where you spend $5,000 a year and the owner never says thank you." He was referring to supermarkets. Major companies jumped into the fray with new, improved, fantastic, terrific computer technology programs that would track customer's purchases at the check-out counter and give the retailer daily printouts of who bought which product at what particular time of the day.

In came the giants: Citicorp with its POS program, Promotion Management Services, GTE Information Services, Marketing Images, Advanced Promotion Technologies. Most failed dramatically with millions of dollars wasted. Although some of the large chains with sophisticated technology would adopt and adapt some of these concepts, rare was the independent retailer who bought in. He saw the daily five-foot-high computer pile and asked, "What am I supposed to do with this?"

Companies didn't understand this independent entrepreneur was concerned with why the specially priced iceberg lettuce he advertised in today's paper didn't arrive in this morning's shipment. Five front-end checkers didn't show up. The pipes in the back room just broke and no one could reach the plumber. Strangers were leaving their cars in the parking lot and not coming to shop. And there were these nicely dressed salespeople standing by the door to his office asking him to sign papers for huge dollar commitment to do direct what?

Yet, these were the same small supermarkets that needed customer loyalty the most. This led to a relationship with Sales Edge, a division of U.S. West, one of the country's six Baby Bells, to design a program for independent supermarkets that would help them not only keep the customers they had but also bring in new customers. Our solution was (you guessed it) direct mail.

Our first suggestion: They should *do everything* for the independent supermarket owner. Create the mailers. Print them. And mail them. All the owner had to do was pick out the specials available to him that month from his wholesaler or manufacturer.

We experimented with one store, starting with a sweepstakes and had a 68-percent return! Regular mailings averaged 12- to 15-percent return. Each was immensely profitable. We expanded the program to 12 stores with the same results. We have now offered this program to 3,000 independent supermarkets across America: small businesses that succeed and prosper because of direct mail.

What began with a small column in *Direct Marketing* magazine from a mimeographed letter we sent to our customers expanded through the years to telling the retail direct mail story internationally.

One day, talking with a close friend, I confide that I'm in the marketing, advertising, and promotion business. Our clients range from the tiny to the huge, and yet our company does no marketing, advertising, or promotion for ourselves. I asked my friend if he didn't feel that was strange.

"Not really," he said, "after all, what do you call it when you stand on a stage in front of a few thousand people. Don't you call that advertising? Isn't that what you're doing?"

I nodded agreement.

I certainly wasn't going to tell him my secret that if it doesn't work with the few thousand, I can follow the advice given to the owner of the hockey team. I can also tell my story one at a time. After all, I am a genuine, 100-percent, tried-and-true Wokabout!

Thirty Things I Learned about Retail Direct Mail in Thirty Years

1. **It's far, far easier to sell to the customer you have than to sell a new customer.** Most businesses spend six times as much money for new customers than they do for the customer they already have. Ridiculous. How do you overcome this wrong direction? Easy—direct mail.

2. **Limited time.** The tighter the time frame of the promotion, the more successful. We were so excited about the success of Neiman Marcus "fortnight" promotions that we duplicated the idea for an Irish sale. We scheduled something every day for the two week period including Atlantic City's first St. Patrick's Day parade. It was the biggest failure we ever had. Our analysis on why-it-failed narrowed down to it was too long a period of time. Three days would have worked. One day would have been terrific!

3. **Running a sale when other stores are closed brings in more customers.** We once ran a "Midnight Madness" sale for a supermarket. They worked with their wholesaler and came up with rock bottom

food prices. The crowds started forming at 10 PM. By 11:00, all the shopping carts were gone and the just-arriving began to bid for carts held by others. By midnight, the carts were selling for $20 each, just to get into the store. This works as well with an "Early Bird Sale" that starts at 6 a.m. And remember our New Year's Day sale?

4. **Running a sale with a sweepstakes increases traffic from 10 to 20 percent.** Or more. When we mailed a notice of a sale to customers on our mailing list, the average response was 5 to 8 percent. The first year we ran a sweepstakes, that jumped to 10 to 12 percent!

5. **Running a sale with a sweepstakes and the customer's name will increase response another 5 to 10 percent.** When we ran the sweepstakes, we told the customers to "fill out your name on this certificate and bring it to the store."

    We then preprinted each customer's name on the certificates and said, "This certificate is exclusively yours (your name is on the certificate). Just bring it to the store to be eligible for one of the 121 prizes." Response jumped from 10 to 12 percent to 15 to 18 percent.

6. **The mailer should "look" like your business.** Use the same type-faces consistently. Is there a color associated with your store (and if there isn't, there should be), use it. Our mailers for our shops became so identifiable that when we did a mailer for a local politician, most people thought it was from our store.

7. **Use your name as the name of your business.** Most people are uncomfortable using their own name. It's like looking at yourself in a mirror. It's okay to do if you're alone, but not if others are watching. Putting your own name for everyone to see is too much "exposure" for most. They tell you "It won't work." And I tell them, 'You're right. But don't tell that to Mr. Macy, Mr. Nordstrom, John Wanamaker, L.L. Bean...." Your name is your name. Through the years it will achieve its own recognition and reputation. And you can avoid the cute names like "The Shop On Corner" (I hope you never move) or the shoe store called "A Step In Time" or, well, walk through your nearest mall and you'll see what I mean.

8. **Give the customer a choice between something and something, not something and nothing.** When was the last time you received a catalogue with only one item? Even the covers of most catalogues have a selection of the most-wanted items. Our mailers listed at least six popular items in each of the shops.

9. **A guaranteed winner guarantees more customers.** We posted "lucky" numbers on all our mailers. (The word "lucky" is a powerful word). Every single number won at least…something. Most were $2 winners. Even though we told the customers (at least six times) in each mailer that everyone was a winner, customers would come in the store and see their "lucky" number as a $2 winner and scream, "I won! I won!" And no, we never said, "Hey, didn't you read the mailer—everybody won!"

10. **Guarantee your merchandise.** Guarantee everything you sell. Regular price merchandise. Sale merchandise. Anything and everything they buy in your store. Each mailer has a "guarantee" that the customer must be satisfied with what they buy. Not just the usual guarantee against wear and tear, but guaranteed to make them happy. Greenwich Workshop is the nation's finest distributor of signed limited edition prints. Many of their dealers increased sales dramatically when they told customers to take the prints home, hang them and if they didn't like them on the wall, bring them back for another print or their money back! The point: A print looks different on a gallery wall than on your living room wall.

11. **If a headline works, repeat it.** I really don't know why a certain combination of nouns, verbs, adjectives and/or prepositions make a customer stop what they are doing and run to buy from you. Every once in a while it just happens. Through the years there are less than a handful of headlines that worked every time they were used. Here's one:

    "Would you buy a $50 Yves St. Laurent shirt on sale for $29?" You can substitute the original price, the name and the sale prices for whatever you want to sell and it brings in customers. We've used it successfully for clothing, stationery shops, supermarkets and a dozen other businesses.

    "The name is Mañana. But at $25, you'd better buy it today." This was for a woman's jacket made in Mexico. We sold out of the 48 pieces the same day the ad ran. We reordered and (with trepidation) ran the exact same ad only ten days later. And sold out again!

    We reordered again and ran the same ad two weeks later. Sold out again.

    Moral: If a headline works, repeat it. There are those who never saw it the first time. There are those who saw it and are reminded. There are those who will tell others.

12. **Cross-sell in your mailer.** If you are a supermarket selling seafood, mention lemons. If you are a clothing store selling snowsuits, mention scarfs, gloves and hats. Things that go together are natural add-ons.

13. **Repeat your main offer many times.** You, your wife or husband, people who work with you and your parents will read every word you write. Your customer does not. They scan quickly. Take your biggest value and repeat it often. If you say it ten times, the first time the customer sees it may be the last time you wrote it.

14. **Co-op with other stores.** Two reasons for this: one, it gives your customer additional reasons for coming to the sale; two, it cuts your cost of mailing since your noncompetitors will pay their share of printing and mailing. We have done many mailings for no printing or mailing costs. We supplied the artist and layout to give the mailer a total overall "look."

15. **It's far, far easier to sell more at busy times than unbusy times.** Those hard to beat figures for Christmas, Easter, Back-to-School are the best times to do more business. People expect to spend money at certain times of the year. Give them reasons to come to you at that time. Creating a Millard Filmore Birthday sale may be different and unusual but it will be tough to have them leave the house and open their wallets. When you fish, you go where the fish are.

16. **Mail customers ahead of time.** Customers want to feel important, separate and receiving-something-special. Telling them to shop the sale before it's advertised in other media is a good move. We once persuaded a stationery shop retailer to send a mailer to their customers telling them of the "private sale for our customers only." Then he became nervous no one would show up.

    He placed a large newspaper ad and ran several radio commercials to announce the sale to the public for the SAME DAY. Later he told me hardly anyone from his mailing list showed up. "I guess Direct Mail doesn't work," he said. And we explained, "No, it doesn't work if you tell someone the sale is for them and then tell everyone else to come the same day!"

17. **Mail more often than you think is okay to mail.** We started out sending mailings to our customer list twice a year for winter and summer sales. Then we went to six times a year. Then we went to every month for our Gold Card customers. Then we sent this select group something twice a month. The percentage of returns always related

more to the offer than the frequency of the mailing. I still like the story when Leon Gorman, grandson of founder L.L. Bean took over the operation and decided the customer should make the decision when to buy instead of him making the decision when to sell. So he increased his catalogue mailings and…did more business.

18. **Calling after a mailing increases store traffic the day of the sale.** A simple "Did you receive our mailer? We wanted you to know before anyone else…" Take your key customers. Give their names and phone numbers to your staff. They call during "down times" when they are not waiting on customers or working on stock. An automatic, never-fails, guaranteed way to bring in more business from your mailing piece.

19. **Write four notes a day.** Each of your staff have "key" customers. In slow times, have them drop a note to their best customers about new merchandise just-arrived or any other plausible reason. The owner of a diner put the postcard received from a salesman in our men's shop on her front cash register. She pointed it out to her customers as "the first time anyone ever wrote me from a store." Yes, she also came in and bought. Would you believe $654.13? Believe it. It happened.

   Make four phone calls a day. Reread #19 and substitute the word "phone" for "notes." It works as well.

20. **Make sure the story isn't better than the store.** Vrest Orton, founder of the Original Vermont Country Store in Weston, Vermont (population, 400) made a success sending his homespun catalogue on turn of the century artifacts (Bon Ami soap, corn cob holders, Walnetto candies). When he began, he went to L.L. Bean in Freeport, Maine and asked for advice. Bean said, "Just remember one sentence: Make sure the story isn't better than the store." His point: Don't exaggerate what you are selling. Use the ancient and honorable technique of "Promise a lot—but deliver more." I once saw an appliance store advertise a TV set with an outline of a man next to the set. The TV set was as tall as the man! I called and asked how this could be and the store owner answered, "Well, the man is only three feet tall."

21. **Have an in-store display of what you featured in your mailer.** Put it in your store where you put it in your mailer. Up front. We once visited a supermarket in Alabama that mailed 20,000 fliers to customers for their giant "Buy One, Get One Free" sale. We walked all around the store and asked, "Where are the specials you advertised?"

"On the shelves where they usually are," said the store manager, "When the customer asks, we tell them to pick out the items in the mailer and bring them to the front counter and we'll give it to them on sale at that time."

The store owner later told me, "You know, that's the best pulling headline in supermarketing but it didn't work for me." Really?

22. **Send your mailer to the postmaster in every zip code you mail.** Enclose a note that explains this is your mailing piece that must arrive at your customer's house before the date shown. Otherwise who comes to your sale? Ask them to please call you when the mailers are mailed. Most will not.

And so, you make phone calls to EACH postmaster AFTER your advertisement is mailed. Did they receive the mailer yet? Was it sent out yet? Are there any problems?

23. **Have extra copies of your mailer available.** If you're running a sweepstakes a certain percentage of your customers will come and say, "I left my mailer at home. How do I know if I won anything?" You quickly give them another mailer with its lucky number and sweepstakes for them to fill out and enter in the store.

The importance of reminding the customers what you have to sell with extra mailers reminds us of the time we did an attractive four color brochure for a supermarket on their attractive sandwich trays. They printed 5,000 to mail and give customers while shopping. When the job was finished I visited the market and couldn't find the brochures. I asked for the owner and they sent me to his office.

I asked him where he was keeping the brochures. He took keys from his pocket, unlocked a cabinet and there were the 5,000 brochures.

"Why don't you have these on counters for customers to pick up?" I asked.

"Are you kidding?" he answered. They cost me 50¢ apiece. If I put them on the counters, people will just pick them up and take them away!" (Now you can't make up stories like that...)

24. **Don't make customers mad.** If you run out of an item, offer them something not on sale for the same price. Whatever it takes. Stew Leonard, owner of two of the world's highest volume supermarkets in Danbury and Norwalk, Connecticut knows the average person spends $246,000 in their lifetime in a supermarket.

He told me, "Every time I see someone coming through the front door, I see stamped on their forehead in big red letters: $246,000. Nothing I'm going to do to have them get mad at me."

25. **Steal!** Everyone in business receives dozens of mailing pieces every day. Which ones made you stop and, better yet, open what-you-received?

    Save That Mailer! And ask yourself, "How can I use this idea in MY business?" There are no new ideas, just new ways of using the successful ones.

26. **Fear of loss is far more powerful than promise of gain.** Those letters you receive in the mail every January from magazine publishers headlined "you have won $10 million" found their sales increased when they changed the words to "you have lost $10 million" (if you did not enter the contest). One of our best sales was one February which we held in Leap Year. The headline: "A sale so great it only happens once every four years."

27. **Use the word "gift certificate" instead of "coupon."** "Coupons" are for supermarket ads.

28. **Use testimonials.** Once, during our New Year's sale, we hired a radio station to come and ask people their thoughts about the sale while they were shopping.

    The station had release forms signed so we could use the commercials at a later date. We did use them for radio commercials in future sales and about 20 of them for the cover of the following year's New Year's Day Sale mailer. If you say something nice about your business, that's you saying it. If a customer says something nice about your business, that carries a lot more believability and is a "makes me want to go there and shop" attraction.

29. **Involve your staff.** Show the folks that work with you a "rough" of your mailer BEFORE it is printed. You'll receive valuable advice. Some of the ones given us in the past include, "You have the wrong date." "The markdown isn't large enough to make anyone come." "I've spotted four misspellings so far."

    In addition, you are accomplishing what people want most from their jobs. When he was a professor at Ohio State University, Ken Blanchard (of "One Minute Manager" fame) did a comprehensive survey on "What Workers Want From Their Jobs." "Higher Wages" came in 5th.

"Being Appreciated" was first and "'A Feeling of Being 'In' On Things" was second. Involve your people if only because your mailer will be more successful.

30. **Give the customer what they want to buy not what you want to sell.** Too many retailers think a sale is having huge markdowns on merchandise that doesn't sell. Your mailer should offer your best-selling items on sale! When they come to the store they'll also buy what you want them to buy. Especially if the store is crowded. That's why casinos bring busloads of senior citizens to play the slot machines. The cost of the trip to the seniors: nothing. Plus a chit for lunch. But when others arrive, they see the huge crowds and say, "Wow! I've come to the right place!"

Bob Stone's
Commentary

Murray Raphel is one of the greatest public speakers I have known. Even experienced speakers shudder to be slotted after him on the speaker platform. As the saying goes, "He's a tough act to follow."

Murray's platform appearances are fired by a single passion, direct mail. His avocation is to help small businesses stay in business by using direct mail. Direct mail is Murray's life.

When Murray started preaching the direct-mail gospel to retailers in the 1960s the church was half empty, so to speak. Today, three decades later, Raphel is the word. Retailers from the smallest to the largest have gotten the message.

The words of wisdom he expresses are devoid of theory: Murray teaches what he has practiced, surviving in a retail business by using direct mail.

Murray Raphel is the consummate retailer. He is the epitome of the entrepreneur who lives by wit, wisdom, instinct, and strategic thinking. To contemplate his strategies is to add to your body of knowledge.

- You can build future sales by inducing consumers to invest in a Savings Club.

- When you write for a publication you automatically gain the status of "expert."

- If you have an altruistic mission in life you benefit likewise.

- Specific words or terms create specific connotations. (Examples: "coupons" are associated with supermarkets; "gift certificates" are associated with department stores.)

- The best day to run a sale is a day when other retailers are closed.

- The top person in an organization is more likely to help you than the subordinates.

- If you are in the consulting business the best way to

attract new clients is to be a featured speaker on a program.

- Because, on average, 80 percent of your business will come from 20 percent of your customer base, wisdom says the priceless 20 percent warrant special treatment and more frequent contact.

- When you find that certain sentences are used consistently in competitive promotions, use them. Don't try to "reinvent the wheel."

- Don't select media on the basis of what you think your customers prefer. Instead find out what your customers really prefer through a questionnaire.

- If your target market is too busy to do their specialized promotions, do *everything* for them.

CHAPTER

13

How a Family-Owned Business Became a Big-Time Publisher
Rodale Press

Robert J. Teufel, President and Chief Operating Officer, Rodale Press, Inc.

*B*ob *Teufel joined Rodale Press in 1961 and was made vice president in 1967 and president in 1979. His position in the industry includes his participation with the Direct Marketing Association (DMA), where he served as board chairman and member of the executive committee. Teufel is in the DMA Circulation Council Hall of Fame. He is a member of the Magazine Publishers of America (MPA), and was elected to serve as MPA chairman in 1992.*

Rodale Press got its start, like many successful mail-order companies, as a reflection of the personal tastes and opinions of its founder. In Rodale's case, it was Jerome Irving (J.I.) Rodale, a successful manufacturer of electrical devices who became bored with his primary business and was looking for a more creative outlet.

In 1934, J.I. Rodale and his brother Joe moved their electrical manufacturing facility from New York to Emmaus, Pennsylvania, taking advantage of an empty textile building offered to them as a tax incentive by the borough. Within a few years, the electrical manufacturing business was clicking along successfully and J.I., who worked as the financial and advertising half of the partnership, was bored to desperation.

The Genesis of the Business

While designing his annual sales catalog, J.I. thought he'd put together a compilation of jokes, witticisms, and miscellaneous factoids. The book was bound two-up along with his catalog and sent along to his customer list. When he got more customer response from his book of witticisms than from his electrical parts catalog, he realized he had an audience and began collecting and distributing books on humor, miscellaneous facts, and other publishing whatnots for the promotional impact on his customer list.

Always unhealthy as a child and overweight as an adult, J.I. was concerned about his health since his family had a long heart history. Reading one of his many international magazines, he came upon the writings of Sir Albert Howard, a British agriculturalist who related soil and health, basically stating that healthy soil led to healthy people. J.I. was so impressed by this philosophy that he bought a farm near Emmaus and began developing it into one of the first organic farms in the United States.

Always a voracious reader, J.I. decided it was time to share this information with his friends and neighbors. He had already published his first book in 1937, a book on contemporary manners that he not only sent to his customer list, but offered to the bookstore trade as well.

Educated as an accountant, he was comfortable with numbers but frustrated as a writer. To polish his own writing skills, he developed the *Synonym Finder, Phrase Finder,* and *Word Finder* lines of reference books, all early Rodale Press successes. From this beginning came "Never Say Said" and a string of writing skill books.

When he had an interest in a subject he devoured every book, magazine, and newspaper article in the field until he became a near expert on it. From this expertise rose his inspiration; "It seems selfish to have all this information and not share it with anyone else." And that was the beginning of his magazine enterprises.

He decided to do a magazine titled *Organic Farming & Gardening*. Certain that the neighboring Pennsylvania Dutch farmers would be willing to subscribe to it, he printed 10,000 copies and had them distributed in surrounding rural mailboxes. He put a solicitation form in the magazine and waited for the response.

There was none. Not a single order came to the magazine, not even an inquiry.

Undaunted, J.I. decided his problem was not the product, but its marketing. He developed a small self-mailer (shown in Exhibit 13.1) put together by himself and the art director of his magazine.

Although there is no record of the response rate for this mailing, it worked well enough for J.I. to continue publishing his magazine embodying the concepts of gardening and health.

By the late 1940s, his successful magazine was torn between two camps. One resented the growing amount of health information in a gardening magazine. The other appreciated the health more than the gardening information. So J.I. decided to cut the baby in half and came up with *Prevention* magazine in 1950.

The launch of *Prevention* was an overwhelming success. A mailing to the *Organic Farming & Gardening* list (he again used a self-mailer as a launch package) was buffered by house ads in the magazine. *Prevention* was profitable from day one and by 1965 it outpaced *Organic Farming & Gardening* as Rodale's largest magazine.

Operational Principles

J.I. and his son Bob, who joined his father's company as president in 1951, early on evolved a series of operational principles that have survived the test of time:

1. **Focus on unique competencies.** Rodale editorial is focused in three areas: home and garden, health and fitness, and active sports. Although these categories may limit some expansion, they help focus the company in its editorial message.

Exhibit 13-1 Self-Mailer Promoting *Organic Farming & Gardening*

Exhibit 13-1 (Continued)

Organic Gardening®
Emmaus, PA 18098

LETTER FROM THE EDITOR

Why Am I "Giving Away" My Best Gardening Ideas?

Dear Friend,

In these pages you'll get just a brief glimpse of what ORGANIC GARDENING® magazine is all about. If you find these tips helpful, why not take a risk-free look at the latest issue of ORGANIC GARDENING?

Robert Rodale
Editor-in-Chief

Just return the attached card, and I'll send you a copy of our latest issue.

I'll also send you a collection of some of the very best gardening ideas we've seen in recent months. The collection is called *Secrets of Master Gardeners* because these "cream of the crop" tips come from some of America's most experienced gardening veterans. And it's free!

You'll get hundreds of "Master Gardener" tips in every issue of ORGANIC GARDENING. Month after month, you'll see how to grow more vegetables, fruits and flowers with less effort and fewer mistakes. That's what makes us the most popular gardening magazine in the entire world!

In the coming months you'll discover how to grow fruit trees in containers on your porch . . . find out about the newest varieties of vegetables, fruits and flowers . . . see how to use herbs for healing . . . learn what you can do with your yard to make it work with your home's architecture . . . get the gardening power-equipment buyer's guide . . . benefit from a step-by-step guide to creating a rock garden . . . learn how to plan a season-long flower garden . . . and much more!

So send in the attached order card today to start ORGANIC GARDENING coming your way. I'll send off your copy of *Secrets of Master Gardeners*.

Act now. The postage is paid and you've got nothing to lose and a great garden to gain!

Waiting to mail your free book,

Robert Rodale
Editor

P.S. Here's your opportunity to find out why ORGANIC GARDENING is the No. 1 gardening magazine in the world—with over one milli subscribers—and get a free gift! Mail the attached order card toda

Bulk Rate
U.S. Postage
PAID
Rodale Press, Inc.

2. **Grow from internally developed resources.** Although Rodale started publishing books before magazines, the ability to cross-mail magazine and book files has led to a unique chemistry.

3. **Use the best talent available.** When Bob Rodale took over Rodale Press, he developed an open mind to outside consultants. House copywriters and creative directors were always tested against the best freelancers. Testing became a Rodale byword.

4. **Use research.** Discover what customers want to read and provide it for them in a user-friendly, accessible format.

5. **Provide high-quality customer service.** Deliver the product or service to the customer faster and friendlier than they expect.

When Bob joined his father in the company, one of his first hires was a recently graduated journalist from Rutgers, Jerry Goldstein. Jerry had been the editor of the *Rutgers Targum,* one of the best student newspapers in the United States, and he had a wide ranging intelligence. Bob put Jerry in charge of *Organic Gardening* editorial and circulation development for both magazines.

When Jerry hired me in 1961, fresh from the U.S. Air Force, I was brought on not only as a direct-response copywriter, but as an assistant editor on *Organic Gardening.* My first summer with the magazine was spent not in doing direct-mail copy but in traveling the country with a staff photographer interviewing organic gardeners and ghostwriting stories for their byline to appear in the magazine.

Doing these first-person stories helped me understand what drove people to garden and why they felt especially strong about *Organic Gardening.* So when I got back to my copywriting chores after the summer tour, I was inspired and focused. When creating a direct-mail package, I could picture the audience. Plus, I gleaned scores of useful testimonials to be used in the brochures.

Jerry was a firm believer in talking not only to your customers, but to your competition as well. In 1961, Jerry, Al Barrett, our person in charge of customer service and list rentals, and I journeyed off to New York to attend our first DMA conference at the Statler Hilton. As the company had slim resources, all three of us shared the same room. And as I was the "new boy," I got to sleep on the rollout cot!

Rodale has consistently maintained support for DMA and other trade associations. Isolated as we are in Emmaus (an hour from Philadelphia, two hours from New York), there was no local DMA or publishing group to share experiences. So we became active in both the Philadelphia Direct Marketing Club and DMA.

The Importance of Copy Testing

It was at that first DMA conference that I learned the importance of copy testing, and when I got back to the office, I questioned Jerry and Bob about our upcoming January mailing for *Organic Gardening*. Where were the test packages that produced the winner we'd be mailing in January? "Oh," replied Bob, "there was no test package."

"But I thought we're always supposed to…"

"Not in this case." Bob related how he was accompanying his wife, Ardie, and children to church and, bored by the sermon, got to playing with the collection envelope. It was a duplex envelope with a perforation down the middle. Half of the space was to hold your contribution for the mortgage fund and the other half for the missions. It was a clever marketing ploy, and Bob thought this could be adapted to an *Organic Gardening* mailing.

"We know that every organic gardener values his soil, and soil tests are an integral part of developing good soil. Our idea is to send out a direct-mail package with a duplex envelope as a response device. Half of the reply envelope will hold the order form and payment, the other half will hold a soil sample. When we receive the soil, we'll have it analyzed and send back results of the test. Who could resist that?"

"But, are we sure this will work?" I asked.

"Of course," Bob said, echoed by Jerry. "This is such a great idea that it just has to work."

The then postmaster of Emmaus, Harvey Eck, was used to getting calls from me since it was my responsibility to schedule work in our in-house fulfillment operation. So, whenever a mailing went out, I would be on the phone to Harvey asking for the count of business reply envelopes so we could get people in that day.

Our *Organic Gardening* mailing dropped the day after Christmas along with a mailing for *Prevention*. By the second week of January we were receiving our first replies to *Prevention*, but no *Organic Gardening* orders. Harboring a vague suspicion that somehow the postal service was holding the *Organic Gardening* orders, I went down to visit the post office. Harvey assured me that not a single order for *Organic Gardening* had been received, and he would process them as soon as they came. Two weeks went by and not another order came in, despite my daily calls to Harvey and his protestations that not a single order had been received.

The last Monday of the month, four weeks after the mailing dropped, my telephone was ringing as I walked through the office door. "Bob, this is Harvey, Harvey at the post office. I thought I'd call you before you called me. You gotta get down to the post office right away, my receiving dock is awash in mud and it's all your fault."

Down to the post office I went, to be greeted by a red-faced postmaster. Dumping out canvas sacks, he showed me pile after pile of dollar bills and paper, all mixed with wet mud and almost illegible. "I could just read enough of this stuff to see that it was your *Organic Gardening* orders," said the stressed-out postmaster.

What seemed like a good idea was actually a terrible tactic. What we overlooked was that many gardeners would walk out to their garden, scoop up a sample of their frozen soil, put it in the package and seal it. We forgot that soil is hydroscopic and, upon being warmed in the bowels of the postal trucks, it began to melt, turning into a sea of mud.

After we went through the chaos and attempted to put together money, orders, and samples, we made a solemn vow that Rodale would never, never, absolutely never, do a mailing again unless it was thoroughly tested not just for copy, offer, and list, but for operational efficiency as well. A few years later, when a *Prevention* writer came up with the brilliant idea of doing a free urinalysis with a subscription order to *Prevention*, we quickly demurred.

Freelancers, Consultants, and Friends

The importance of seeking and following the best freelance and consultant advice solved another problem for us. In 1968, certain that our one-shot book operation was not enough to sustain a major publishing effort we determined to go into the book club business. There was a feeling among senior executives at Rodale that there was something just a little bit wrong with a negative-option book club. "You know, that form of selling is illegal in England. It's called inertia marketing over there, and if it's not legal in England, I don't think we should do it here."

At that time, our J.I. Rodale Limited operation in England produced almost 50 percent of the revenue and the majority of our profits, and our experience there had substantial impact. Further, Rodale had a tradition of holding itself to a higher standard. I, of course, felt that a positive-option book club didn't have a chance of working, but went ahead to develop the test packages anyway. Of course, the project failed, and we were just about to give this up as a bad idea when I attended the 1969 DMA conference in Boston.

The creative track that year offered a free 15-minute consultation with any one of ten top direct-response copywriters. Because I had been impressed by the work Walter Weintz had done while he was at Reader's Digest, I joined the long line of folks clutching direct-mail packages waiting for Walter's words of wisdom.

The package I handed him was our positive-option book club test. "This doesn't have a chance of working," smiled Weintz, always a gentleman. "I wouldn't waste a cent trying to retest this, as the concept is invalid. I don't know how you could ever make a positive-option book club work in this country."

"But," I explained, "my management will not allow me to test a negative option."

"Let me come down and talk to them," he replied. "I'll be happy to explain the facts of book club life to them."

And he did. Walter's eloquence in stating all the plusses of negative-option book clubs was such that he was retained to develop test packages for both *Prevention* and *Organic Gardening* book clubs. His marketing concept and copy approach clicked, and we began our two book clubs, which have since grown to seven. All thanks to Walter's ability to convince Rodale's management that there is nothing unethical about negative option! Is there?

Walter, joined since by his son Todd, has been working with us since that date and has developed scores of winning packages and concepts for us. During the course of our business relationship, a lasting friendship has evolved.

The Megantic Club in Maine is the quintessential old-time flyfishing club. Barbless hooks only, catch and release mainly, all developed in splendid isolation from your fellow man. And Walter Weintz invited me there for some fishing.

The group Walter put together as an added incentive included two of my fellow Lehigh University alumni: John Canova, then vice president, advertising manager of Time-Life Books, and Andy Swenson, then with Meredith Corporation. John had been in my class, and Andy and I had worked together on the school newspaper.

While sharing a canoe one evening with John, he asked if Rodale was into regression. "John," I replied, "I know you quite well but not well enough to dwell on the sexual preferences of my fellow employees."

"No, no, no," John blurted, "you know, multivariate regression analysis. The stuff we studied at Lehigh in Math 40 Statistics class."

"You mean you can actually apply something you learned in college to your job?" I queried.

"Well, if you're not using it already, you should call a fellow named Gordon Grossman who's doing some consulting work for us at Time-Life Books. He has made the most meaningful contribution to our marketing efforts than anything in recent years."

When I got back to the office, I gave Gordon a call and he came down to visit. That was a pivotal day at Rodale. Before Gordon's arrival, we had used the usual recency, frequency, money equation in evaluating house lists. We also used affinity as a predictor, but we were still not able to use our vast number of expires with any degree of confidence, nor could we successfully mine large files that had no apparent affinity. Gordon changed all that.

Working with Gordon, we established a separate and discreet marketing database apart from our active subscriber and book buyer files. Use of our marketing database is one of the key factors to our continued success. Many folks have worked for the success of the operation, but our focus on database integrity has been a singular success.

Once again, our strategy of reaching past our own limitations to worthwhile outside advice more than paid off, and we have been working with Gordon Grossman, to our great benefit, for more than 15 years.

Internal Training and Development

Perhaps because we are so isolated from major metropolitan areas, Rodale has always had a commitment to internal training and development programs. It is described in our company as "the ethic of constant improvement." Gordon Grossman, Walter Weintz, Mike Michaelson, and other consultants worked with us over the years not just on individual projects, but as leaders of in-house training seminars as well. Other programs by Joan Throckmorton and Bob Hemmings have helped our creative people develop as well.

We have had great success in developing in-house copywriters and art directors. Our in-house copy and creative staff has expanded from the Bob Teufel and Carl Manahan department that we had in 1971 to well over 60 copy, creative, and production people working on direct marketing. This is the size of a decent direct-response agency. Last year, we put 5,761 jobs through our production system. Surely a daunting amount of work.

When I came on board at Rodale, I was the first almost full-time copywriter. Previous to that, Jerry Goldstein wrote most of the copy using an outside writer, Paul Minor, who ran a small New York agency specializing primarily in union public relations. Paul had a special feeling for Rodale products, and often he, Jerry, and I would work on developing package and premium concepts.

Fighting the Federal Trade Commission

Because of our early success with health-related products we developed a special feeling for this market. Copy had to be loaded with benefits and always topped with a premium (as illustrated in Exhibit 13.2). Writing health copy is especially tricky, because you must be absolutely sure that the claims made for the magazine, premium, or book are truly a reflection of the product itself.

From 1961 through 1965, Rodale Press fought a battle with the Federal Trade Commission (FTC) when it took issue with the contents of a book called *The Health Finder* and several premium books. The FTC asked Rodale to sign a consent agreement saying it would stop advertising *The Health Finder* using aggressive direct-mail techniques. Apparently, members of the medical community felt only they were qualified to write on health issues.

At that time, Rodale was barely getting by financially, and it would have been an easy decision to cave in to the FTC rather than put the entire company's financial standing at risk, but Bob Rodale decided this was the only thing to do. Rather than rely on local representation, Bob hired the prestigious law firm of Arnold & Porter. The Rodale case was led by Thurman Arnold, one of the deans of the Washington legal profession and one of the original Roosevelt Administration "trust busters."

Rodale felt that the FTC position would put the entire health-publishing initiative at risk. As the FTC attempted to spread its case from *Health Finder* to *Prevention* magazine advertising, he was especially concerned.

In 1965, the hearing examiner recommended to the FTC that it file a cease-and-desist order against certain Rodale health books and any similar books. This would have had a devastating impact on health-book publishing operations. Thurman Arnold appealed to the full Commission, and the ACLU filed an amicus brief supporting Rodale's position. Contemporary press accounts viewed the FTC position as an assault on the first amendment.

The FTC was silent on this issue for some time, but issued a press release in 1971 that basically set the precedent for advertising claims of health publications. It stated that if the advertising copy is a true reflection of the contents of the book, the copy is covered by the same first amendment protection as the book itself. This was a true victory for Bob Rodale and Rodale Press.

Customer Service

Timely customer service for magazine and book orders for many small publishing companies meant using service bureaus. Basically big-city–based firms looked at customer service, or fulfillment as it was then called, as a back shop

Exhibit 13-2 Envelope Promoting Doctors' Health Cures

Doctors' Astounding
Secret Health Cures!

FREE BONUS GIFT!

• Rub aspirin *on* bee stings to stop pain! PAGE 558.

• Heal a cut faster with table sugar! PAGE 175.

• Cure athlete's foot with ordinary baking soda! See how, PAGE 35.

• Why wet tea bags stop canker sores! PAGE 112.

• Ease back pain with two pillows! PAGE 44.

• Secret ingredient in Italian foods slashes cholesterol! PAGE 141.

• PLUS: *2,450 ASTONISHING HOME REMEDIES from America's top physicians and health experts!*

PREVENTION® MAGAZINE
HEALTH BOOKS
Emmaus, PA 18098

Bulk Rate
U.S. Postage
PAID
Rodale Press, Inc.

Open this envelope immediately . . .

Exhibit 13-2 (Continued)

Brought To You By PREVENTION® Magazine Health Books.

PREVENTION HEALTH BOOKS

Dear Friend,

Even doctors now say it's true.

There are certain foods so powerfully healing, they can

SLASH CHOLESTEROL LEVELS!
PREVENT STROKE!
REVERSE YOUR CHANCE OF A HEART ATTACK!
EVEN SAVE YOUR LIFE!

Now, the nutritionists at the famous Rodale Food Center have combined the top 50 super-healing foods on earth into an astonishing collection of intensive healing meals that can redeem -- even reverse -- a lifetime of bad habits.

Now this amazing Meals That Heal Cookbook is yours absolutely free when you mail the enclosed card!

Just mail the enclosed reply card today. Hurry -- before all copies are gone!

Mark Bricklin
Mark Bricklin

YOURS FREE!
"MIRACLE MEALS"

PREVENTION'S
MEALS THAT HEAL
COOKBOOK

No purchase of anything required. No commitment. No strings attached.

● Meals that cut heart-attack risk. PAGE 42.

● Cheesecake that controls blood pressure. PAGE 45.

● Stroke-preventing gourmet dinner. PAGE 32.

● PLUS MORE: See inside now . . .

Printed in USA

factory type operation. But as Rodale had its beginning in a manufacturing environment, clerical and production functions came as second nature.

From the beginning, we had in-house magazine customer service facilities and took special pride in its timeliness. In fact, Publishers Clearing House used to issue an annual report card with a bonus check to the companies that exceeded their timely fulfillment specifications, and it was a special treat for our director of customer service to present this customer service report card rebate to management.

Bob Rodale had a special concern about customer service that he articulated in a memo to his executive group in 1971. This formed the essence of our customer service philosophy:

> Mail order is a procedure which offers convenience of a sort to the purchaser. He or she can buy something without leaving home, except to go to the mailbox, but in exchange must wait a varying period of time for receipt of the merchandise.
>
> Mail order offers a tremendous convenience to the company selling merchandise. The company does not have to make provisions for physical handling and comfort of the customer. The customer appears "in an envelope." As we all know, it is much nicer and more profitable to deal with customers in envelopes than in person.
>
> We know that it is impractical to keep a customer waiting when he or she appears personally. To keep him waiting in an envelope is completely unjustifiable from a philosophical point of view. Since the company has already enjoyed the tremendous convenience of not having to put up with the customer face to face, I can see no excuse whatever for making him sit around in written form for even as long as one week.

In 1989, the complexity of our magazine operation required a second look at in-house customer service. The files varied from *Prevention*'s 3 million subscribers to 100,000 for some of our smaller startups. Also, the increasing complexity of split editions and Christmas-gift promotions made it essential that we consider options other than our in-house–developed fulfillment software package. After waves of consultants and in-house circulation managers looked at the options, we determined to outsource magazine fulfillment to Communication Data Services, who specialize in magazine fulfillment, while keeping our book and newsletter fulfillment in-house.

Also, we decided to retain our marketing database inhouse as this is our significant corporate asset and we determined inhouse control and focus was essential for this to continue success.

Where Rodale Press Stands Today

Today, the revenues of Rodale Press are $150 million in the magazine and newsletter division, and $250 million from the book division. As a great deal of our book division revenue comes from health books, it would be difficult to see how we would be able to sustain our vitality had we buckled under the FTC consent order.

It is difficult to separate the business success of Rodale Press from the philosophies of J.I. and Bob Rodale. Bob especially was a visionary manager who set a personal tone and direction without micromanaging and was able to attract, hire, and retain the best people because of this policy.

When a test didn't work or a new product flopped, there was no search for victims to blame as in some companies. Rather, Bob would simply ask what we had learned from this experience, and how were we to insure this would not happen again. This developed a culture of risk taking throughout the company that has paid off in a succession of successful product developments.

Rodale book division, led by Pat Corpora, has developed an effective strategy for new-product testing, development, and marketing. Pat's business strategies are as follows:

1. **Excellent editorial products that are well researched.** This means that our editorial people come up with good, creative book concepts that are focused toward the customer. However, it also means that they have the flexibility to have those concepts researched and surveyed, so the books we eventually publish are the books that our customers want the most. Our editorial people produce almost 500 concepts a year, but they have the open-mindedness to leave it up to the customers to choose which titles will actually be published.

2. **Benefit-oriented promotions with inviting offers.** We place a high level of investment and time into the development of our promotional materials. The creative selling approach is one of the most inviting offers in the industry (21-day examination, send no money now, installment billing, merchandise return labels, and so on). My direction to the marketing people is to put the product into the customer's hands. If the customer decides to return it, that is an entirely different issue, and we need look at the value of that product. The combination of strong creative and inviting offers allows us to get the maximum number of copies into customers' hands.

3. **Sophisticated name and information selection technique.** Our marketing database is a key strategic advantage that we enjoy. Being

able to select customers by past history, interests, and demographics allows us to pinpoint our promotions more accurately.

4. **Timely responses and efficient customer and distribution services.** This is an area that's often overlooked; however, it is vitally important that we do these things well.

This discipline and focus has enabled Rodale to successfully sell one-shot books, an accomplishment not easily imitated by others. A recent success, *The Doctor's Book of Home Remedies,* has already sold over 8 million copies using all forms of direct response from television to supermarket take-ones to package stuffers to radio.

Further direction from Bob Rodale to "grow the earning assets of the company, not just profits" has also put the company in good strategic positioning. One of the joys of working at a privately held company is the independence from stockholder pressure to increase quarterly earnings. Anyone involved in a direct-marketing business knows your success rate is dependent on such vagaries as variable monthly response rates, postal-rate increases, and new product tests. Thie cyclical nature of the direct-mail business makes it especially vulnerable to these concerns.

Rodale's commitment to developing an internally diversified company and sticking to our three prime market niches has worked well over the years. We have been able to grow these areas by startups and acquisitions, and have had strong growth over the past 10 years.

Bob Rodale was killed in an automobile accident in Russia in September 1990. His wife and partner, Ardath Rodale, picked up his title of Chairman of the Board and most importantly for a family-owned company, continued to focus on basic values.

In fact, we just finished our annual corporate officers' retreat and, instead of focusing on the usual number-driven analysis most companies go through, we focused on what we felt were the primary values of Rodale Press, the values that give us our unique philosophical underpinnings and a strategic advantage as well. These values are:

- We deeply care and show concern about our family at Rodale Press by encouraging a healthy lifestyle, being sensitive to their personal needs, and providing opportunities for people to develop to their fullest potential.

- We are committed to constant improvement of our products, processes, and ourselves.

- We are committed to an internal culture of cooperation, courtesy, honesty, and respect.

- While we realize we must be profitable to exist, we don't just exist to be profitable.

- We are committed to practicing these values as we reach out to our customers and our partners throughout the world.

Bob Stone's
Commentary

Can a successful manufacturer of electrical devices become a successful publisher? The Rodale Press story answers that question with a resounding *yes*!

Can a desire to share knowledge with friends and neighbors serve as the catalyst to sharing knowledge with strangers? It can, and it did.

Can a family businessman in a little town in Pennsylvania compete with the giant publishing industry in the Big Apple? An annual revenue of $500 million puts this question to rest.

But the $64,000 question is, can a small family business grow to the size of a major publisher and still retain the original principles and philosophies that launched the business in the first place? Hardly ever, except for Rodale Press.

Bob Teufel is the epitome of a dynamic chief executive officer, who uses all the sophisticated tools direct marketing has to offer, but does so within the confines of the philosophies and principles that formed the company culture since the outset.

In weaving the fascinating Rodale Press story, Bob Teufel has identified the major strategies that have led to continuous growth.

- ☐ Don't try to be all things to all people. Focus on unique competencies.

- ☐ Develop products and services to which you can cross-sell other products and services.

- ☐ Don't limit yourself to in-house creative talent. Always test in-house talent against freelance talent.

- ☐ Don't produce what you think your customers want. Instead, use research to learn what your customers really want.

- ☐ To create lasting relationships, deliver the product and service to the customer in a faster and friendlier manner than they expect.

- The best way to picture the audience is to talk to customers to learn how they feel about your product or service.

- Share experiences with your competition; both of you will benefit.

- The more you circulate among consultants and competitors, the more you will add to your in-house body of knowledge.

- The better your in-house training program, the more likely you are to develop and keep talented employees.

- Hire the best legal firm you can, even at financial peril, if giving in on a principle would seriously impact your business.

- Be a visionary manager who sets a tone and direction, but to attract, hire, and retain the best people, avoid micromanaging.

- Make it as easy as possible for the prospect to try your product or service (21-day examination, send no money now, installment billing, merchandise return labels, and so on). If customers, in abundance, decide to return the merchandise, take another look at the value of what you are offering.

- Being able to select customers by past history, interests, and demographics makes it possible to pinpoint promotions more accurately.

Twenty-Five Years of Growth
Direct Marketing Association

Bob DeLay, President, The DeLay Group

Bob DeLay is editor and publisher of The DeLay Letter, *reporting news, analysis, and trends in direct marketing. He was previously president of the Direct Marketing Association (DMA) for 25 years. DeLay is secretary-treasurer of the DMA Educational Foundation and was one of its original founders in 1965. He received the Miles Kimball Award in 1978, the Ben Gurion Award in 1980, and the Robert Alex Jones Award in 1984. In 1988, DeLay was inducted into the DMA Hall of Fame.*

On a cold winter night in January 1959, I sat thoughtfully, in a suite at the Chicago Sheraton Hotel. Although I was attending a Direct Mail Day reception, my thoughts were totally consumed by a decision about my future. At the time, I was with a Chicago advertising agency. My dream was an exciting and lucrative career that would lead to Madison Avenue.

But into this dreamy future had come a challenge cloaked as an opportunity. I had been offered the position of president of the Direct Mail Advertising Association (DMAA). It was New York—the center of the advertising world. But it was direct mail, better known outside the profession as the J--- mailers!

Sitting beside me that evening was a man I had already learned to respect, a man who knew direct mail. I approached him with the problem. He simply said, "Take it."

So in March 1959, I took over as president of the DMAA. There was a small staff of five people. The location was a loft on 57th Street, and the income was $158,000, not quite enough to cover expenses. But it had a core product, direct mail, that was destined to become an essential ingredient in advertising and marketing.

Admittedly, direct mail was held in low esteem. The association, itself, had little to offer in the way of benefits other than a central source for the exchange of information, and even that was limited.

But, over the years, the medium attracted some exceptional people, most of them crusaders. For many years, they gave more than they got. But with some leadership and planning, the goals of making direct mail a needed force and a respected partner in marketing have been accomplished.

My 25 years with the association covered many pitfalls, but achieved rather exceptional growth in the use of the medium and the broader aspects of direct marketing and direct-response advertising. In the succeeding pages, I have tried to briefly outline a generation of strategies and goals that formed the underpinnings of today's direct marketing and the trade association that represents this dynamic discipline.

Unfortunately, this book was not the appropriate place to record the humor or heartaches that were almost daily fare during this period. Those stories involve hundreds, if not thousands, of marvelous volunteers, staff members, and unsung zealots of direct mail. They could add much color, dynamism, and even some romance to this factual recounting.

From DMAA to DMMA to DMA

The association's name change was an evolution that cannot be regarded as a planned strategy. The change was a careful, studied approach to ensuring the eventual path of direct mail and, eventually, direct marketing, and to placing the organization in the right position for continued service and growth. The strategy was to serve this evolving discipline as it continued to seek its place in the advertising and marketing community. This was accomplished slowly for some. Yet, for many, it became an abdication of its basic roots.

For many years, there has been a strong disagreement over what direct marketing, by definition, really is. Les Wunderman, a founder of Wunderman Cato Johnson, must be given credit for introducing the terminology. He mentioned direct marketing in a speech before the old Hundred Million Club in New York City in 1961. Then, in 1967, he explained his concept in an historic address at the Massachusetts Institute of Technology. He was also realistic enough in later years to admit that direct marketing was an evolving discipline.

For the DMAA, this new discipline was both an opportunity and a problem. Veteran direct-mail users felt the association should stick by its roots and continue to orient its services to direct mail. In a bold step, Pete Hoke, publisher of *The Reporter of Direct Mail Magazine* changed its name in 1970 to *Direct Marketing.* Even founder Henry Hoke, Sr., was alarmed at what his publisher son had done.

Nevertheless, the association had carefully crafted a board of directors that truly represented the membership. The Board was not pushed into action, but, in deference to its membership's feelings, it proposed in 1973 that the organization's name be changed to the Direct Mail/Marketing Association (DMMA). It was a bow to both sides. And it served its purpose—to move the association forward without losing many of its constituency.

There were a number of vendors in the direct-mail community, like list compilers, who felt betrayed by the change. Several chose to cancel membership. But, the change opened up new opportunities on the user side. Many advertisers and marketers didn't feel they belonged in a strictly direct-mail–oriented organization. And, whether the association appreciated it or not, the junk-mail syndrome kept many major companies from placing their names on the DMAA roster. But print, direct-response television, telemarketing, and computer-service bureaus found a new home for the exchange of information and education. The "new" association also offered a platform for these companies.

In the next 10 years, it was widely acknowledged that direct mail, as important as it was, represented only one of the media that direct-response marketers were using. And there was further acknowledgment that direct marketing was not just an advertising discipline, but a new way of marketing that offered a new channel of distribution.

As an example, catalogs began to appear in large numbers. Shopping from home in the 1980s became the right time and the right place for companies using direct marketing. The credit card, 800 numbers, and computers had changed the shopping world.

In 1983, the association positioned itself to serve an even broader constituency by becoming the Direct Marketing Association (DMA). It was an acknowledgment of the change that had taken place in both advertising and marketing. This evolvement couldn't have been a planned strategy because no one could rightly foresee the change. But certainly by recognizing change and reacting to it in a carefully orchestrated manner, it placed the association in its rightful position, the center and the voice of direct marketing.

Changing the Face of the Membership

In the late 1950s, the DMAA membership pattern had little relationship to the DMA of today. In fact, the association was a medium-sized group of individuals (not companies) who paid dues of $36 per year.

Most of the members were people from industrial products companies (National Cash Register, Dow Chemical, Eastman Kodak, DuPont) who used direct mail to get leads for salespeople (yes, salespeople!). And most were not advertising managers, but persons who planned and, most often, executed campaigns for distribution systems.

Consumer mailers? Mostly circulation people from publishing companies. It was often charged that the publishers "ran" DMAA. There were few mail-order types (Sunset House, Miles Kimball). But no Sears, Montgomery Ward, JC Penny, or catalogers as we know them today.

The supplier side was heavily weighted. Yet there were only 15 list brokers in those days, and they had their own association (Professional List Brokers Association). Some smaller advertising and promotion agencies, such as Sackheim, Dickie-Raymond and James Grey, were members. Stone & Adler wasn't yet a dream. The direct marketing agency of today, a vital segment of the industry, did not yet exist. it was all direct mail.

Printers and paper and envelope companies belonged to the association because DMAA members used their products. And once each year they could exhibit at the association's annual meeting and exhibition. In those early years, the DMAA and the Mail Advertising Service Association (lettershops) had to schedule exhibits together in order to get sufficient attendance and avoid having the vendors exhibit twice!

There was a group of fund raisers who had no other home and thus clung to DMAA because it was at least a source of direct-mail knowledge.

Thus, in the early 1960s DMAA, if it were to survive both financially and as a service organization, had to change its face. The strategy was to initiate a company membership program and extend the base of the membership into the consumer products and services field. It was a bold strategy, and the only option that appeared to have a chance of rescuing the association as a viable entity. At the time, there were about 1,900 individuals who belonged. Many of them were behind in their dues payments, and many were on a six-month, or even a three-month, trial membership.

To compound the problem, the membership was heavily weighted toward suppliers. The goal, and thus the strategy, was to obtain a 70-percent user majority.

Fortunately, the association had the benefit of some strong officers and board members who believed in the concept: Bernie Fixler (Creative Mailing), Red Dembner (Newsweek), Angelo Venezian (McGraw Hill), and Giles McCollum (Reuben H. Donnelley). They agreed on the hiring of Jim Kobak of J.K. Lasser to design a company membership program with an appropriate dues scale.

The Company Membership Plan was a tough sell, but it received membership approval at the annual meeting in Pittsburgh in 1963. One year later, the association had lost 600 members, but the dues base was increased by more than one third. The plan was modest. One hundred dollars for the minimum scale and $2,000 for the top scale depending on revenues spent (consumer) or revenues earned (vendors) from direct mail. Previously dues had been $48 for each individual. Each dues unit entitled a company to one member. Although the numbers have changed, the basic plan that brought financial security and credibility to the organization remains in place today.

A significant part of the strategy was to enlist the growing numbers of consumer mailers. They were beginning to mail millions rather than the hundreds and thousands common to the business-to-business (then called industrial) mailers, which were mainly in the mail for lead generation. Stability, growth, and proper representation depended on recruiting large mailers. It was a slow process, but it was a strategy that sparked the growth of the association and made it truly representative of the mailing industry. And, when the smoke cleared away later in the 1960s, DMAA could also boast that it was a user organization with 68 percent to 32 percent of vendors.

Selecting a Board of Directors

One of the most politically dangerous strategies is that of selecting a board of directors. And yet, over the 40 years that I have observed this process at DMA, it has been one of the least controversial issues.

In the early days, a strategy was established that included only two basic tenets: (1) The Board should reflect the geographical membership of the association; and (2) the Board must represent the major categories of membership.

These requirements proved sufficient and equitable until the early 1960s, when changes in the character of the membership prompted additional criteria, if not a more serious look at what the association represented. For instance, in 1954, I was elected to the Board because I was an advertising manager of an industrial company in Louisville, Kentucky. The nominating committee needed an industrial advertising person from that area. However, my other qualifications of experience, knowledge of trade association politics, and time available to provide useful input, were subject to question, to say the least.

Another criteria that was examined was length of terms. Some members of what was then the Board of Governors, stayed on the Board as long as 12 to 15 years. And often companies with big lists (such as Reuben H. Donnelley or Reader's Digest), believed they should always have a representative on the Board. Admittedly, these companies contributed greatly, not only financially, but in experience and credibility. And many trade associations (for example, Magazine Publishers of America and Audit Bureau of Circulations) have unwritten rules that allow some of the larger members continuing representation.

But that strategy and policy were not workable or desirable for a trade association that represented the variety of interests that has always made DMA a complex organization.

Therefore, it was necessary to establish terms of office as a valuable criteria. And it was necessary to recognize that the organization now represented many direct-response media, not just direct mail. Telemarketing, radio, television, and print became important marketing tools. Packaged goods, catalogs, and even retail were areas that wanted representation in the direct-marketing arena.

Having presumably done "all the right things" to make the selection process fair and equitable, we instituted one additional strategy to the eventual building of a strong board of directors. We agreed to select the highest officer within a company whether they were direct marketers themselves or not. This raised the level of people on the Board. It provided people who could "sign the check" or authorize it and people who could speak for their company. This turned out to be a key ingredient.

The growth in both media and categories dictated a change in the size of the Board. Board membership was increased from 24 to 30 to 36 and included permanent representation for each immediate past chairman, the Direct Marketing Educational Foundation, and the chairman of the Government Affairs Committee. Also, two elected members had to be from the international membership. The total provided a sounding board that reflected itself in few power struggles and led to continued growth for the association.

These actions, which were the evolvement of a continuing strategy of change, have now stood the test of time.

Establishing a Washington Presence

Although the DMA always had a volunteer or a committee responsible for Postal Affairs, the association had no official representation in the nation's capital until the mid-1950s. And then the representation consisted of a part-time consultant whose primary duty was to write an occasional newsletter for the membership.

At that time, the committee consisted of a chairman, the paid head of the association (named "president" as of 1957), and the Washington consultant. When a postal-rate case was imminent, visits were made to key congressmen and an appearance was made before the congressional committee in charge. Those were the tactics used. There was no strategy.

In 1963, the association retained the services of a man who also worked for the Printing Industries of America. Space, time, and work were shared equally. In fact, this person was not even a registered lobbyist at the time since the term "lobbyist" had as bad a connotation as "junk mailer."

But, in 1966, DMAA decided the time had come. The association had to have a physical full-time presence in Washington and a strategy for representation. After all, representation was like education, clearly part of the mission of the association.

Like most things in Washington, the office grew in both size and influence, mainly due to the aggressiveness of the vice president of government affairs, John Jay Daly, and the pressures of membership to thwart continuous postal-rate increases.

In 1962, Postmaster General (PMG) Edward Day appeared at the annual DMAA conference in Chicago. That was significant since it was the first time (according to a search for historical records) a PMG had appeared before a DMAA conference.

In 1964, DMAA scheduled a "postal parley," a one-day programmed session in Washington to familiarize members with postal problems. And, of course, to meet some postal officials who were considered "adversaries." It was the birth of an annual event that brought users and top postal officials into head-to-head meetings.

At this juncture in its history, DMAA added a strategy that set it apart from the traditional lobbying of Washington representatives. In 1965, Board member Reed Bartlett of Procter & Gamble initiated a meeting with Postmaster General John Gronouski and his top staff. The DMA Government Affairs members and the postal officials were elated with the results of the two-hour meeting. The PMG himself cited the need and desirability of continuing such exchanges. Although it sounds like a simple strategy, it must be remembered that the Postal Department rarely talked to customers in those days. Thus, this session for mail users bordered on the historic!

Subsequent meetings determined the exchange should be formalized. Also, it was agreed that other groups representing advertising mail should be present. Shortly after Lawrence A. O'Brien became PMG, he formalized the Mailer's Technical Advisory Committee. This committee, through its representation and regular meetings (six times a year) has been a forum for the exchange of ideas. It has also been used effectively as a sounding board for major changes in the U.S. Postal Service. It has eliminated most of the surprises that traditionally frustrated the mailing community.

As with most trade associations, the Washington presence has been responsible for improved and continuing relationships with not only Congress and the postal service, but regulatory bodies such as the Federal Trade Commission (FTC), the Federal Communications Commission (FCC), the Postal Rate Commission, and others. Beyond that, the Government Affairs office has been the focal point for privacy concerns, use tax problems, and expansion of legislative activity within the 50 states.

With the growth of power in Washington and the manner in which it shapes the future of many businesses, DMA's strategy of making representation a priority became a primary reason for its membership growth. The association's chief lobbyist, Richard Barton, has 14 years of service with DMA and a lifetime in the nation's capital. Continuity of service has supported the vital strategy of representation.

Establishing a Spring Conference

Sometimes strategies evolve from an idea. This was certainly true back in 1962, when the DMAA Spring Conference was born. The concept of a spring conference that would draw international attendance was not in the minds of its creators.

Actually, this first event was called a Western Regional Conference. It was held in San Francisco. It's real purpose was to show West Coast members that DMAA was not just a New York organization. Strangely enough, with some members, the New York perception still exists today.

Registration for the two-day event was only $48 (but so were the annual dues). To stage a meeting on the West Coast loomed as an unusual burden. The event must not lose money. At that time, our office manager was also my secretary/assistant, in charge of meetings and seminars, and the board liaison. There wasn't any money for advance travel, so site selection was accomplished on advice from a volunteer committee.

The key to the success of the meeting, both from a financial and informational standpoint, was the Board of Directors. They agreed to be on the program. With this wide diversity of talent, plus some West Coast professionals, we staged a successful meeting for more than 300 registrants. And we broke even. Just three staff members, myself, my wife Bonnie, and my secretary/assistant, plus the West Coast committee ran the show.

The West Coast Conference continued to be held each year until 1966, when we began to promote it as the Spring Conference. Strength and growth were attributed to the fact that the meeting attracted mostly high-level executives and managers. Although that motivation may have come from the high cost of travel, it nevertheless served the purpose.

Like most "trial events," the Spring Conference had its ups and downs (such as arguing for a half day with committee chairman, Len Carlson of Sunset House, about raising the price to $52.50). Those were tough days!

There was also the ill-fated 1975 Spring Conference in Mexico City. Unfortunately, that was the year of a strong recession. And to complicate matters the President of Mexico made some anti-Semitic remarks that received broad publicity. The result for DMMA was a couple of hundred cancellations. The 225 who attended always referred to it as "one of the best." Pleasing people, especially members, can defy strategies!

Although the establishment of the Spring conference could easily be looked on as an event rather than a strategy, it was significant in that it opened the way for much broader thinking in building a bond with more distant membership. And it had a noticeable impact on the exchange of information, the extension of education, and a leadership in networking that has made DMA a close-knit group of professionals.

Initiating a Global Presence

Although I had served overseas during World War II, it took me nearly 10 years to realize that advertising and marketing were global opportunities. And before DMA adopted a strategy to become a truly international organization, I had to go through a learning process that happened quite accidentally.

In 1963, I received an invitation to join a panel of U.S. "experts" to conduct a group of advertising seminars in Australia. It seemed like an appropriate time to visit other direct-mail enthusiasts and some of the DMAA members around the world. So I contacted the British Direct Mail Association (BDMA) and its counterpart in France to arrange speaking engagements, a chance to meet larger groups of people.

My colleagues in Australia were well-known U.S. advertising men: John Cunningham (Cunningham & Walsh), Art Nielsen, Jr. (The A.C. Nielsen Company), and Rod Erickson (Universal Broadcasting). We completed full-day seminars in Sydney, Melbourne, and Brisbane. Audience attendance ranged between 200 and 300. I sensed later that the trip was worth it, if only for the fact that my fellow speakers got a first-hand glimpse of how useful direct mail was.

After layovers in Hong Kong and Rome, I made many direct-marketing contacts in London and addressed a large crowd at the BDMA meeting. The visit to Paris seemed equally rewarding; I even met a few DMAA members.

Between that eventful trip and 1973, new opportunities to visit members and address direct-marketing audiences occurred each year. It was a thrill and a learning experience to visit overseas members on their own turf. It was at this time that U.S. members began to evoke interest in Europe. In 1967, we arranged the first Mail Marketing Mission to Europe, visiting London, Paris, Rome, Frankfurt, and Amsterdam. In each city, we spent two days meeting with direct-mail members and two days sightseeing.

These marketing missions attracted our quota of 30 participants. We conducted them in 1967, 1969, 1971, and 1973. A visit to Russia in 1973 was notable. On the agenda was a stop in Lucerne, Switzerland, where we attended the Schmid Symposium. Walter Schmid and I had first met in Geneva during the 1969 marketing mission. He was an invited speaker.

However, during the 1973 Schmid Symposium, many of our DMAA members, not totally satisfied with the program, suggested that we hold a regular DMAA conference in Europe.

By this time, experience had taught me to think globally so the suggestion fell on willing ears. We promptly organized the first full-fledged DMAA European Conference and held it in Montreux, Switzerland, in the spring of 1974. Although only 176 people attended, it provided the seeds for a significant future membership in Europe. These meetings, held each year, were moved to other venues in order to give the program exposure in various countries. Subsequent meetings were held in Amsterdam, Paris, Munich, Vienna, and London.

Although attendance never grew beyond 375, our members in Europe and many other countries found the meetings a learning experience. And for the Americans, it was an eye-opener to discover the expertise that existed in many far-away lands.

In 1982, the European meeting was held in conjunction with the annual DMA conference in Los Angeles. It was the first opportunity overseas members had to have their own meeting in the same location as the DMA annual meeting. It was an artificial, but meaningful, merger that brought global interests more closely together. And it proved immensely popular with more than 600 overseas delegates attending. Similar joint sessions in Miami, Chicago, and Montreal through 1985 brought continued large overseas participation and learning rewards.

During the 1970s and 1980s, there were many opportunities to provide the global experience that started so accidentally in 1963. Numerous visits to Japan, Australia, and Far Eastern countries stimulated membership and worldwide exchange of direct-marketing information. A landmark event was a joint meeting in 1980 in Singapore sponsored by the associations from Australia, the United Kingdom, Hong Kong, Japan, and DMAA. The Scandinavian members, always enthusiastic travelers, hosted many events in Finland and Sweden that cemented those relationships.

In the excitement and difficulty of "pulling" the direct-mail world together, most people overlooked the strong relationship that DMAA had established with its northern neighbor, Canada. Canada did not have its own association until 1967. Before that, as many as 150 Canadian companies were DMAA members. But the time came when, mainly because of postal and governmental relationships, Canada needed its own organization. The DMAA was cooperative in extending the privileges of the U.S. library, traveling leaders exhibit, and regular member rates for conference registrations. Although these might seem like trivial benefits now, they were extremely helpful to the fledgling Canadian association in attracting members.

The global strategy was furthered in the 1970s when the association's constitution was changed to permanently include two international members on the Board of Directors. Daniel Hauguel (France) and Alfred Gerardi (Germany) were the first "internationals" outside of Canadians to have official recognition as global partners. This move was further evidence that direct marketing was truly a global discipline.

Credibility through Self-Regulation

Perhaps the one strategy that brought survival to direct mail as we know it today was the decision in 1970 to create and implement a proactive program of self-regulation and image enhancement.

There was a public, anti–direct mail fire burning. Even the Chief Justice of the Supreme Court, Warren Burger, had publicly denounced "the flood of junk mail." Vocal members of the association added to the crisis. With the atmosphere so charged, it was quite possible direct mail would face legislation that could destroy some of its practices.

Procter & Gamble, through its DMAA Board representative, Reed Bartlett, offered to have the renowned public relations agency of Hill & Knowlton conduct a study of the problem. And the agency agreed to make recommendations for a program for the association; indeed, for all mail users.

Internally, DMAA had two staff members—Bob Hanford and John Jay Daly—who played a vital role as we formulated the program. Bob Hanford was our promotion manager. In a memo to me in the spring of 1970, he suggested we enlist the aid of the major list compilers (Donnelley, Polk, Metromail, and Mail Advertising Corp.) to gather a "troublemakers list." Daly called it a "dissident list." It would be made available to members for "cleaning" their mailing lists of anti–direct mail consumers. That suggestion was the seed that, with much study and many added features, became the Mail Preference Service (MPS).

In September 1970 at the Annual Conference in Miami, the Board of Directors approved the concept and plan for implementation of MPS. This was accomplished only after a dramatic meeting, since several of the more influential companies opposed the action. In fact, the Board representative of one of the largest list companies swore his company "would never adopt MPS as long as I am president!" Subsequently, many companies canceled their membership in the association. Fortunately, Board member John Yeck suggested we also introduce an "add on list" for people who wanted to get more mail. That proved decisive in the subsequent public relations program. Advertisements like the one shown in Exhibit 14.1 gave consumers the opportunity to reduce or increase the amount of mail they received.

The public relations firm of Daniel Edelman was hired to implement an image program using MPS and the Guidelines for Ethical Business Practice as a cornerstone. A barnstorming tour of 25 major markets featuring television, radio, and newspaper interviews brought new credibility to the use of direct mail as a vital advertising medium. Media coverage was nothing short of phenomenal and, strangely perhaps, most of it was positive.

Thus, when President Gerald Ford appointed the Privacy Protection Study Commission in 1975, DMAA was ready. In addition to MPS, the association also started Mail Order Action Line (MOAL). Its implementation was an answer to the constant inquiries from a *Washington Star* reporter to the DMAA's John J. Daly about why the association wouldn't do something about the "bad guys" in the mailing business. John Daly's recommendation to me was to set up a complaint office. That seed sparked the initiation of MOAL. It was a self-regulatory plank in the program that started in 1975 and is a vital part of the DMA structure to this day.

Fears expressed by members in regard to MPS and MOAL never became significant factors, although MPS was the most controversial. But it immediately began to evidence three times as many people who wanted to get more mail

Exhibit 14-1 Advertisement Giving Consumers the Opportunity to Reduce or Increase Mail

Want to get LESS advertising in the mail? MORE?
The DMMA gives you a choice!

Who's the DMMA? We're the 1,800 member companies comprising the Direct Mail/Marketing Association. Many of the manufacturers, retailers, publishers and service companies you've come to trust most over the years are among our members. ☐ And we think you deserve a choice, as to how much—and what kind—of advertising you receive in the mail. If you'd like to get less, mail in the coupon on the left. We can't stop all your mail,

but you'll see a reduction in the amount of mail you receive soon. ☐ If you'd like to receive more mail in your areas of interest— catalogs, free trial offers, merchandise and services not available anywhere else—mail the coupon on the right. Soon, you'll start to see more information and opportunities in the areas most important to you. Let's hear from you today!

LESS mail

I want to receive less advertising mail.

Mail to: DMMA Mail Preference Service
6 East 43rd Street
N.Y., NY 10017

Name (print)

Address

City   State   Zip

Please include me in the Name Removal File. I understand that you will make this file available to direct mail advertisers for the sole purpose of removing from their mailing lists the names and addresses contained therein.

Others at my address who also want less mail—or variations of my own name by which I receive mail—include:

MORE mail

I want to receive more advertising mail.

Mail to: DMMA Mail Preference Service
6 East 43rd Street
N.Y., NY 10017

Name (print)

Address

City   State   Zip

I would like to receive more information in the mail, especially on the subjects below (circle letter):

A All subjects	J Health Foods &	R Sewing, Needlework,
B Autos, Parts	Vitamins	Arts & Crafts
& Accessories	K HiFi & Electronics	S Sports & Camping
C Books & Magazines	L Home Furnishings	T Stamps & Coins
D Charities	M Insurance	U Stocks & Bonds
E Civic Organizations	N Plants, Flowers &	V Tools & Equipment
F Clothing	Garden Supplies	W Travel
G Foods & Cooking	O Photography	X Office Furniture
H Gifts	P Real Estate	& Supplies
I Grocery Bargains	Q Records & Tapes	

(add ons) than less. This was a public relations coup. President Ford's Privacy Protection Commission grilled me and other witnesses at the hearings in 1976 and 1977. The facts stood up. A widespread advertising program, in which the magazine industry provided millions of dollars in free advertising space, was dynamic proof that the association was trying to reach all of America. A 12-page *New York Times* insert in 1973 was additional testament to the openness of the campaign. It was in that historic document that the famed Isaac Asimov authored an article on the thesis that numbers (social security, and so on) were more personal than names. Advertising by member companies paid for 90 percent of the cost ($120,000) of the insert.

A strategy for making direct mail respectable as an advertising medium was not new. Traveling road shows initiated back in the 1930s by Henry Hoke, Sr., when he was the executive director of DMAA, attracted many businesses to use the power of direct mail. And, in 1959, the formation of the Business Mail Foundation by Reuben H. Donnelley's David Harrington and other vendors of that era, was an attempt to produce a favorable image for the medium.

But the 1970 strategic initiative, despite disbelievers even today, positioned direct mail as the cornerstone of the expanding discipline that was beginning to be recognized as direct marketing. Without doubt, it showed the power of self-regulation in thwarting harmful legislation. And it truly set the stage and helped to preserve an even playing field for the privacy concerns of the 1990s.

The Formation of Councils

One significant principle in running a successful trade association is to stimulate involvement. A successful strategy for membership involvement must be predicated on maximum participation and minimum control. A delicate balance must be reached where staff has ultimate authority for decisionmaking. Those decisions should almost always be bsaed on the will of the majority.

In its long history, DMA, like most organizations, used a committee system to gain participation and move projects. It had as many as 20 committees in operation in the 1960s and early 1970s. An ethics committee, formed in 1954, eventually led to the Standards of Practice and, later, Guidelines for Ethical Business Practice, a set of standards that brought considerable stature to the use of direct-mail advertising. Unfortunately, in those early days, most DMAA committees met twice each year on "all Committee Day" in New York City and were almost moribund the remainder of the year. It was obvious that DMAA needed a new strategy for involvement.

In the late 1960s, DMAA had formed an "In Plant Production Council" consisting of six companies (DuPont, Kodak, Dow Chemical, Youngstown Steel,

U.S. Steel, and National Cash Register) that met periodically to discuss planning, production, and use of direct mail. The like-interest concept was successful. When the committee system became suspect, it was decided a new strategy of "like-interest councils" was a possible solution to getting members involved and creating useful information, research, statistics, and educational value.

The first "full-fledged council" that appealed to a broad section of the association's membership was the Insurance Council, later named the Direct Marketing Insurance Council (DMIC). Despite a rocky start in its first two years in the early 1970s, DMIC has become one of the largest, most active, and most productive of the council programs. The councils provided a networking opportunity that really didn't exist before. By 1984, eight councils were active, and the expansion in segments and members has been the lifeblood of modern DMA.

Although the council concept was a strong strategic move, the implementation was fraught with problems. The question of how the council activities should be financed was the classic example of the chicken and the egg debate. Without separate funding, activities were limited.

Finally, the bullet had to be bitten. Separate council dues were voted by the membership. Thus, benefits such as newsletters, statistics, and other industry information evolved.

One of the significant advantages of the council concept to an association as diverse as DMA was uniting self-interest groups like catalogers, computer-service bureaus, direct-response agencies, and other categories of members that previously had to use a conference or an occasional seminar to network with colleagues. The council concept proved ideal to serve these multi-interests.

Professional Ethics

Ethics has never been a sexy subject, but a set of standards for behavior had become vital for DMAA and particularly for direct mail and telemarketing.

Fortunately, this truism was realized early by the DMAA. After years of bickering, a "General Standard of Practices" was presented at the annual business meeting in Boston in 1954. The Public Policy and Ethics Committee was surely what we would call today a "blue-ribbon panel." Jess Roberts (Commercial Credit, Atlanta) headed the committee. Other members included Elon Borton (American Federation of Advertising), C.E. Larrabee (Printer's Ink), Sid Bernstein (*Advertising Age*), Henry Hoke, Sr. (*Reporter of Direct Mail Magazine),* Edward N. Mayer (James Grey, Inc.), Fred Michaels (Sears Roebuck), William Sproul (Burroughs, representing the National Industrial Advertisers Association), James

Mosley (Mosley List Service), Bill Power (Chevrolet), Jasper Rolland (National Better Business Bureau), Eliot Wight (U.S. Envelope), Robert Whitney (National Sales Executives), Maxwell Sackheim (Maxwell Sackheim, Inc.), Bill Henderson (DMAA Executive Director), and John Yeck (Yeck Brothers), who headed the subcommittee that wrote the final standards.

The "Code" was adopted at the 1954 annual meeting, and an implementation committee was appointed. The Code was incorporated into a new application for membership.

My first involvement (beyond being a member and sitting on the Board of Directors from 1954 through 1957) was attending some rather boisterous meetings during the early 1960s as committee members argued about "putting teeth into the enforcement of the Code."

But, in 1962, the committee was reformed. Fred Decker of Printers Ink became chairman. Upon his retirement, Bob Hutchings (IBM) became chairman. As Hutchings noted, the committee relied heavily on the Better Business Bureau to handle complaints, most of which were generated by the committee itself. And, to further block progress, our lawyer was always on hand at the meetings to remind us about violating the antitrust laws.

However, these restrictions did not satisfy the committee. Nor, indeed, did I feel we were vigilant enough and forceful enough to police our membership and the field of direct mail.

The committee was assigned to develop a strategy and implementation procedure to handle complaints. Hutchings, as chairman, appointed a member of his staff (Dick Petrocy, later director of marketing for the Book-of-the-Month Club) to develop a decision map. This turned out to be a step-by-step procedure for handling a complaint. Although the Postal Inspection Service offered some assistance to the committee, the major source of help continued to come from the Better Business Bureau.

A frustrating blow to the committee's determination was a case brought before the Board of Directors in the late 1960s. The committee had followed the decision map and arrived at the recommendation to expel a member. The Board took a dim view of the proposed action. One member not only walked out, but he directed the minutes should show he was absent during the discussion. It turned out he was a competitor of the company being "tried."

Bob Stone took over the chairmanship in the early 1970s and succeeded in getting more results from the Postal Service. Pornography was the big target and biggest complaint in those years. It was a tough problem to deal with no matter what strategy was undertaken. However, the pandering law took that burden off the shoulders of the association and its sometimes futile attempt to "clear out the bad guys."

Persistence paid off. Eventually, the ethics responsibility was broken into two separate committees, a planning committee and an operating committee. This strategy, together with the growing importance and credibility of the direct-marketing field brought results.

A second case for expulsion was brought before the Board. This time, the Executive Committee of the Board had already recommended expulsion, and we had the votes to take this crucial action. However, as the Board met and before it could take action, a messenger delivered a letter of resignation from the member.

By the early 1980s, most complaints were handled by the operating committee. And most often, the company charged with wrongdoing agreed to cease and desist.

Facing the Educational Challenge

In the mission statement of DMA's constitution, education is clearly cited as a primary goal of the association.

The association's bow to solid direct-mail education was twofold: a once-a-year institute for professionals held at the University of Illinois and the once-a-week (two semesters a year) course at New York University (NYU). This was later taken over by Nat Ross and NYU.

For years the association depended on master educator Edward N. Mayer, Jr., to teach the basic course in direct mail. The annual Circulation Seminar was a fixture in the 1960s. And a series of computer seminars taught by Leo Yochim was, in the minds of the association, a step forward in the educational program of the mid-1960s.

In 1976, Board Chairman Francis S. Andrews set up a series of task forces to evaluate and recommend activity areas of DMMA. One of these, of course, was education. The task force, headed by IBM's Bob Hutchings, recommended a new "department of education" be set up and a new vice president for education be hired to implement a program. Board approval followed as a budget agreement was reached.

Within 90 days a professional educator, Dante Zacavish, was hired and three professional educators (Pierre Passavant, Richard Hodgson, and Paul Sampson) had committed to the new program. Even more significant, a business plan was approved, initial courses were outlined, and the first programs began.

The educational program was quickly accepted by the membership. The program was soon looked on as the most credible training opportunity for professionals in the field of direct marketing.

Meanwhile, a program to bring direct-mail knowledge and, thus, career opportunities for bright, young college students had been underway since 1966. Lewis Kleid, a leading list broker, contacted Edward N. Mayer, Jr., and me to devise a project for college students that he would fund. The result was a week-long institute for 20 college students. The DMMA Board Chairman, Reed Bartlett (Procter & Gamble), had the foresight to enlist John Yeck as chairman of what became the Direct Marketing Educational Foundation (DMEF). Although it was separately incorporated, it relied on DMMA, its sister nonprofit organization, for administrative assistance.

For the first 10 years, Yeck was an invaluable right hand in the teachings of Ed Mayer. Mayer spent innumerable hours teaching courses to college and university students. It bred a trickle of talent from the college ranks into the professional field. The progress was slow.

The DMEF fulfilled another useful strategy in the steady growth of the use of direct mail and other direct-response media. If the field were to continue to prosper, it must have bright, young people, not only to replace aging veterans, but also to bring "new blood" into the direct-marketing discipline.

Plagued with inadequate finances, DMEF carried on its mission with the aid of a DMMA staff member, who also worked in the professional education department.

But, in 1980, the foundation moved forward by hiring its first full-time president, well-known educator, Dr. Richard Montesi. Yeck had almost religiously given time and effort from his company to keep the foundation afloat. But the hiring of Montesi brought dramatic results. A fund-raising drive brought $1.7 million. And the addition of scores of new "members" brought a steady stream of operating funds. Seed money from the foundation started a degree program at the University of Missouri—Kansas City and assisted the program at Northwestern University (Evanston, Illinois). Programs for professors as well as students brought direct marketing into the curriculum of hundreds of universities.

Thus, the two-pronged strategy for education in the field of direct marketing has spawned an educational level that provides quality professional training and has brought thousands of new college and university graduates into the direct-marketing field.

Attacking the Junk-Mail Syndrome

Perhaps the most pervasive lifetime problem facing the direct-mail/direct-marketing field is the "junk-mail syndrome." Detractors and advertising media rivals were persistent in their attacks. Naturally, DMA was continuously haunted to do something about the problem.

In late 1958, a group of direct-mail suppliers headed by Dave Harrington (then head of Reuben H. Donnelley) formed the Business Mail Foundation (BMF). The BMF avowed its purpose to try and bring about a more credible image for the direct-mail medium.

When I came to DMAA as president in early 1959, this separate entity existed mainly because the association seemed to lack the finances and other motivation to assume the problem. My strategy was to try to meld the BMF into the DMAA public relations program. Working with the BMF Board and its public relations agency, we accomplished the union in 1962. The educational materials created by the BMC proved helpful. But the problem needed a bigger, well-funded solution.

With DMAA experiencing growing pains, including the change to a company membership structure, the larger plan to improve the image of the medium did not take shape until 1970.

At that time, the attack had escalated because the newspaper industry saw advertising dollars moving over to direct mail. The Scripps-Howard chain of papers, then a strong force in major U.S. markets, carried out a periodic editorial blast at junk mail. There was also a public clamor against pornography in the mail, which we discussed previously.

After a study by the Hill & Knowlton public relations firm in the spring of 1970, members of the DMAA staff spent considerable time producing a program that would gain Board approval in September. I well remember taking two weeks away from the association office to plan the strategy and outline some 26 tactics we could use to implement the program.

Financing the new program proved relatively easy. The Board had voted on a voluntary assessment to accompany each dues invoice. Sensing the need, members supported the program. More than $250,000 was received the first year. The assessment continued for several years until the association was able to maintain the program through regular dues adjustments. This "voluntary assessment" was a strategy used earlier to fund a heightened government affairs program. As my treasurer, Kent Rhodes of Reader's Digest remarked, "DeLay, you've got more tin cups on your belt than anyone I know."

After Board approval in September (not an easy task since a stringent self-regulation program featuring MPS was included), public relations agencies were reviewed. The Daniel J. Edelman firm was hired. Its official duties commenced in January 1971. The program was extensive and broad based, even though its targets included government officials, Congress, and the advertising profession.

But the public was vital to the strategy. Education was necessary. The public had to be convinced that people liked to get mail; they opened most of what they received and read thoroughly or partially a high percentage of their advertising mail. This had been proved by an historic A.C. Nielsen study sponsored by the association back in 1964. But little research had been done since that time.

The strategy of the Edelman firm included a single, bold stroke to take the word to the public that advertising mail was a valuable source of information for them; television, radio, and newspaper interviews were given in all major U.S. markets. It was with considerable trepidation that two staff members (Celia Wallace and John Daly) and I made the initial visit to Hartford, Connecticut. The television, radio, and newspaper media responded in full force. After all, the junk mailers were in town.

Yes, there was some negative newspaper publicity. Like the *San Francisco Chronicle*'s headline: "Junk Mail White Knight Visits SF!" But the television and radio interviews were amazingly fair. We stressed MPS as a way to get off national mailing lists. We also encouraged people to sign up if they wanted to get more mail. When we hit Chicago and seven television stations turned out for our press conference, we felt we had struck gold.

Admittedly, the "road show" was our loss leader. But we were supporting it with educational material and an awareness campaign that got results. Hundreds of local radio stations picked up our commercials as a public service. We used well-known personalities, like Steve Allen, Jane Meadows, Don Knotts, and Louis Nye, in light-hearted spots that urged listeners to "get off or get on" mailing lists. My interview on the popular "60 Minutes" was not as successful. CBS wanted a "hatchet job" and they got it by taking our 52-minute interview with Morley Safer and splitting the tape into three 90-second "on camera" tapes! But other national television shows used Celia Wallace, John Daly, and myself in hundreds of newscasts.

The other significant part of the program was a credit to our publishing members. Time-Life, Meredith, Reader's Digest, and more than 20 other magazine publishers contributed millions of dollars in space for our MPS and MOAL ads. Our fine relationship with the magazine industry paid off in spades.

The result: During the 10 years the Edelman agency shepherded our image program, there were three times as many people asking to get on mailing lists as there were to get off. It was a public relations coup. Those results were invaluable at the Privacy Protection Commission hearings in 1976–77. Of the seven areas of investigation by that Presidential Commission, mailing lists was the only one where no legislation was recommended!

The image program continued in the 1980s. It was staff-oriented rather than directed by a public relations agency. Both methods were effective. Not that the "J word" has been exorcised. But, certainly, the credibility of direct mail and direct marketing has increased dramatically.

Conclusion

In early 1985, I handed over the reins of DMA to Jonah Gitlitz, an experienced trade association executive. I had hired Jonah in 1981 to head the DMMA's Washington, DC, office. He had spent the previous 11 years with the American Advertising Federation as executive vice president.

The 1980s were a period of tremendous growth in many fields. Direct marketing, although facing increasing pressure in many areas, was no exception. With experienced leadership and a growing acceptance of direct marketing as a fundamental discipline, the stage was set for rapid growth of the association.

Yes, the problems of privacy were resurfacing. Environment became a new force to deal with. The use tax problem that had lain dormant since the mid 1960s suddenly became a major threat to mail users. And, despite a firm foundation that had been built to improve the image of direct mail, its competitors and opponents seemed to have touched a vital nerve in the consumer.

Despite all of these problems, the DMA of today is a vital force in the advertising and marketing world. With more than 100 million consumers having bought by mail or phone in the United States alone, its contributions to the economy and its power to create sales have been well documented.

For those of us who had a hand in the association's progress over 25 years, we are especially proud of the DMA of today.

Bob Stone's
Commentary

This chapter is more than a story about the 25-year growth record of a trade association: It also reflects direct marketers and DMA growing together in cadence.

It is no coincidence that all the other success stories in this book feature individuals who have contributed to and benefitted from DMA. It is this bond, this giving and receiving, that has resulted in success beyond fondest dreams.

I can speak with intimate knowledge about Bob DeLay, for it was I who urged him to "take it" that cold January evening in Chicago when he asked whether I thought he should accept the offer of the DMAA presidency.

Gentleman that he is, Bob didn't tell you just how glum the situation was at DMAA when he ascended to the loft on 57th Street in New York for the first time.

Here are some snapshots of what he faced. A small staff. No money to invest in expansion or better services. A medium—direct mail—that was held in low esteem.

Considering the sobering fact that there was no money to invest, challenges were so great that only brilliant strategies could meet the challenges. Let's look at two of the challenges and the strategies that were applied to solve them.

Challenge: How can we mount a membership drive without money to cover the cost of mailing?

Strategy: Get an outstanding salesletter writer to do a mailing package on a pro bono basis and induce suppliers to produce and mail at their expense.

Challenge: How can we run a first-class annual convention in a host city without a staff to develop the program?

Strategy: Review membership in the host city and select the "movers and shakers" to serve as general chairman, program chairman, promotion chairman, and exhibit chairman. Then monitor their progress from headquarters.

So many of Bob's strategies came under the category: "Necessity is the mother of invention." Here's a checklist of his strategies, expressed as universal strategies, that can be applied to any line of business.

☐ Change the name of your association (or firm) when the present name no longer reflects the scope of what you do.

☐ Knowing that many people resist change, *do it* even though you know some will abandon you.

☐ Change is the one constant in business. Keep up with change and anticipate future changes.

☐ If your membership (customer) base isn't fueling growth, change the face of your operation so that income feeds growth.

☐ Establish a board of directors that reflects your membership (customer) base. Limit the term so you can have a steady flow of new directors who reflect changing times.

☐ If your organization is subject to legislation in Washington, make sure your interests are represented in a professional manner.

☐ Recognize the trend toward global marketing. Ask yourself how your organization can capitalize on this trend.

☐ Self-regulation is the best deterrent to government regulation.

☐ Cater to the special interests of your members (customers).

☐ American businesses are measured by the ethics they practice. Establish a code of ethics that puts your organization beyond reproach.

☐ Organizations who support industry education are the beneficiaries of talent that would not otherwise be available.

☐ Never hide from attack on your industry. Instead, take the offensive with a professional public relations program.

Afterword

As editor-in-chief of *Direct Marketing Success Stories,* I became obsessed with the idea that even though each story is unique unto itself, there must be a number of outstanding traits shared by these heros and heroines, each of whom has reached the pinnacle of success.

A questionnaire was designed and sent to each author, and common traits emerged. From the results of the survey, we can create the profile of one person who closely resembles all the successful people who contributed to this book.

I have a college degree with a B.S. in Journalism. I'm a strong believer in continuing education, having participated in over 60 direct-marketing seminars and workshops.

I've been a member of the Direct Marketing Association throughout my career. I've attended 32 national conventions. I'm a supporter of the Direct Marketing Educational Foundation.

I read around 34 books a year, half of which are business related. I also read at least 12 trade and business magazines each month.

I am indebted to others who have generously shared their knowledge with me. I, in turn, have shared my knowledge with others. I have spoken before direct-marketing clubs and national conventions on innumerable occasions. I've written about 30 articles over my career. I've also lectured occasionally at the college level.

It's not all business and no play. Family activities have a high priority in my life. I get my exercise. Golf and travel rank high on my list of hobbies. Vacations total about three weeks a year.

The profile survey ended with a request: "In 50 words, or less, please write your formula for success in business." What follows is a cross-section of advice which, as the saying goes, you can take to the bank.

- Always consider yourself a student and maintain a hunger to learn.
- Be persistent.
- Be resourceful in gathering information; there are valuable lessons all around you.
- Transplant successful business practices into your own needs.
- Balance your professional life with your family/leisure life.
- Treat time as your most precious resource.
- Your customers almost always hold the answers to your questions.
- Invest in your people and your network.
- Listen carefully to an experienced opinion and to children.

Hire the best people you can find to do the best job. Make sure you have clear and achievable goals. Remember that the customer is the heart and soul of your business and to please the customer from a product, price, and service viewpoint is your number-one goal.

Believe in your work and your company. Always do your job better than it was ever done before. Develop skills of leadership: personal skills, motivating, and delegating responsibilities to other skilled people. Be a dreamer, think big. Be a long-range thinker and planner.

Never reach the point where you think you know it all. We all learn on the job through observation, communication, and trial and error. Successful executives recognize the need to refine their knowledge, skills, and instincts on a continuing basis to generate fresh ideas.

- Stay focused.
- Stay involved.
- Stay informed.

- Network.

- Ask lots of questions.

- Take responsible risks.

I strongly believe that actions have consequences, and we each are responsible for our own actions. I also feel that through continuous effort we can make good things happen. You should make every effort to do what you do very well and be selective in what you choose to do.

Consider the Parable of the Talents. There are many lessons here. For business, one of them goes like this. Do what you are given to do. Whether it is a small task or a large one, do it well, do it on time, do it responsibly. Once you gain a reputation for getting the job done, done well, done on time, you will find that your responsibilities will grow, the measure of your recognition will expand, and your rewards will surely take care of themselves.

About the Author

Bob Stone
Chairman Emeritus, Stone & Adler, Inc.

Bob Stone is one of the true pioneers of the direct-marketing industry. His distinguished career spans more than 40 years, and during this time he has played a formative role in the growth of direct marketing, both in the United States and internationally.

In addition to his two highly successful books, *Successful Direct Marketing Methods* and *Successful Telemarketing,* Stone is author of more than 200 articles on direct marketing, which have appeared in *Advertising Age* magazine since 1967.

He is also an eight-time winner of the Direct Marketing Association's Best of Industry Award. The firm he cofounded, Stone & Adler, has received the Direct Marketing Association's highest honors, including the Silver and Gold Echo Awards as well as the International Direct Marketing & Mail Order Symposium's Bronze Carrier Pigeon Award. Stone is a member of the Direct Marketing Hall of Fame, and a recipient of the Edward N. Mayer, Jr., Award for contributions to direct marketing education, the Charles S. Downes Award for direct marketing contributions, and the John Caples Award for copy excellence.

His affiliations are numerous: former director of the Direct Marketing Association; former president of the Chicago Association of Direct Marketing; former membership chairman of the Direct Marketing Association; former president of the Associated Third Class Mail Users; board member of the Direct Marketing Educational Foundation; and adjunct professor at the University of Missouri.

About the Contributors

Bill Baker's first job was as a catalog copywriter for Sears. Then he had the good luck to be hired by one of the great "wicked old mail-order men from Chicago," Paul Grant. Another bit of luck brought him together with Tom Nickel, the founder of the Baldwin Cooke Company.

Baker wrote the company's first direct-response copy, and he insists there are whole paragraphs that are still being used today. He moved to general advertising, first at Leo Burnett and then at FCB, where he became executive creative director and executive vice president. Baker had the good sense, some 27 years later, to return to direct response and the Baldwin Cooke Company.

Jock Bickert is the chief executive officer of Looking Glass, Inc., a Denver-based firm that provides client companies and organizations with real-time customer feedback about how customers regard their products and services. Within 24 hours, clients can learn which of their customers have had positive or negative experiences with their company; how customers respond to new products, product enhancements, or promotions.

In 1960, Bickert joined a fledgling survey research firm, Frank N. Magid Associates, where for three years he performed audience research for radio and television broadcasters. He then joined the University of Denver Research Institute and for seven years headed the survey research function there. In that capacity, he conducted numerous studies for government agencies, including the National Science Foundation, the National Aeronautics and Space Administration, the National Bureau of Standards, and the Bureau of Indian Affairs.

In 1970, Bickert contracted a severe case of entreprenosis, mitigated only when he and two colleagues from the university, Ted Browne and Dean Coddington, formed their own research and consulting firm, BBC. In 1973, their company received an *Esquire* magazine "Business in the Arts" award for assisting in the startup funding and planning for several minority performing arts groups. After five successful years, he sold his interest in BBC and founded National Demographics & Lifestyles in 1975.

Tom Collinger was named senior vice president of Chicago-based Leo Burnett Company and the company's director of direct marketing in November 1990. His responsibilities cover all Burnett clients.

Collinger's direct-marketing background began at age 13 in the warehouse of his father's direct-marketing firm in St. Louis, Missouri. There, he got a taste of the "backend" of the business. Once he earned his Bachelor of Science degree from the University of Colorado, Collinger joined a St. Louis sales-promotion agency, Bowers and Associates. Following a two-year stint there, he officially rejoined his father's firm, Marketing Associates of America, where he worked in the marketing department for four years. His next three years, in Los Angeles, were spent building a direct-marketing business that was later sold to Time-Life Books, and events took him to Chicago.

Collinger entered the advertising agency business in 1981, as vice president and general manager for Ayer Direct, where he stayed until 1983, when he was made general manager at Ogilvy & Mather Direct. Almost five years later, in 1987, he joined Leo Burnett to become one of a group of direct-marketing professionals who bring these skills to the over 2,200 Burnetters and their 34 clients.

Collinger has been a guest speaker at local and national Direct Marketing Association (DMA) conferences, the Professors' Institute of the DMA's Educational Foundation, the Advertising Research Foundation, and Northwestern University's Kellogg Graduate School of Business.

Bob DeLay is president of The DeLay Group, a consulting firm headquartered in Westport, Connecticut, and specializing in direct-marketing communications. DeLay is editor and publisher of *THE DELAY LETTER,* reporting news, analysis, and trends in direct marketing, and having a paid circulation. It is published 22 times a year.

DeLay was previously president of the Direct Marketing Association (DMA) for 25 years and served as DMA's vice chairman in 1986. He is secretary-treasurer of the Direct Marketing Educational Foundation and was one of its original founders in 1965.

As president of DMA, DeLay initiated the DMA government affairs office in Washington, DC (1963), organized the first Government Affairs Conference (1965), created the first and largest resource library serving the field, published the annual *Fact Book,* and began such consumer services as the Mail Preference Service and Mail Order Action Line.

DeLay received the Miles Kimball Award in 1978, honoring the individual who has contributed the most to the industry. In 1980, he won the Ben Gurion Award, presented by State of Israel Bonds, and in 1984, the Robert Alex Jones Award honoring those direct-marketing professionals who have made exemplary contributions to the field.

The South Dakota State University Alumni Association bestowed its Distinguished Service Award for Professional Achievement on DeLay in 1985, and the Direct Marketing Club of New York gave him the Silver Apple Award. In 1987, DeLay received the Ed Mayer Award in recognition of outstanding educational leadership in the field. In October 1988, the DMA inducted DeLay into its Hall of Fame.

John Goodman is nationally recognized for his advances in retail direct marketing. His areas of focus are database segmentation and creative execution. He maintains a well-balanced understanding of applying database-driven marketing strategies within the retail marketplace. As Vice President of Marketing for Helzberg Diamonds, he is responsible for all advertising, marketing, strategic planning, direct marketing, sales promotion, and credit marketing for this specialty retailer which operates 150 stores nationwide.

Goodman has extensive retail marketing experience in developing and executing successful marketing strategies over the past 15 years. His direct-marketing experience includes running his own retail direct-marketing agency where he developed direct-marketing strategies for Helzberg Diamonds, the National Collegiate Athletic Association (NCAA), and many other national retailers.

He has served as president of the Kansas City Direct Marketing Association, is on the Steering Committee of the Retail Marketing Group of the Direct Marketing Association (DMA), is a member of the Retail Advisory Task Force of the DMA, and is frequently called on to speak at universities and marketing organizations throughout the country. He graduated from the University of Kansas with a Bachelor of Science degree in Journalism and also holds the Professional Certificate of Direct Marketing from the University of Missouri—Kansas City.

Rose Harper began her career at The Kleid Company as controller. She was the first woman president of a division of Dart Industries, Inc., when Kleid was a subsidiary of Dart Industries (a Fortune 500 company). In January 1994, after 40 years, Harper turned the top position in The Kleid Company over to Mike Manzari, a long-time associate. She has stayed on as a company consultant and is continuing her industry activities.

Harper has served as chairman of the board of the Direct Marketing Association (DMA) and was treasurer for four years, the first woman to serve in either capacity. She was inducted into the Direct Marketing Hall of Fame in 1985 (the first woman so honored), received the Silver Apple Award from the Direct Marketing Club of New York and the Ed Mayer award in 1986 for outstanding contributions to education, was chosen Direct Marketer of the Year in 1987 by Direct Marketing Day in New York, and received the 1987 Direct Marketing of the Year Award from the Women's Direct Response Group.

She serves on the Board of Trustees of the Direct Marketing Educational Foundation, as well as on the Board of Direct Marketing Idea Exchange and the NYU Center for Direct Marketing. Harper is a member of the Committee of 200, an organization of top female executives and entrepreneurs. She is listed in the current editions of *Who's Who in American Women* and *Who's Who in America.*

Harper has lectured over the years at various industry functions such as NYU School of Continuing Education; Direct Marketing Educational Foundation Collegiate Institutes; Direct Marketing Days in New York, Chicago, and Los Angeles; DMA seminars and programs; and Direct Marketing Idea Exchange. Her book, *Mailing List Strategies: A Guide to Direct Mail Success,* was published by McGraw-Hill in March 1986 and received excellent reviews in both the United States and Europe. It is now in its fifth printing and was selected by *Library Journal* as one of the best business books published in 1986.

Henry A. (Hank) Johnson's career spans 40 years—all of it in the catalog direct-marketing industry. He started after high school as an office boy at Montgomery Ward and worked his way up through the ranks to the position of buyer.

After World War II, Johnson joined Aldens and spent 25 years there, advancing to executive vice president/merchandise and advertising manager. Johnson joined Spiegel in 1976 as president and chief executive officer (CEO); he retired as vice chairman in December 1987.

Johnson is recognized as one of the most knowledgeable and creative direct-marketing entrepreneurs. As Spiegel's president and CEO, he engineered a completely new marketing strategy designed to posture Spiegel as the world's leading woman's fashion catalog store: a true department store in print, with products and services to meet the needs of today's busy woman. During his tenure, sales increased from $260 million to $1 billion.

In 1983, the Horatio Alger Association of Distinguished Americans selected Johnson to receive the Horatio Alger Award. On November 4, 1991, he was named to the Direct Marketing Association's Hall of Fame.

In July 1990, Johnson's book, *The Corporate Dream,* was published and has received favorable reviews in such notable publications as *Crain's Chicago Business,* the *Chicago Tribune,* and the *Washington Times.*

Johnson presently serves as a business consultant, specializing in helping companies redirect their marketing strategies.

Lester B. "Dusty" Loo went to work in his family's business—Current on graduation from the University of Kansas in January, 1961. It was a very small business at the time, operating out of a basement. Loo didn't know it at the time, but a mail-order course he took in college gave him knowledge and insight that contributed immensely to the phenomenal growth of the family business. Even he could not dream of what his dedication to direct marketing would accomplish in the long term.

Starting early in his career, Loo set a course for becoming both an industry statesman and a civic leader. His dedication to direct marketing led to his appointment as chairman of the Direct Marketing Association (DMA) in 1980. He has served on the DMA Long-Range Planning Committee and the Direct Marketing Educational Foundation.

All the while, Loo has given generously of his time and money in support of civic and business organizations. His activities and positions have included membership in the University of Colorado's Business Advisory Council, member of the Chief Executive's Organization, director of the National Association of Greeting Card Publishers, member of the World Business Council, and president of the Colorado Springs Symphony Orchestra Association.

Following the sale of Current on December 31, 1987, Loo became chairman of a private investment group, High Valley Group, Inc.

Jack Miller was born in Chicago in 1929 and worked his way through college to graduate from the University of Illinois School of Journalism in 1950.

After six years of experience as a traveling salesman and sales promotion manager in specialty foods and sample cases, Miller started his own office supply business in 1956 with a $2,000 loan and a phone in his father's chicken store. Brother Harvey joined him a year and a half later and, in 1974, brother Arnold left his accounting practice in Los Angeles to combine forces in the company.

The first mailing was a penny postal card to 156 people Jack had called on. Additional mailings followed until, four years later, mail order had become their way of doing business.

Miller was elected a Fellow of the Illinois Business Hall of Fame and has been honored with the Spirit of Life Award for the Office Products Council of the City of Hope, the Torch of Liberty Award from the Anti-Defamation League of B'nai B'rith, and the Industrialist of the Year Award from the American-Israel Chamber of Commerce. In 1991, he received the first Lifetime Achievement Award from the Direct Marketing Association (DMA) and, in 1992, was named Man of the Year by *Office Products Dealer Magazine.* In 1993, he was honored as the Direct Marketer of the Year during Direct Marketing Day in New York.

Murray Raphel is a speaker, writer, and consultant to major business organizations including retailing, the food industry, insurance companies, and financial institutions.

He writes monthly columns on marketing for *Direct Marketing* and on supermarket retailing for *Progressive Grocer.*

Raphel travels nearly 200,000 miles a year speaking on marketing, advertising, and promotion across the United States, Canada, Mexico, Europe, Australia, New Zealand, and the Far East.

He developed Gordon's Alley, a multimillion-dollar, center-city pedestrian mall in Atlantic City. His annual seminars at the International Marketing Symposium in Montreux, Switzerland, and at the Food Marketing Institute Convention in Chicago attract large crowds and high ratings. He was given the prestigious Montreux Award for his international contributions in the field of direct marketing.

Raphel is the author of *The Great Brain Robbery, The Do-It-Yourself Direct Mail Handbook, Mind Your Own Business, Tough Selling for Tough Times,* and *Customerization.*

Jerry Reitman joined Leo Burnett Company as executive vice president in January 1987 to fully integrate direct marketing worldwide into the agency's general advertising function.

Prior to his move to Chicago, Reitman was chairman of the Reitman Group, a full-service direct-response agency. He was the founder and chief executive officer (CEO) of Scali, McCabe, Sloves Direct. Prior to that, he was executive vice president, international of Ogilvy & Mather Direct, where he developed its international network from 2 to 28 agencies over a five-year period.

Reitman has found time to distinguish himself with a variety of industry activities. He is past chairman of the DMA Ethics Policy Committee; a member of the Advisory Board of the Montreux Symposium for Direct Marketing Communication; a member of the Executive Committee for the Publishing Hall of Fame; an outside director for Scandinavian Airline Systems (SAS) Publishing and Distribution Services; past president of the Direct Marketing Club of New York; past chairman of the John Caples Awards; and a member of the Board of the Creative Guild.

He has lectured on direct marketing, creativity, and advertising in 32 countries around the world, and his articles have appeared in *Advertising Age, Fund Raising Magazine, Folio, Direct Marketing,* and the Dutch advertising magazine, *Adformatie.*

Bob Teufel joined Rodale Press in 1961 and was made vice president in 1967 and president in 1979. Rodale Press, a family-owned publishing company, has approximately 1,000 employees and is headquartered in Emmaus, Pennsylvania.

Teufel's position in the industry includes his participation with the Direct Marketing Association (DMA) where he served as board chairman and member of the Executive Committee. He received the Marketer of the Year award from Direct Marketing Day in New York, "Man of the Year" from the Philadelphia Direct Marketing Club, and the Lee C. Williams Award from the Fulfillment Management Association; he is in the DMA Circulation Council Hall of Fame. Teufel is a member of the Magazine Publishers of America (MPA) and was elected the MPA's chairman in 1992. He was chairman of The American Magazine Conference in 1983, and chairman of The American Magazine Congress in 1988, 1989, and 1990.

A graduate of Lehigh University in 1959 with a B.A. in Journalism, Teufel was an Information Officer in the U.S. Air Force and a captain in the Air Force Reserve until April 1961.

Lillian Vernon is the founder and chief executive officer of Lillian Vernon Corporation, a specialty catalog company that markets gift, household, gardening, decorative, and children's products. Born in Germany, Vernon fled to the United States with her family before the onset of World War II and settled in New York City. She started her company in 1951 with $2,000 of wedding-gift money. She placed a $495 advertisement for a personalized purse and belt in *Seventeen* magazine and received $32,000 in orders, and her business was launched.

Over the last four decades, the company has experienced exceptional growth. Revenues for fiscal year 1994 were $196.3 million. Last year, the company received more than 4.4 million orders and employed over 2,000 people during its peak season.

About the Contributors

Always willing to give of herself, Vernon donates funds and merchandise to over 500 charities each year. She serves on the boards of several nonprofit organizations, including the Virginia Opera and the Girl Scout Council of Virginia. She enjoys speaking at universities and has received several awards including the Ellis Island Medal of Honor, the Big Brother/Big Sisters National Hero Award, and Gannett Newspapers Business Leadership Award.